Modern Newspaper Practice

Titles in the series

Series editor: F. W. Hodgson

Modern Newspaper Practice

A primer on the press

Fourth Edition

F. W. Hodgson

Focal Press

To Yvonne, who made this book possible

Focal Press
An imprint of Butterworth-Heinemann
Linacre House, Jordan Hill, Oxford OX2 8DP
225 Wildwood Avenue, Woburn MA 01801-2041
A division of Reed Educational and Professional Publishing Ltd

A member of the Reed Elsevier plc group

OXFORD   AUCKLAND   BOSTON
JOHANNESBURG   MELBOURNE   NEW DELHI

First published 1984
Reprinted 1986
Second edition 1989
Revised reprint 1992
Third edition 1993
Reprinted 1994, 1995
Fourth edition 1996
Reprinted 1997, 1998, 2000
Transferred to digital printing 2001

British Library Cataloguing in Publication Data
A catalogue record for this book is available from the British Library

ISBN 0 240 51459 9

Printed in Great Britain by Antony Rowe Ltd, Eastbourne

PLANT A TREE

British Trust for
Conservation Volunteers

FOR EVERY TITLE THAT WE PUBLISH, BUTTERWORTH-HEINEMANN
WILL PAY FOR BTCV TO PLANT AND CARE FOR A TREE.

www.focalpress.com

Contents

List of Illustrations

Preface to Fourth Edition

The fourteen years since I first wrote *Modern Newspaper Practice* have witnessed huge changes in the way newspapers are produced. Having seen web-offset litho replace the rotary press, and photosetting replace hot metal – bringing with them full run-of-press colour – we are now into the final stage of the total system: electronic pagination, or the making up of newspaper pages on screen.

The computer technology that has brought this about is breathtaking to anyone seeing it for the first time. Journalists have tools of unimaginable accuracy and sophistication to enable them to create newspapers of a quality, at a speed and with an economy never before possible. Moreover, it is a control that is totally within their own hands.

This is the world we examine in this new edition of *Modern Newspaper Practice*, the standard introductory text on the press used by journalism and media courses. It has been revised to cover the very latest developments in technology and their effect on various areas of practice. It also offers important updates on courses and career training. A new glossary and illustrations are included.

It remains for me to offer a familiar warning: however good the electronic tools at their disposal, journalists should remember that they are still only tools. They are the means of making better and – one hopes – more newspapers. How good those newspapers are depends, as it always did, on the professional skills and integrity of those who write, edit and put them together.

I am indebted to an increasing list of colleagues and ex-colleagues in what we used to call Fleet Street and in the provincial press for their help. I should mention the editors of the *Manchester Evening News*, the *Evening Standard*, *The Times*, *The Sun*, the *News of the World* and *Kent Today* for permission to reproduce pages (and layouts in some cases), and the editor of the *Daily Telegraph* for allowing me to quote extensively from a leader in Chapter 1. Keith Hall, ex-Chief Executive of the National Council for the Training of

Journalists, and Rob Selwood, his successor, have given me their time and advice.

Tom Crone, Legal Manager of News Group Newspapers, never minds me pestering him; Richard Beamish, Head of Training at the Newspaper Society, has discussed training issues with me, and Alan Shanks, their technical officer and his assistant Gary Cullum have helped with their knowledge.

Among organizations who have given much appreciated services and information are: the Press Association, Advertising Association, National Union of Journalists, Audit Bureau of Circulations, Media Society, National Readership Surveys Ltd, the Association of Free Newspapers and the Press Complaints Commission. I hope the again amended bibliography reflects the many writers on the media whose ideas I have looked at and who, in many cases, I have worked with.

F. W. Hodgson
Ninfield, Sussex
March, 1996

1 A newspaper's role

The vigour of newspapers as a medium of mass communication in the face of competition from radio, television and latterly electronic news-sheets has confounded media prophets of earlier decades. A reason for this was advanced by the *Daily Telegraph* in an editorial opinion published when the paper re-appeared after a strike which had stopped national papers for several days.

The editor apologized to his readers for having left them to television and radio for their news coverage. It was no substitute, he said, for a newspaper whose readers,

> 'get an average daily amount of news on a vast variety of subjects which, if read out on radio or television at the normal speed of 120 words a minute, would take ten hours to read . . . This figure is for news alone. It does not include any form of feature article or advertisements, though these last may often be regarded as news in their own right – news of jobs vacant, of new products available, of theatres and concerts, of births, marriages and deaths.
>
> 'The idea of broadcasting trying to match this is grotesque. If it made the attempt, it could do nothing else. And all its audience would have to hear everything. In a newspaper the reader can pick or choose – the sports enthusiasts go to their pages, the moneyed or would-be moneyed to theirs, each man to the story or feature which interests him most. With broadcasting no such personal selection is possible.'[1]

It was a piece of propaganda for the *Telegraph* but it explained in essence why newspapers continue to be bought in large numbers and read. National dailies, for instance, despite gloomy predictions over the years, and one or two changes of title, are not that much different in total circulation from what they were at the end of the 1939–45 war when, for the first time, they reached 15,000,000. In 1955 they were 15,167,700, in 1961 they were 15,757,800, in 1971 they had dipped to 14,318,000; in 1983, by which time breakfast TV

had become a new rival, they were up again to 14,992,953. By 1990 a
buoyant economy had pushed daily sales back up to 15,295,000, with Sunday
sales at 17,828,000. Inevitably, the years of recession thereafter took their toll
and 1992 showed dips in daily sales to 14,113,000 and Sundays to
16,161,000. By the end of 1995 daily sales stood at 14,474,184 and Sundays
at 15,796,040.

The *Daily Telegraph*'s piece is a reminder also of the range of content of
the modern newspaper. From being originally a journal of record or a journal
of opinion, it has broadened in scope so that today advice and entertainment
have become as important to readers as news and opinion. The newspaper,
provincial and national, has also become a forum where readers themselves
can express their views and even influence the paper's content.

This broadening of range was present to some extent in the popular Sunday
papers which began in the mid-19th century (the *News of the World* is a
survivor from 1843) and were aimed at the less affluent classes for whom the
heavily taxed daily press was too expensive. The removal of Stamp Duty in
1855 and, more important, the arrival of universal education with the passing
of the 1870 Education Act, paved the way for the mass circulation daily and
the expansion of local papers. Lord Northcliffe's *Daily Mail*, launched in
1896, in particular established the broad pattern of modern newspaper
content in response to the demands of the new readership.

Structure of the press

Both historical and geographical reasons play their part in the structure of the
press. The main division in Britain today is between what we call the national
press and the provincial and local press. At one time all newspapers were, in
essence, regional or local papers in that they circulated in an area bounded by
the limits of distribution. Thus, while London had *The Times*, the *Morning
Post* and other prestigious dailies, Manchester, Glasgow, Birmingham and
Newcastle also had important daily papers with their own reader catchment
area.

The development of the railway system in the mid-19th century, coupled
with the relatively small area of the country, made national distribution
possible and the stronger and wealthier papers such as *The Times* and the
Daily Telegraph (from 1855) and one or two others became the first truly
national dailies. With the addition of the new popular mass circulation
newspapers at the end of the 19th century (the *Daily Express* for instance, in
1901), Britain had acquired a vigorous national press.

At the same time, the smaller provincial papers continued to serve the
needs of local news and advertising. Thus a two-tier system emerged with
national, foreign and political coverage appearing in the national papers and
mainly community interests being served in the provincial press, with town-
based evening papers becoming dominant.

A like structure can be seen in Japan and the Scandinavian countries where similar geographical and transport factors apply. In the United States, on the other hand, and in India and many larger countries, size and distribution problems make a strong centralized press difficult to sustain and papers tend to be more regionalized, each city and area having its own.

In Britain and similar sized countries the intense competition for readers among rival national papers has resulted in a greater emphasis on visual impact as competition is transferred to the news stands. Increases or decreases in national sales often reflect the extent to which a newspaper can influence the impulse buyer.

In the provincial press, and in the press of those countries where newspapers tend to circulate on a regional basis, this competitive element applies much less since the newspapers publish mostly on solus sites.

A distinctive aspect of the national press in Britain is its division into 'popular' and 'quality'. This broadly reflects the historic factors mentioned. The quality, or what is sometimes called the serious, press describes papers founded mainly before 1896 which follow the tradition of the journals of record and opinion of the 18th and early 19th century. They are strong on political, industrial and cultural news and devote some pages to international news and also to financial matters. Their layout is restrained with a concentration on longer texts; their readership lies in the more educated section of the market and there is less competition for the impulse buyer. There is usually an 'upmarket' social flavour to their content, even though there may be political differences from paper to paper. Examples are: *The Times, Financial Times, The Guardian, Daily Telegraph, The Independent, Sunday Times, The Observer* and the *Sunday Telegraph.*

The popular press is represented by those papers founded mainly after the launching of the *Daily Mail* in 1896 and influenced by its popular 'down market' approach and working-class and lower middle-class appeal. Today such papers are largely tabloid, or half size. The dominant influence behind their bold layout and wide human interest content was set in the 1930s and 1940s by the *Daily Mirror*, the first paper to reach a high circulation with the tabloid format. Among the popular press are: the *Daily Mirror, The Sun, Daily Star, Sunday Mirror, The People* and the *News of the World.* The differences in layout and style between quality papers and the popular tabloids will be dealt with in later chapters.

There is some merit – supported by readership surveys – in placing the remaining two British national tabloids, the *Daily Mail* and the *Daily Express*, and also the *Sunday Express*, in what press commentators call the 'middle ground'; that is the area that falls, in content and social flavour, between the quality press and the popular press. The *Mail*, though it can claim to be the first popular daily, has occupied this middle ground for many years under the 1st, 2nd and 3rd Lords Rothermere. The *Express* has been less consistent, edging its readership appeal at times towards the

Daily Mirror's market and at other times towards the *Daily Telegraph*'s market. The *Sunday Express* has pursued a more deliberate middle-class, middle ground approach from the time of its launch by Lord Beaverbrook in 1918.

The increasing polarization of Britain's national papers between 'quality' and 'popular' has worried Royal Commissions. The 1949 one observed in its report that in general 'the press provides for a sufficient variety of political opinion but not for a sufficient variety of intellectual levels. The gap between the best of the quality papers and the general run of the popular press is too wide and the number of papers of an intermediate type is too small.'[2] The extinction since then of several titles and the launching of new ones has increased this polarization and has reflected a tendency by advertisers to influence the balance by favouring with their business those papers whose readership falls into clearly identifiable social groups.

In the provincial and local press, the terms popular and quality have no real significance, though old-established morning papers like the *Yorkshire Post*, the *Northern Echo* and the *Glasgow Herald*, tend to be more up-market in their content and approach than town evening papers. Likewise there are noticeable differences in market approach between city suburban weeklies and those in the counties.

Factors in mass communication

The development and varied role of the press has made the newspaper the archetype of modern mass communications media, which are the means by which messages containing ideas and information are transmitted by communicators to a mass audience.

There are two factors common to all mass communications messages which need stressing at this stage for two reasons:

1 They are relevant to newspaper practice.
2 They are of value to students who may in the future work in various media or move from one medium to another.

These factors are the limits of *space* and *time* within which a communicator works, whether he or she is concerned with spoken or written material, advertisements, publicity hand-outs or Government leaflets.

Space might be said to be the boundaries or shape taken up by a message. In the case of a newspaper news story this would be the available length on the page which, in its turn, reflects its news assessment in relation to the other stories on the page or in the paper. The writer and sub-editor have to contain the essential facts in this prescribed space and gain the maximum effect from the words (and in some cases the pictures) that can be contained in the space.

A radio news item has even more critical boundaries in the number of words that can be used. These are governed by the speed of news reading, the air space that is available for the news programme and the number of items that the programme contains. The length of the items is fixed by a word count which seldom exceeds 100 words a minute, averaged out over pauses.

A newspaper or magazine advertisement is similarly limited in content by the shape and size of the space that has been bought. In this space must be included the slogan, or 'selling line,' sometimes an illustration, a description and price of the product or service and the reasons for buying it. In the case of a television advertisement, where sound competes with vision, 65 words is about the maximum that can be allowed in a 36-second spot.

A publicity handout allows more scope for words. Yet here there are important psychological boundaries to word content: the time and tolerance of the reader (usually a journalist) into whose hands it falls. In a similar category comes a Government information leaflet. As with a printed handout, excessive length and size can be counter-productive if the intention is to catch and hold the reader's time and attention.

Time: This involves gathering, compiling and presenting of message so that it reaches its audience within a time limit which will ensure its maximum effectiveness and relevance. A news item, either in a newspaper or on radio, must obey a deadline which will allow the information to retain its newness by the time it is read or listened to.

The technology of mass communications – the use of the electric telegraph from the 1840s, and later of the telephone, teleprinters, computer systems and facsimile transmission – has always been designed to speed the communication of information and ideas.

Time can mean timeliness. Advertisements on television, radio and in newspapers and magazines are invariably timed to phase in with sales campaigns, and the date for advertisements is booked as well as the space and format. Most publicity hand-outs aim to gain the maximum effect from the timely exposure of information to the press or public.

It can be seen, therefore, that a communications message is not just a case of arranging words and pictures but of getting the maximum effect from them within allowed disciplines of space and time. These two disciplines should be kept in mind during our examination of modern newspaper practice.

The language of mass communication

The constraints of space mean that in any form of mass communications language must be used with care to get the maximum effect. It must be clear, unambiguous and to the point. When a reporter and a sub-editor are working to a tight space there is no room for unnecessary words or 'waffle'. School-room English must be rigorously pruned so that every sentence serves a purpose.

In radio journalism, reporters and news writers work to an even tighter schedule. An item more than two minutes long is a liberal allowance in a news programme that might have to be contained within ten minutes' air time.

The person who puts together the words of an advertisement – the copy-writer – knows that every word must earn its keep when a client is paying perhaps thousands of pounds for the space and is expecting to see results in terms of sales. In public relations a printed handout that waffles is destined for the waste bin.

How can we get the best out of language in these difficult circumstances?

The answer is certainly not to sacrifice good grammatical construction or to use jargon. Both these faults can cloud the meaning of what is written. Nor need good style be thrown overboard.

A clear mind and a sound knowledge of the languare are the first essentials. English is a flexible tongue and, as headline writers and sub-editors discover, there is usually a simpler way of saying things than might at first appear. Simplicity, in fact, is the vital step on the road to clarity, though it has to be worked at.

There are various ways of spelling out the do's and don'ts of language for communicators but they are probably most usefully summed up, for those using written words,[3] under the following ten headings:

1 Go for the shorter word where there are alternatives. This is a general rule, not an invariable one. Beware of trying too hard and relapsing into stilted prose. Stay close to popular speech. You will hear plenty of good short Anglo-Saxon words still in use. Harold Evans says: 'Sentences should be full of bricks, beds, houses, cars, cows, men and women.'[4]

In particular, use one word in place of wasteful phrases:

near	not	adjacent to
now	not	at this moment in time
now	not	at the present time
during	not	not in the course of
before	not	prior to
because	not	in consequence of
save	not	effect a saving
from	not	as from
watched	not	kept observation
although	not	despite the fact that

Call a spade a spade and a cat a cat, not a feline creature, nor a bird a feathered friend.

2 Avoid foreign or little-used words. For rendezvous why not meeting? Or fight for fracas? Resist the temptation to garnish your account with 'de rigeur', 'bête noir' and 'sine qua non'. Don't pop in a Franch or Latin phrase just because you have seen *The Guardian* do in in their editorial opinion. As a journalist starting out on a career you should not be trying to baffle your readers with learning.

3 Avoid excessive use of adjectives and adverbs – especially those that add nothing:

broad daylight	really good
wholly truthful	rather fine
blazing inferno	completely untrue

or those that have lost all meaning:

luxury flat	stunning blonde
shock move	brutal murder
vital clues	pretty girl
neat semi-detached	burly policeman

and, above all, double adjectives:

deep blue sea	full, unabridged account
long, tedious journey	nice big kiss
fine sunny day	clear unambiguous statement

An adjective must extend the noun, not prop it up. A sentence in which every noun is preceded by an adjective is tedious and clumsy and loses pace. If you are seeking to trim the words, see how many adjectives you can take out without damaging the meaning.

4 Avoid excessively long sentences. This does not mean that you must never use sentences of longer than seven or eight words. The deciding factor is clarity and there is less chance of departing from clarity or losing the subject in a shorter sentence. The longer it is the more complicated becomes the structure and punctuation.

Try to use an active, or transitive verb: i.e. 'The boy told the truth' not 'The truth was told by the boy.' And 'The boy caught the man,' not 'The man was caught by the boy.' You can see how the sentence is strengthened – and saves on space.

5 Avoid lesser-used tenses where you can. They lead to difficulties in phrasing. Be consistent in the use of tenses. Present, past and future can serve most purposes.

6 Beware of jargon. Giving active consideration to ... should be left to town halls and ministries. Likewise transportation (for transport), proliferation (spread), blueprint (plan), and in short supply (scarce). End products and ongoing plans should remain in their bureaucratic pigeonholes along with downturns, upturns, formal approaches, finalizations, maximizations and, for that matter bureaucratizations. Have none of them.

7 Avoid parentheses as far as possible whether between brackets, dashes or dots. They strain the eye, stretch the brain and impair the flow of the sentence. If commas do not do the job adequately, take out the parenthesis and make a new sentence of it.

8 Banish clichés or at least, if you must, ration them sparingly. Newspapers should have done with burning issues, towers of strength, putting things in a nutshell and blessings in disguise. Sports writers should, in particular, pension off: in at the deep end, in the heat of the moment, Wembley-sized roar, in the thick of the action, over the moon and absolutely choked. Only very old ladies should be allowed to say: 'it was just like the Blitz.'

In popular tabloids there might be just room for an occasional sweet smell of success, knickers in a twist or alive and well and living in. . . .

Clichés can damage the text by lulling or boring the reader/listener and turning situations into stereotypes.

9 Keep punctuation simple. It should be used only where without it the meaning is in doubt. Punctuation which causes the readers to go back and read the sentence again has failed. If an 'and' or a 'but' seem to need a comma or a semi-colon before them it is often better to start a new sentence at that point.

If a sentence contains a lot of commas and semi-colons it is better to split it into separate sentences. Keep exclamation marks for exclamations.

10 Keep paragraphs short. They ease the eye by avoiding solid slabs of type setting. Remember that a line of reading text in any average newspaper column width will take only four or five words.

A word of warning, however, from *Fowler's English Usage*: 'The paragraph is essentially a unit of thought, not of length; it must be homogeneous in subject matter and sequential in treatment.'

Words are the capital of the communicator. Even pictures, valuable though they are in newspapers and magazines (and even more so on television) cannot stand without them. Precious time has to be taken on television news to explain newsfilm. It is essential that the best possible use is made of words within the allowed limits of space and time. Every word has a job to do. There can be no passengers.

What is news?

Before we go further in our examination of modern newspaper practice we must question and define what we mean by news, the commodity from which the newspaper derives its name.

Much ink has been expended over this knotty problem. Norwegian sociologists Galtung and Ruge[5] have made a much quoted definition which sees news as a crisis of variable intensity which is assessed by factors of 'personalisation' or 'cultural proximity'. Another popular sociological concept is the gatekeeper theory – that news consists of those events specified by a news gatekeeper, who is the executive strategically placed on a newspaper to decide from the varied input of material what is news in terms of the paper's requirements. The gatekeeper, or senior processor, thus becomes the definer of news and exerts a total influence on the information placed before the readers – or so the theory goes.

'Dog bites man – no interest. Man bites dog – news,' is an old chestnut presented to young reporters, while Harold Evans puts forward the definition 'News is people.' Some authorities stress the element of the exceptional or the marvellous: 'News is anything that makes a reader say gee whizz,' says an American editor quoted in Daniel Boorstin's book, *The Image*.

The fault with all these attempts is that they are defining what *makes* news rather than what news *is*. Much closer to the truth is the simple definition of news given in the Concise Oxford Dictionary: 'Tidings, new information, fresh events reported.' This demonstrates the fallacy of most definitions: that they confuse the event with the report of the event.

Events covering a wide range of descriptions involving people, animals and things, some marvellous, some mundane, become news only through their existence being made known. An event which no one knows about – a secret marriage of a famous person, for instance – cannot be news. It becomes so only when it is disclosed to the public, maybe many years afterwards.

In a similar category were the treaties and campaigns of long ago which became news only after the information had been carried for days or weeks by messengers across oceans and continents to the editorial office of a newspaper. A big story might have wide coverage in a country's press and yet the following day one newspaper could pick up some facts of the story that had been previously overlooked. By disclosing these factors the paper is able to run a 'follow up' story. It is publishing news.

It is worth recalling that as long ago as 1852, John Thaddeus Delane, the famous editor of *The Times*, in the course of a quarrel with Lord Derby over the paper's political coverage, wrote in a leading article: 'The first duty of the Press is to obtain the earliest and most correct intelligence of the events of time and instantly, by disclosing them, make them the common property of the nation . . . The press lives by disclosure.'

By this token, any event or facts that have already been disclosed to the public thereafter cease to be news. We thus have a yardstick by which news can be recognized.

It can be argued that the disclosure of an event which makes news in one country, or in one area even, might not be considered newsworthy in another. It could equally be said that the disclosure of information of a highly specialized nature to one group of readers – the discovery of ancient field systems, for instance, reported in an archaeological magazine – might be of no news interest to other readers. This is true and it demonstrates an important characteristic of news – that there is no absolute value judgement by which new information is selected and published. It might be news by our abstract definition but it must be the sort of news that is likely to be of interest to the readers of a particular publication in order to be selected.

The job of editors is to assess and choose news for their readers. The choice in an average newspaper may cover a wide range of events involving what people say and do and suffer and achieve. An item's eligibility for use, however, depends broadly on two factors, the geographical and the personal – the 'where' and the 'who'.

The geographical factor: We notice when we are abroad that there is far less news of our country and its business in the press there than we find in newspapers at home. Overseas students might be affronted to see so little reference to their country – Nigeria, New Zealand, Malaysia, say – when they first open British newspapers.

This demonstrates the geographical or proximity factor at work.

News, in general, loses its impact the further it is from a newspaper's distribution area. A change of Government in Bolivia will be a front page 'lead' story in that country's newspapers. It might be given good inside placing in a British newspaper that specializes in international news such as *The Times* and *The Guardian*. It might get only a paragraph or two in a popular tabloid, or maybe no mention at all. A local weekly paper will ignore it.

Equally a wedding of a local businessman might get a picture and half a column of description in a local weekly paper, to whom the event is close. Nationally it would not be considered.

Newspapers serve a particular area of readership. The limits on available space demands a process of selection. The geographical or proximity factor helps in this.

The personal factor: An examination of newspapers in general will reveal that a number of the people concerned in news stories are well known. Of the people that are not well known there have to be good reasons – the facts or the circumstances in which they are involved – for their being mentioned.

Where speeches or comments are quoted they are often from people such as politicians, industrialists or trade unionists whose views make news.

A fairly minor accident or illness can become a news story in a national newspaper if it concerns a public or well-known figure. In the case of a shop manager or a postman it would be of news value, if at all, only in a very localized newspaper in the area. The events in which a person-in-the-street is involved have to be unusual or special to be included in the pages of any newspaper.

This is the personal factor at work in news choice.

Special interest: The above two factors are, of course, simplifications. Though they are valid in nearly all cases it will be seen that they work on a sliding scale. The geographical factor is not absolute. A foreign political event might get a reasonable mention, as we have said, in a British newspaper that gives space to international news. It is less likely to appear in the popular tabloid which does not normally publish such news unless the event is of exceptional importance to Britain or of special interest, for some reason, to its readers.

The sliding scale works equally with the personality factor. A speech by a local political figure might not rate coverage in the national press but it might be covered in a national publication specializing in those particular views or the activities of a political party out of which they arise.

Some provincial weekly papers have a strong agricultural bias in their content. Some evening papers cover news of certain industries because it is part of the employment pattern in their area. Here, personality news might be selected because it relates to these special interests.

Even in national papers there are special interests at work. *The Guardian* is strong on educational matters, *The Observer* on African news, the *Financial Times* on technology, energy and the economy, the popular tabloids on everyday human interest stories. In weekly publications and magazines the degree of specialization becomes more pronounced.

Thus, while news can be defined as the first disclosure of a fact or an event, there is no absolute scale of value by which it can be measured. For the purpose of selecting news for the readers, an editor takes into account the geographical and personal factors of each story and then qualifies these by relating them to the special interests of the newspaper and its market.

It is because there are no absolutes in news assessment that newspapers, while in agreement on some stories which are of fundamental importance on the day, display such diversity of content.

Further reading

The reports of the three Royal Commissions on the Press, 1947–49, 1962–63 and 1976–77 (HMSO, London), though dated, contain good material on the structure of the press as a whole, and have informative charts. Simon Jenkins's *Newspapers, the Power and the Money* (Faber & Faber, London, 1979) covers aspects of recent national newspaper history. Ian Jackson's *The Provincial Press and the Community* (Manchester University Press, Manchester, 1971) analyses the role of provincial and local newspapers.

On communication English there is sound advice in Ted Bottomley and Anthony Loftus's *Journalists' Guide to the Use of English* (Express and Star Publications, Wolverhampton, 1971). An essential text now available is Nicholas Bagnall's *Newspaper Language* (Focal Press, 1993). Some amusing but sound advice on the pitfalls of newspaper English can be found in Keith Waterhouse's *On Newspaper Style* (Viking, 1989). Robert Burchfield's *The Spoken Word, a BBC Guide* (BBC, London, 1981), is invaluable on grammar and pronunciation and can help both radio and newspaper journalists. *Fowler's Modern English Usage*, Second Edition, revised by Sir Ernest Gowers (Oxford at the Clarendon Press, 1982) is an essential standby.

References

1 Sir Michael Swann, then chairman of the BBC, developed this point further at a seminar at Leeds University in March, 1975: 'First, and most formidable, is the extremely slow pace of the spoken word as a means of informing ... TV slows things down by a factor of two or three or four with its pictures and necessary explanation of what the pictures are. *The Times* turned into a TV news bulletin, therefore, would last for two, three or four days solid.'
2 *Royal Commission on the Press*, 1947–49 (HMSO, London, 1949).
3 For those in broadcasting, see: BURCHFIELD, ROBERT: *The Spoken Word, a BBC Guide* (BBC, London, 1981).
4 EVANS, H., *Editing and Design, Book 1: Newsman's English* (Heinemann, London, 1963).
5 In a contribution to: TUNSTALL, JEREMY (ed), *Media Sociology* (Constable, London, 1970).

2 Finding the news

A newspaper looks to its staff reporters for its main news content. There are other sources such as local correspondents, or stringers, who are, in effect, part-time contributors; freelance writers of various types, and news agencies which provide a continuous supply of national, provincial and foreign news. The use of staff reporters, however, gives a newspaper the best control over its news gathering and provides the greatest likelihood of exclusiveness, or of getting stories which no other paper has. The element of exclusiveness is especially important to national newspapers in Britain which, as we have seen, publish in a highly competitive market.

A national daily might have, in its head office and other news-gathering centres, from thirty to sixty reporters, and a provincial evening perhaps a quarter of that number. Figures depend on the area of a newspaper's coverage and on what it can afford. In some towns there are sharing arrangements between newspapers to ease the staffing burden of covering the many forms of static news such as courts, councils and various committees. Some newspaper groups have pooled services.

The reporter's job

Most reporters are general reporters (for specialists, see Chapter 3). They may be assigned to cover any sort of story, either singly or as part of a team. During their training they are taught to assess news value in various situations so that they can be relied upon to identify it for their readers as they go about their assignment. Such news might arise from investigating an entirely new situation: for instance the disclosure of contamination at a lead works or first indications of an outbreak of fowl pest on a farm. Or it might consist in checking facts and personal details relating to a known news situation: for instance a chat to the wife of a newly appointed Cabinet Minister or the family of a soldier who has won a medal.

Whatever the circumstances, the reporter is in charge of the facts once he or she has been briefed by the news editor or chief reporter and has set off on the assignment. Some briefings can be very helpful where detailed information has already reached the newspaper. Sometimes it happens that information on which the assignment is based is wrong and the story 'falls down'.

Come the deadline for filing the story, the reporter must have checked the facts, talked to the people concerned and have put together the account in a readable form.

Checking the facts. There are many facts which the reporter must check in reference books, archives and newspaper cuttings files or by a telephone inquiry. These include the spellings of names and places, the style and titles of well known people, geographical information, business and literary backgrounds of people and information arising from references in previous news stories which are relevant. The reporter should check the cuttings files in the office library before leaving to cover a story and use reference books when filing the story. If the reporter cannot get back to the office he or she can telephone a request for a particular fact to be checked by the subeditor.

The most important facts, however, may be verifiable only during the coverage of the story, which must stand or fall on the clear descriptions and careful note taken of interviews with people concerned, or of evidence given in the case of court hearings. In seeking information the reporter must go to the people who are competent and qualified to give it. If there are two sides to be considered both must be allowed to offer views. Good relations with functionaries such as the police, hospital staff and people in public life are most important.

Local news patterns. The closeness to the community gives local newsgathering a pattern which differs from national newspapers. One of the earliest jobs for a young reporter is to make 'calls' – to visit, or telephone, contacts in local life such as the police, the hospitals, local councils and public services through whom news stories in the area might first break. Such contacts are usually cultivated at a social level and become, in effect, listening posts dotted around the community. Sometimes a reporter might be able to do a contact a favour in return. Thus a personal contact book is built up which becomes one of the most valuable parts of the reporter's equipment as he or she gathers news in the area.

Courts, inquests, local councils, amateur dramatic productions, meetings of many sorts, human interest stories of local people and local sport – these are the stuff of a town evening paper (Figure 3) or local weekly. But equally a young reporter might become involved in the features side of a small paper, writing entertainment and shopping guides, helping out with the sports coverage and contributing to marketing supplements. It is in this wide spectrum of activity that techniques are learnt and the seeds of specializations first sown.

Local papers carry important news that a community cannot get from the national press and get only marginally from local radio. A report on local paper content presented to a conference of the Newspaper Society (which covers provincial proprietors) at Brighton in February, 1983, came to the conclusion that what people wanted was more local news. It stated: 'We must give the reader more news – more local, more relevant and more exciting news and more hard news. It is a sad fact that over the past 50 years the number of news stories on the front pages of our papers has dropped by up to 80 per cent. An exception – one small paper with an old fashioned layout crammed with news stories – has seen its circulation go up from 70,000 to 80,000.'

Interviewing. Facts, even in what seem the simplest of stories, can be sometimes difficult to uncover. People may have a vested interest in concealing information. They may be unaware of the significance of what they have seen or know. Meeting, talking to and dealing with people is a vital part of the reporter's work. It requires tact, patience, psychology – and courtesy – to conduct an interview.

It is usually quite wrong, for instance, to wave a notebook about or to ostentatiously play the part of a reporter. This can close doors or frighten people. There is much to be said for the quiet drink with someone in a convivial bar or the inquiry about their job or family to put people at ease. A shorthand note or a tape recording, where appropriate, should be taken once the person has agreed to talk, not only for accuracy but for the record in case the statement is challenged. Where a lengthy text is expected to result, a tape recorder has much in its favour.

There are now some handy miniaturized tape recorders available, yet the circumstances are often not suitable for taping nor are some people keen to talk if they think they are being taped. Another point is that a shorthand note is still more likely to be accepted than taped statements in the event of court proceedings arising out of a newspaper report. Tapes can be objected to in court unless they have been accepted as agreed documents by both sides or can be proved authentic. The reason usually given for objection is that tapes can be tampered with, though it is possible to argue that a shorthand note could also be tampered with.

If the statements or conversations are of great importance, with possible legal implications, it is better to have a colleague present at the interview for corroboration.

The following points are a useful guide for reporters for a newspaper interview.

- Where possible research the person beforehand in reference books and cuttings so that you know something about him or her. It helps to produce rapport and gives the questioner credibility.
- Prepare the questions you wish to ask beforehand. It can prevent time-wasting. You can always add questions when you see how things are going.
- Let the person do the talking. Intervene only when the remarks are going off the point.
- Do not put words into the person's mouth.
- Do not ask the person to give views on something about which he or she is not competent to talk. Be certain you are talking to the right person for the information you want.
- Do not press questions if the person is reluctant to answer or is showing signs of distress.

These points apply also to telephone interviews which are often necessary when the person from whom you seek information cannot be reached in any other way, or if time is short. In such cases remember that an abrupt telephone manner can be very annoying to people who might be able to help you.

The above procedure applies, of course, to the ideal situation. Often there is no time to prepare a set-piece interview. Nor is it necessarily just a case of knocking on a door and showing a press card. Sometimes a reporter has to endure long hours of waiting to get to someone and the vital quote might be just a few words spoken over the shoulder as the person rushes off.

Intrusion. Pursuit of a story and, in particular, attempts to reach and talk to people involved in news stories, have resulted at various times in charges that the press has intruded into people's private lives or has 'hounded' them.

The decision on how far a reporter or photographer can go in this direction can be difficult to take in the case of people such as politicians and showbusiness personalities who live very public lives. There are cases where public figures pointedly use the press for publicity purposes but are less forthcoming when the press is trying to follow up a story in which the public interest is involved.

Attempts have been made in Britain to have rights of privacy defined but have met with opposition both in and out of Parliament. Cases of alleged intrusion were submitted in evidence to the 1947–49 Royal Commission on the Press. Its Report, in effect, put the matter aside to be dealt with by the Press Council whose setting up was one of its recommendations (see Chapter 10).

The various adjudications made by the Press Council on complaints of intrusion were finally embodied in an important Declaration of Principle published by the Council in April 1976. This referred to attempts by MPs to define the right to privacy by statute law and declared that 'any attempt to legislate on privacy would be contrary to the public interest.' It then went on:

'The following statement represents the policy which the Press Council has and will continue to support and which accords with the practice of responsible journalists:

'1. The publication of information about the private lives or concerns of individuals without their consent is only acceptable if there is legitimate public interest overriding the right of privacy.

'2. It is the responsibility of editors to ensure that inquiries into matters affecting the private lives or concerns of individuals are only undertaken where, in the Editor's opinion at the time, a legitimate public interest in such matters may arise. The right to privacy is, however, not involved if the individuals concerned have freely and clearly consented to the pursuit of inquiries and publication.'

The Declaration insisted that the public interest must not be 'only a prurient or morbid curiosity,' and it added that 'in the public interest' does not mean the same as 'of interest to the public.'

The document took into account intrusion by bugging and other devices and went on: 'Invasion of privacy by deception, eavesdropping or technological methods which are not in themselves unlawful can, however, only be justified when it is in pursuit of information which ought to be published in the public interest and there is no other reasonably practical method of obtaining or confirming it.'

The declaration finally instructed journalists that 'the Council expects the obtaining of news and pictures to be carried out with sympathy and discretion,' and laid the responsibility squarely upon editors for the actions of reporters and photographers.

Complaints of intrusion continued to come before the Press Council, however, and the problem was one of the issues, along with demands for a right of reply by complainants, that dominated the anti-press Parliamentary agitation of 1988–89 which led to the setting up of the Calcutt Committee.

It was on the recommendation of the committee that 'to strengthen voluntary self-regulation to the maximum degree,' the Press Council was replaced in 1990 by the Press Complaints Commission. The new commission at once issued a mandatory Code of Practice for editors of which Section 4 dealt with privacy as follows:

Intrusions and enquiries into an individual's private life without his or her consent including the use of long-lens photography to take pictures of people on private property without their consent are not generally acceptable and publication can only be justified when in the public interest.

Note – Private property is defined as any private residence, together with its garden and outbuildings, but excluding any adjacent fields or parkland. In addition, hotel bedrooms (but not other areas in a hotel) and those parts of a hospital or nursing home where patients are treated or accommodated.

On the subject of harassment, the Code laid down:

(i)   Journalists should neither obtain nor seek to obtain information or pictures through intimidation or harassment.
(ii) Unless their enquiries are in the public interest, journalists should not photograph individuals on private property without their consent; should not persist in telephoning or questioning individuals after having been asked to desist; should not remain on their property after having been asked to leave and should not follow them.
(iii) It is the responsibility of editors to ensure that these requirements are carried out.

(For full Code of Practice see Appendix B).

Trespass. Though there is no general right to privacy under the law, people can bring an action for trespass against a newspaper if it can be proved there has been wrongful interference with possession of land – i.e. a house – through unauthorized physical entry.

Privilege. Newspapers frequently handle stories such as court hearings and sittings of Parliament and public bodies where serious allegations are made about people which, if made and reported elsewhere, could lead to actions for libel. Under British law the need for freedom of speech in the public interest on such occasions is recognized and a newspaper's reports in these circumstances are deemed in law to be 'privileged'. However the report must be 'fair and accurate' and should be published contemporaneously and without malice. Nor would a report of a court hearing or public body be privileged if it concerned matter gleaned from documents that had not been read out in court. Misrepresentations of court proceedings or carelessness or inaccuracy in a headline or story can result in the withdrawal of the protection of privilege should an action result.

A complex schedule published as part of the 1952 Defamation Act specifies the occasions when a newspaper is covered by absolute or qualified privilege and thereby free from prosecution over any statements reported.[1]

News writing

All stories written for publication, whether news, features or any other, are referred to as 'copy'. Reporters' work can be taken down over the telephone by keyboard operators who are called copytakers (they can also be called telephone reporters); copy is read and sorted by copy tasters.

Presentation. When close to a deadline an experienced reporter might telephone a story straight from notes or from a rough draft. This is a skill that only long practice in news writing to a paper's requirements (and using notes) can teach. In this case the copy-taker keyboarding the text will present it on screen in the way required. More usually these days, the reporter will use a laptop workstation, or return to the newsroom, and compose the story straight on to the screen.

The rules of presentation have not changed much from earlier days. The story still needs the reporter's name at the top and a one-word catchline of a distinctive sort (the computer will reject any that has already been used) by which it can be called up for checking and editing.

The story, when finished, must still be marked END – or MFL if more is to follow later – and any specific instructions to the subeditor bracketed into the text. Later text can be catchlined, say, ADDGEM or INSERTGEM where GEM is the original catchline. Alternatively, if there is time, the reporter can re-nose the story with new material, showing by its catchline – say, NEWGEM – that it is a later version. Following through, the subeditor will perhaps give the subbed version the catchline ZGEM so that it is not confused with the original story where both are retained in the system.

The reporter does not have to worry about line spacing or margins; these are allowed for automatically by the computer. It is important to capitalize or use quotes for any words or parts of the text that require it.

A warning (also mentioned elsewhere): do not type in abbreviations for words. They could finish up in the paper like that.

Construction. A well written news story should have an introduction, or 'intro', that takes and holds the readers' attention. This should contain the most essential point of the story and the one on which the sub-editor (see Chapter 7) will probably base the headline. A story in which the essential details, in terms of news value, are buried in the middle will need drastic editing and probably rewriting and will result in delay.

A reporter should not try to cram everything into the intro. He (or she) should not start with a quote; it is better given in the second paragraph. The place and occasion are also better left to the second or third paragraph unless they are themselves of news value.

An example of the wrong approach would be:

At Manchester yesterday the Archbishop of Canterbury said: 'I see advantages in a closer working arrangement with the Roman Catholic Church. I hope to make a statement to Convocation shortly about this matter.'

This would be more effective rewritten thus:

The Archbishop of Canterbury called yesterday for what he termed 'a closer working relationship with the Roman Catholic Church.'

He told a gathering of clergy in Manchester: 'I hope to make a statement . . . etc.'

A reporter should not begin an intro with details of the place and time, nor begin the story with a subsidiary clause:

Speaking at Manchester yesterday, the Archbishop of Canterbury said: . . . etc.

It slows the story.

A 'delayed drop' intro can be successful in an unusual or funny story – i.e. where the scene is set in low key to accentuate the contrast of the main fact when it is introduced perhaps in paragraph three.

Once the intro has been drafted (it can take some thought!) the story should thereafter run in logical sequence, giving first the details which the reporter considers the more important, with the lesser important facts towards the end. This will enable the sub-editor to cut the story from the end if the need for shortening it arises. With some stories of the more human interest or whimsical sort it is possible to have a deliberately contrived last paragraph which 'rounds off' the story.

Quoted sections should be clearly indicated and the names, style, titles and addresses checked and given in full. Words should not be abbreviated.

It might be asked what is the right length for a particular story? In some cases the news editor or chief reporter will give a general briefing where advanced information is available. Sometimes a story can be lengthened or shortened by consultation depending on how it develops during the coverage. With a number of stories of a fairly routine nature such as local inquests and court hearings, the reporter will be able to judge from the general news pattern of the newspaper the approximate worth of the story.

All guidelines have to be approximate. The input of news can be variable and there are days on some newspapers when the news flow seems almost to dry up and others when there is a rush of good stories. Either situation can force a quick reassessment of the length of some stories that are already being written.

Entering text. The use of direct input as a result of the change to computerized printing systems means that reporters now enter their text by the use of VDUs (visual display units). This enables the text to be stored directly in the newspaper's computer memory to await recall for editing and typesetting.

This should pose no difficulty to a reporter who has basic typing skills. A VDU (sometimes called a VDT, or visual display terminal or simply a terminal), has the same QWERTY keyboard as a typewriter, but has a monitor screen alongside it on which the words appear as they are typed, and on which the story can be scrolled back for checking. The device, in fact, is a great improvement on the typewriter since, by the use of simple keyboard controls, the work can be corrected and revised on screen so that a clean version can be filed without the need for retyping. This makes for faster presentation of text. More complex keyboards are used by sub-editors and those involved in the typesetting and page composition part of the system.

Where, because of urgency or lack of time, a story is telephoned in from a rough draft prepared on site, or from shorthand notes, it can be taken down by a copy-taker using a terminal, so that it is immediately entered into the office system. Many newspapers, however, now use portable work stations, which are mini terminals, complete with fold-down screens, which can be linked to the office computer by means of a modem attached to a public telephone line. The reporter simply dials for copy at the office and then enters the story. These devices are also useful for correspondents or freelance journalists who, for various reasons, might want to file copy from home.

Some special points for news reporters:

- Keep in touch with the news editor when you are out of the office covering a story. Telephone any new developments, changes or warnings of later copy. It can help in page planning.
- Draw the attention of the office lawyer to any point in your story which you think is legally worrying.
- Keep a copy of your story in your screen 'basket', and check it with the final version in the paper. Much can be learned by this.
- If you are not going to be in the office after writing your story, leave a telephone number where you can be contacted if any queries arise.
- Always carry your press card and a pencil and notebook. News can happen anywhere, any time.

The modern newsroom

The newsroom is the hub of a newspaper. It accommodates the reporters, each at a desk with a terminal and telephone, and is centred around the newsdesk at which sit the news editor (sometimes chief reporter on a local paper), the deputy, with perhaps senior reporters standing in and usually a

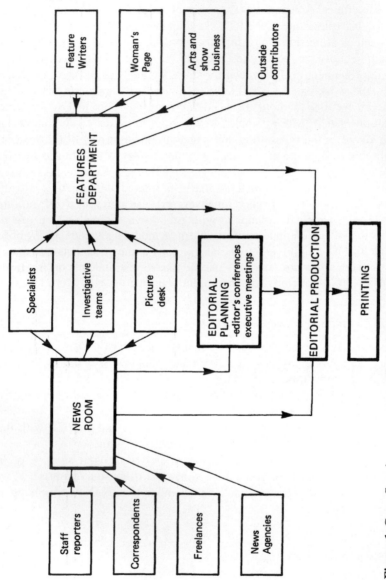

Figure 1 Copy flow in a newspaper office. The arrowed lines show the copy flow into the news room and features department, and thence to editorial planning and production

secretary. It also houses recent newspaper files and a few shelves of reference books and telephone directories. It has a regular messenger. As edition times approach, it is the scene of great noise and activity as keyboards clatter, instructions are given and telephone conversions are carried out (see Figures 1 and 2).

Role of the news editor. The news editor's job is to organize the news gathering and news writing activity of the day by assessing information at hand, briefing reporters and local correspondents, planning the coverage of stories in the light of the day's known schedule of news, and checking the finished work before it is passed to the sub-editors.

From the news diary the news editor prepares a daily news schedule for the information of the editor and senior colleagues. This shows the stories that are being covered and by whom. The news editor must also authorize any expenditure by reporters such as rail and air warrants for distant stories, payments to informants and requisitions for day-to-day funds.

The news desk spends a lot of time assessing the value of information telephoned in by correspondents, or even by members of the public, discussing the development of stories with reporters who ring in from locations, and reading agency copy. The extent and thoroughness of a paper's coverage is the responsibility of the news editor and as edition times approach his or her contribution to the copy flow is crucial.

On morning papers, both national and provincial, the newsroom works a long day, usually from about 10 a.m. until after the last edition has gone to press, maybe at 3.30 a.m. the following day. The duties of the news editor and deputies, and of the reporters, are divided into shifts, with some on early shift, a few on the 'night watch' and the bulk of shifts overlapping to give maximum coverage for the main part of the day.

Figure 2 A newsroom on line: terminals at the *Manchester Evening News*

News coverage. Despite the popular notion that news is the unpredictable, the likelihood of many news stories is known some time before and it is thus possible to assign reporters to them in advance. Such assignments are known as *diary jobs*. They include sittings of Parliament and courts, tribunals, committees, local councils and inquests, State and Royal visits, opening ceremonies, political speeches, the announcement of election results, sports fixtures, weddings, funerals and follow-ups to known news situations. What actually happens at these events, especially statements, decisions, results and speeches, is certainly new in the real sense of news value and the disclosure of this information will form a large part of the news content of the pages.

Tip-offs from the public or from local correspondents can alert the news desk to some newsworthy situations such as an unusual human predicament or a potential crime story. This sort of news may only be disclosed as a result of information from someone on the inside.

A considerable segment of news is, of course, impossible to predict. Under the general heading of *the unexpected* are stories of Government changes, sackings, industrial trouble, accidents, fires, sinkings and abductions, arrests, deaths and even wars.

The coverage of big stories such as general elections and types of disaster needs very detailed planning with the various 'ends' of the story allocated to reporters and investigators, pictures laid on, and copy and edition times plotted in advance. Often local correspondents will be asked to help in coverage.

Local correspondents: These are local paper journalists who are accredited by national papers, many provincial papers, and the news agencies (and also BBC and ITN News) to cover stories in their area as and when needed. This usually means when a staff reporter is not available or when the event is some distance from a branch office. Local correspondents are usually paid an annual retainer, a fee in return for which they make their services available when needed. They are also paid lineage for each story. This is a payment calculated on the number of lines of text published. Some correspondents will offer stories for use. In other cases they will write to an order from the news editor. Ordered stories are paid for whether they are used or not.

It is not usual for a local correspondent to work for two rival papers where a conflict of loyalties might occur. The idea is to obtain their exclusive services when needed.

Where to find it. News rooms have a collection of reference books most likely to be needed for checking information. If these are not sufficient the

Figure 3 All the news: sixteen news stories give good local paper value in this well filled *Kent Today* page. End-column briefs provide an eye-catcher for the busy page turner

office reference library will have an even more detailed collection. Such books will include for example:

The Arts:	*Who's Who in the Theatre*, the *Oxford Companion to Music*, the *Oxford Companion to English Literature*, *Encyclopaedia Britannica*, *BBC Year Book*.
Military:	The *Army List, Air Force List, Navy List*. Jane's *Fighting Ships*, Jane's *All the World's Aircraft*.
English Language:	The *Oxford* and *Webster's Dictionaries*, Fowler's *English Usage*, *Roget's Thesaurus* (good for headline words).
Geography:	*The Times Atlas*, Bartholomew's *Gazetteer of Great Britain*; any world gazetteer, *AA & RAC Handbooks*.
Business:	*Stock Exchange Year Book, Directory of Directors*.
Local Government:	*Municipal Year Book*.
Parliament:	Vacher's *Parliamentary Companion*.
Society:	*Debrett, Burke's Peerage, Who's Who?*
General:	*Whitaker's Almanac* (a treasure trove of national and political statistical information), L. C. J. McNae's *Essential Law for Journalists, Willing's Press Guide, Brewer's Dictionary of Phrase and Fable*, and *Crockford's Clerical Directory*.

Pictures

Pictures were part of news pages even before 1904 when the *Daily Mirror* began publishing actual news photographs rather than portrait studies which had been appearing in newspapers for about fifteen years.

Pictures give important information such as how a person or a place in a news story look, or what actually happened, more effectively than words in some cases and they thus supplement and extend the text. They can also be news in their own right.

Great news pictures like the shooting of President Kennedy, tower over the words. Many pictures which are good simply because of the combination of luck and skill on the part of the photographer, rather than because of their news value, equally earn their place in a newspaper.

Yet, with very rare exceptions, a picture, unlike the text, cannot stand alone without words to give it explanation and meaning. Sometimes a caption can make a picture. Pictures, however, can also be used – and misused – to create an emotive or conditioning effect in the reader's mind.

Picture desk. The picture set-up is a small-size replica of the newsroom with the picture editor (or chief photographer) presiding over the staff photographers who are assigned jobs in a similar way to reporters, and usually in conjunction with the newsroom.

The old plate camera had a long mileage with press photographers who prided themselves on its use, but today nearly all press work is done with advanced 35mm cameras, often with 'saturation' footage of the subjects.

Picture sources are supplemented by syndication agencies who give a daily service of pictures, and by office picture files when just a 'head shot' or a stock picture is needed.

Picture handling

The old idea of a wire-room handling the input and output of pictures has gone by the board as a result of computerization. As recently as the 1980s if a photographer were given a job away from the office he had to take with him a wireperson to operate the heavy transmitter, while back at the office a darkroom printer waited to unscramble the picture signal on the receiving drum and turn it into a print. Now it is all done by the photographer (see Figure 4).

The film is developed on the spot and the photographer uses a portable, highly miniaturized mobile transmitter (simply called a 'mobile'), connected by a modem to a telephone, to send the pictures in negative form down the line to the office. Transmission time varies but takes typically seven or eight minutes. On remote overseas locations a satellite telephone might be used. Soon, filmless cameras using only a chip will speed the process even further.

At the office, the images are received on an **electronic picture desk** (EPD), which in fact is a desktop computer, and are viewed by the picture editor on a television monitor. A choice having been made, the required shots can either be printed out on paper for conventional editing or be passed on electronically to the next stage in the production process.

The picture images are next sent to the scanning studio for electronic retouching as required, and for separations to be prepared in the case of colour. Where, as is now increasingly the case, newspapers are being made up on screen, the pictures are then 'imaged' into the pages to fit the spaces. In fact it is possible to.transmit pictures from anywhere in the world directly into the network of computers used in page production so that the first time a picture is seen as a print is when the newspaper comes off the presses.

News agencies

News agencies perform a useful service collecting and syndicating news and pictures to subscribing newspapers on an annual contract basis. Most countries nowadays have their own national news agency, some jointly

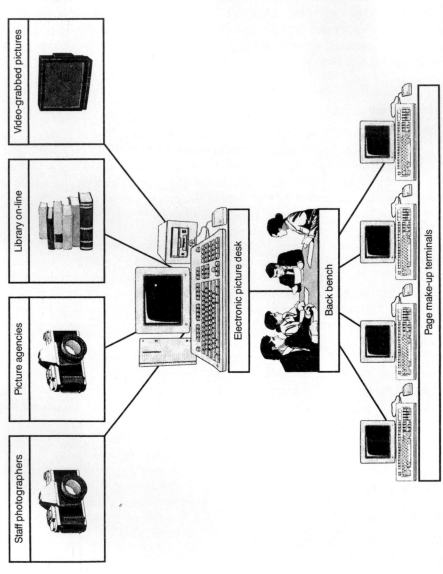

Figure 4 Pictures for the page: the electronic path that leads to the page terminals in a totally computerized system

owned by the various newspaper companies, others subsidized by the State. In Britain the principal national agency, the Press Association (PA), is co-operatively owned by the main provincial newspaper companies.

News is gathered through correspondents around the country and is edited and transmitted to newspapers from the PA's London headquarters on four services: news, financial news, sport, and pictures and graphics, plus a world news service of items concerning Britain and Ireland edited from Reuters and Associated Press. All services are on line in computer-ready text, with made-up screen-ready setting offered to subscribers for TV listings, city prices, sports statistics and weather details. In addition, the main services are available by teleprinter, now mainly for non-newspaper customers.

There is also a service for teletext screens and a faxback facility linked to PA's live news and sports databases by which newspaper readers can dial in for information updates.

The *big four* international agencies used in Britain – Reuters, United Press International and Associated Press from America, and Agence France Presse – provide for a world daily newspaper circulation of more than 450 million and a world broadcast audience in excess of 1,500 million. Reuters and UPI are the world's leading suppliers of newsfilm for television. They also sell directly to data banks and private subscribers, and their computerized financial services bring in important revenue.

Volume usage of international agency copy is heaviest in America where it is fed straight into newspaper computers or delivered directly to listeners by the 'rip and read' news services of local radio stations.

In Britain, most of the bigger newspapers take Reuters as well as the national agency, Press Association, and some perhaps one foreign agency. Staff writers are usually given preference by editors if they have covered a story, with the agency service either filling in the gaps in coverage or being used as a news monitor or to check stories. National newspapers with large reporting staffs use least agency copy.

Press Association is the main provider of national news and sport for provincial papers.

The international agencies are useful as initial spot news tipsters, which helps papers which are interested but who do not have a man on the spot. A newspaper may then send in a roving 'firefighter' correspondent. The reduction in recent years in the numbers of foreign correspondents maintained by Western countries has increased dependence of newspapers of all types on news agencies for news from abroad and the role of news agencies generally is expanding.

Agencies developed originally in the 19th century as part of the expansion of news coverage made possible by the building of the railways and the introduction of the telegraphic service in the 1840s. The first was the Havas Agency, which began business in Paris in 1837, eventually to be absorbed by Agence France Presse. Reuters was established in London in 1851.

Copy distribution. Agency copy enters the newspaper as part of the daily news input. The standard practice is to give each story numbered catchlines, and a dateline to show place of origin. A story might be followed by *Adds* i.e. later material – and maybe eventually a *New Lead*.

The more important running stories are transmitted under the following codes:

Flash:	The first brief indication of the story – maybe half a dozen words.
Rush:	The first actual details available – maybe a couple of paragraphs.
Snap:	Short messages giving brief details as they become available.
Rushfull:	The first full account based on the details so far available.
Full:	The full authoritative version.

Other news sources

The remaining input of news stories comes mainly from freelance contributors, foreign correspondents, material based on press hand-outs and official reports, and from pooled services within newspaper groups, to which reporters on each paper contribute.

Freelance contributors are self-employed journalists, often specialists who sell their work to various newspapers either for a one-off payment, or on a contract basis for a fixed programme of work, or for payment for shifts worked. Their main use is on work for which a staff reporter is not normally available. They might also work on stories such as those covering crime or medical or technological matters where their special skills are useful.

A few freelance writers might sell an idea to the editor and then be paid to write the story, but more often they are employed on a regular contract over a period because of their skills or contacts for a particular type of work. Sometimes they might work as part of a team including staff reporters. In other cases they might be engaged for holiday relief work on a casual basis for payment per shift worked.

Whatever the arrangement, most freelances, even the most successful ones, seek to establish themselves by a number of regular connections with newspapers, sometimes accepting an annual retainer in return for an option on their services when needed.

Foreign correspondents are mostly staff journalists, though they can be freelances. In a newspaper giving a good deal of space to foreign news such as *The Times* or the *Daily Telegraph* foreign correpondents are part of the network of coverage of key centres around the world and work under the direction of a foreign editor. In the provincial press and most popular national papers, foreign news is considered less important and full-time correspondents are rare and are often part of a group sharing arrangements, with direction coming from the news editor. In such cases while the correspondent will file the main stories, coverage is often ordered to suit the needs of particular news situations.

Hand-outs and reports. There is a steady flow of hand-outs and official reports into newspaper offices from company press officers, public relations agencies, nationalized industries and Government departments. In cases where their contents might contain information of news value to the readers they are given to a reporter or, in some cases, a specialist sub-editor, to form the basis of a news story. Official reports on social issues such as racism, poverty, unemployment and housing can be very important news stories in their own right by reason of their publication.

Geoffrey Harris and David Spark note in *Practical Newspaper Reporting*:

'You will find in the course of time that it is not unusual for someone to drop a 50,000-word report on your desk and expect a 1,000-word report by lunchtime.'[4]

Such writing requires a rapid assimilation of the material and an eye for those parts of it which are of concern to the readers – plus the ability to render this material quickly into a news story.

Objectivity and comment

The charge of bias in news coverage, which is made about newspapers from time to time, is difficult to refute satisfactorily. As we have seen, the very act of news selection involves a bias towards a certain content. Factors of geography, personality and a newspaper's special interests all play a part in this selection. No newspaper can say, therefore, that its pages represent an unbiased selection of world or national news. Nor can newspapers published in any other country, or under any other political system, claim this.

The problem of bias in the writing and handling of news emerged anew during the sittings of the 1976–77 Royal Commission on the Press in the course of a Working Paper commissioned from sociologist Professor Denis McQuail, which examined sociological writings on the Press.

Professor McQuail suggested that news bias had something to do with acceptance of 'standardized models' for news situations and the growth of 'news stereotypes' to which certain types of news were subconsciously made to fit. This situation was a consequence of the pressure of putting a newspaper together.

He quoted one source, G. Gerbner, who in a study of the French Press in Journalism Quarterly (1964), took the extreme view that 'there is no fundamentally non-ideological, apolitical, non-partisan news gathering and reporting system.'

Professor McQuail's own conclusion, after looking at a good deal of evidence, was that in view of the pressures at work in newspaper production 'it would be unrealistic to expect a newspaper to match the criteria of other branches of inquiry', which seemed to suggest the revolutionary theory that branches of academic inquiry were free of bias.

The sociologists' discovery of 'news stereotypes' – which, if they mean anything, mean an accepted framework of recognition against which news happenings can be spotted and classified – need not imply bias. Such 'stereotypes' can be merely shortcuts in copy-tasting or 'gatekeeping'.

The accepted political partisanship[5] of a newspaper, if it has one, need not inhibit a reporter from doing an objective job on his assignment provided he or she remembers that the function is to uncover facts and not to prove something.

To some extent newspapers have themselves to blame for the suspicion of bias that exists in the public's mind. An editor, if challenged, would say that the aim in news writing is to be objective, to present the facts as they are found, any arranging of them being for the purpose of readability. This is the reporter's job. Comment and analysis are reserved for experts who write articles, mostly under their own name, about the news or as background to the news. These are called features.

In practice this division is not sustained. Editors tend, on news pages, to present reports from experts writing under their own name which are more correctly pieces of comment and analysis and are therefore strictly features. The increasing use of news by-lines is an invitation to reporters to impose their own personalities and analysis on news situations and thus aspire to the rank of experts.

Thus a blurring of news with comment begins to take place which can give rise to accusations that the newspaper is guilty of bias in its news reporting.

It is unlikely that the human mind can ever be rid totally of subconscious bias. Nevertheless, where the reporting of news is concerned, the public has the right to expect objectivity as far as is humanly possible and a journalist has a duty to exercise it as far as he or she is able to.

Further reading

G. Harris and D. Spark's *Practical Newspaper Reporting* (Focal Press, 2nd Edition, 1993) remains a sound instructional manual for young reporters.

Interviewing is covered on pages 36–48 and news story structure on pages 49–74. The work of news agencies is considered in Oliver Boyd-Barrett's *The International News Agencies* (Constable, London, 1980), and of foreign correspondents and the news room in Jeremy Tunstall's *Journalists at Work* (Constable, London, 1971).

Terry Fincher's *Creative Techniques in Photo-journalism* (Batsford, London, 1980) and Martin Keene's *Practical Photojournalism* (Focal Press, 2nd Edition, 1995) are comprehensive on their subject. On the legal side, McNae's *Essential Law For Journalists* (Butterworth, 13th Edition, 1995) and Tom Crone's *Law and the Media* (Focal Press, 3rd Edition, 1995) are indispensable.

References

1 McNAE, L. C. J.: *Essential Law For Journalists* (Butterworth, London, 1995).
2 See Chapter 8 for use of VDUs in copy input under computerized systems.
3 BOYD-BARRETT, Oliver: *The International News Agencies* (Constable, London, 1980) p. 15.
4 HARRIS, G., and SPARK, D.: *Practical Newspaper Reporting* (Focal Press, 2nd Edition, 1993) p. 175.
5 See Chapter 10, pp. 160–2, on political partisanship.

3 The specialists

Non-news editorial content is traditionally classified as features. Under this heading come such strange bed-fellows as Lobby correspondents, in-depth investigations, readers' letters and horoscopes.

The one thing that newspaper features usually have in common with news is the element of timeliness. In the case of background or 'situation' features, which explain and give context to the news, the timeliness is obvious, even though a good deal of the content is already known or accessible. Such features would not have been written had the subject not been in the news.

Yet the link of timeliness extends beyond this type of feature. Take a regular motoring column for example. Here the writer is often concerned with the details and performance of a newly launched car or with the problems of motoring relative to the season, such as holiday arrangements, budget provisions, energy saving and so on.

Season is likewise relevant in gardening and fashion features. Cookery recipes are frequently concerned with seasonal ingredients and home decorating is usually tied to spring cleaning. Holiday articles are published when readers are planning their holidays and the paper is full of holiday advertising. Even the horoscopes centre around the forecasts for the day or the week. Above all, showbusiness features and sports gossip are pegged to the current shows and fixtures.

The element of timeliness can still apply where the serialization of a controversial book is concerned. The timing of its publication is the news peg. Diary, or gossip columns rest on their topicality.

There are exceptions – crossword puzzles and comic strips, for instance, which usually come under the features department. Even cartoons, however, often have news angles, and so have many readers' letters.

It can thus be said that in most cases timeliness is an element in newspaper feature writing which it shares with the news content.

There is another element present in a feature, whether it be a news background article, a profile of a new public figure, a personalized column or even an article on slimming, which divides it sharply from news writing. This is the presence of a point of view.

Developing a point of view requires an approach far removed from that in the news writer's mind. The feature writer assembles a number of facts, some current, some perhaps old, and some figures, quotations and descriptions and weaves from them a pattern of argument in order to come to a conclusion. The conclusion can be the explanation that lies behind a news story, behind some Government policy or current economic problem or simply behind someone's success.

A feature writer, you will notice, still requires facts and quotations from people though their newness is no longer the paramount consideration. The writer is still concerned with what people say or do, but for more selective purposes. He or she may produce some interesting new statistics, but these are a means to an end. Here the purpose is to illustrate a point of view. It is the argument and the conclusion that count.

A feature, in its broadest sense, is a piece of explanatory, deductive, writing from which bias is inseparable. It is a view of something printed under the writer's name, as opposed to a piece of news writing, which is an objective first-time disclosure of facts.

This does not mean that clarity and directness of language can be put aside. The language in its words and phrasing, however, does take on a more personal role as a result of the relationship between the writer, who is putting over a view, and the reader whose support he or she is soliciting.

Here is an example by John Beattie, in *Plus* magazine, of how argument and direct appeal to the reader can colour feature writing:

'If you feel like shedding a tear for the giant panda because it is one of nature's endangered species, then cry your eyes out for the latest victim – the humble dormouse! For this cheeky little fellow, bright-eyed and bushy-tailed, has been hit by years of intensive farming which have wrought an insidious change on the face of the British countryside, so altering the landscape that old wildlife habitats have been irrevocably damaged. Endless clouds of pesticides and chemical fertilisers, hedgerows ripped up in the name of agricultural efficiency and countless lost acres of toppled woodland – all have taken a steady toll of the common dormouse *muscardinus avellanarius* which has undergone a depressing decline over a number of years. . . .'

In a different market, this example from *The Times* Spectrum column shows how facts and figures can be harnessed as a means to an end:

'Patricia Healy and her husband Danny remortgaged their home to do it. Pauline and Ray Williams spent their £16,000 savings during a legal fight which lasted three and a half years. It took Leslie and Rose Hatcher two years to overcome the might of official indifference. And only last month

Robert and Carol Awcock tasted victory after spending £7,000 over 27 months. All the couples had proved, literally, that they have the courage of their own convictions.

'They have several things in common. All have suffered the tragedy or death of a son. None of them was prepared to accept an erroneous official decision not to charge the killer. And each family started a private prosecution. . . .

'As such prosecutions become more common . . . etc.'

Style

News writing style has a more universal texture than other forms of newspaper writing because of its factual and objective nature. Good news writing should not differ markedly from the *Daily Telegraph* to the *Daily Mail* or from the *Financial Times* to the *Birmingham Mail*. Popular tabloids such as the *Daily Mirror* and *The Sun* have the tightest construction because of the extreme strictures of space resulting from the type of layout. Here can be discerned a 'tabloid style' in which vocabulary appears at its most basic and usage at its most colloquial, particularly in human interest stories. Yet the general run of hard news in the popular tabloids has good pace and a texture not much removed from good news writing in the qualities. The main difference arises from the attempt in the popular tabloids to humanize situations through the use of colloquial words and selected facts to increase a story's acceptability to its readers.

Difference in style is more marked in features. Here the writing in quality papers and in certain provincial evenings and mornings rests on a wider vocabulary and a more sophisticated construction than in down-market papers. In either market choice of words is vital in the process of persuasion and presentation required of a feature. The writer uses words to play on the sensations of the readers, to give colour and rhythm. The length of the words and the use, or otherwise, of adjectives help the writer to inject either pace or languor into the writing.

The real movement in the writing, however, comes from sentence construction, from the harnessing of grammar to push forward the argument. The right words allied to fluent construction can give a sense of clarity, pace and commitment that carries the reader with it and makes the best feature writing – be it popular or quality – compulsive reading.

A feature writer, and particularly a freelance feature writer, having acquired the ability to harness words and sentence construction to his or her needs, must also develop an awareness of the readers at which the writing is aimed. A good feature writer is adaptable, knows or has researched the subject, and has reader-awareness, and should be able to address himself or herself to a variety of newspaper audiences.

Selling features involves a precise study of the market and a publication's requirements. A current copy of the *Writers' and Artists' Yearbook* (A. & C. Black) is useful for this, but publications should be bought and inspected before submitting material. Once achieved, a regular connection is the best source of a reasonable income.

The features department

Because of its many-sidedness, the features content in a newspaper often exceeds the space taken up by the news. In the supply of this material the features editor of a big daily performs a similar function to that of the news editor in the newsroom (see Figure 1, page 22).

The features editor briefs staff feature writers, orders material from freelances, sees to payments, discusses articles with writers, checks the finished product, and keeps a schedule of the day's or week's work and of forward projects for the information of the editor and senior colleagues.

Yet there are signs that this arbitrary division of editorial activity is no longer tenable. A number of features specialists – the staff fashion and motoring writers, for instance – might cover actual news events in their field and write an opinionated assessment that defies classification as news or as a feature. Staff reporters might be moved to in-depth investigations that tie them down for weeks and involve much detailed assessment of a situation which might have a 'news peg' but is a news feature rather than a report. We are entering here the area of the specialist and it is a long way from the features department of cartoons and crossword puzzles.

The difference is being recognized by the growth in national papers, and some of the bigger provincial ones, of such titles as assistant editor (special projects) and the creation of semi-autonomous departments for carrying out investigative work.

It is more suitable to examine these various aspects of newspaper practice under the heading of 'The Specialists' than that of feature writing.

Investigative reporting

Investigative reporting is the name usually given to detailed in-depth examinations, extending over a period, into given news situations. Examples might be gang protection rackets, practices in the used car trade or allegations of corruption in a local council, but the work can also involve 'social' situations such as drugs and sub-teenagers or loneliness and the aged.

The essence of this type of writing is the close attention to detail and the systematic interviewing of people involved and combining of documents so that a dossier is built up. It often involves skating near to the law in the search for information where the public interest is of over-riding importance. Frequently the information sought is being with-held by people who have a vested interest in its concealment or who are willing to utilize the law to stop their activities from being revealed.

Such work requires skilled and well-informed investigators who are really operating in the role of detectives. The work and the writing in a big project may be split up among members of a team, which can include staff writers and freelances, under the direction of a project editor who collates the material and welds it into the final report. It requires close legal checking.

The history of in-depth reporting goes back a long way in such Sunday papers as the *News of the World* and *The People*, where investigators examined a criminal's activities or a social problem over a period and finally produced a 'special report'. The technique was given a new meaning by the highly organized Insight investigations which began to appear in the *Sunday Times* in the 'Sixties. This was the first newspaper to allocate a team of reporters under a project editor to carry out investigative work on a regular basis with continuous forward planning. The investigation into the Thalidomide drug, which had caused the birth of deformed babies, was one of the great successes of Insight, and one which resulted in long litigation before the paper was allowed to print the results. Insight reports have won many awards.

Space is the limiting factor of the Insight method. The idea is to present text and pictures over two or more pages with the text running to 6,000 words or more. It is a form of journalism more suited to the fatter and leisure-orientated Sunday papers. Yet the influence of Insight techniques – what Harold Evans calls 'horizontal team work' – has been considerable in modern newsroom planning.

Parliamentary journalism

Nearly all daily and evening papers, national and provincial, cover Parliament either directly with their own staff or under group arrangements, the size of the team varying from one to as many as five according to a paper's requirements.

There are two sorts of specialist. First there is the Parliamentary reporter who sits in the press gallery of the Commons and takes a shorthand note of the debates which are of interest to the paper. Parliamentary reporters, with shorthand speeds of around 200 words a minute, work in teams, relaying copy either by telephone, typescript or direct wire and computer input in time for the various editions.

Secondly, there are the Lobby correspondents. They may attend some debates but more frequently they move around the corridors of the House of

Commons on the look-out for exclusive political stories. Lobby correspondents, of which there are about 80, some newspaper writers and some broadcasters, are so called because they are licensed by the Commons Serjeant-at-Arms to stand about in the Members' Lobby in order to make contact with MPs. They have a room of their own at the Commons and also their own association.

A lot of their information comes through private dealings with politicians and MPs and some from Whitehall press officers. Lobby correspondents are allowed to see in advance Government White Papers, Bills, announcements, reports and MPs' Written Questions. They also have meetings, sometimes twice daily, with the Prime Minister's press staff.

The understood thing about many of these encounters is that journalists may use information given to them without attributing it to a named source. This serves two purposes. Politicians can air views or policies without being held to them, and newspapers can get useful advance warning of political events or of likely legislation.

Lobby correspondents are only as valuable as their contacts. Each one has special sources which can be 'tapped' in the bars, restaurants or lobbies of the House. It is a world in which leaks and rumours abound, where today's speculative piece of Government intentions may become tomorrow's hard news, or where a disgruntled Minister may plant an off-the-record Cabinet 'leak' to serve his own ends.

Political newsgathering is described by a Lobby correspondent questioned by Jeremy Tunstall[1] as a 'market place' which involves both the giving and receiving of information. Mediating in this activity are the Whitehall PROs who might appear to be funnelling information to correspondents but who at the same time are protecting their departments.

Loyalties are important to Lobby correspondents, too, for a natural keenness to break a story must be tempered by the need to protect their sources with whom they may share certain confidences.

Some newspapers also have a Parliamentary 'sketch writer' who contributes a regular personalized or humorous column on activities in Parliament.

Showbusiness

The coverage of showbusiness news and gossip, particularly of television and the 'pop' music world, is especially characteristic of the popular national dailies and Sunday papers. It is part of their market strategy for attracting young buyers, and at the same time responding to the interests of the sort of family groups which form the bulk of their readers.

In seeking to rationalize a coverage which, to some, might seem disproportionate, it needs to be said that in bringing a wide range of experiences into the home by way of the screen, television has itself become a news factor. Its personalities and the controversy and discussion surrounding its programmes impinge on some people's lives probably more than any other activity. Items that appear on TV become talking points and spark off further news investigations and discussions. Thus television, as did the cinema in its heyday, becomes a source not only of gossip but of hard news stories with which many readers feel they can identify. Programme guides are a vital part of this coverage.

In like fashion the world of 'pop' music yields up personalities and news situations which are of interest to a significant number of young readers.

To cater for this demand most newspapers employ showbusiness reporters and gossip writers whose job is to seek out stories and features about the people in this field. It is a thriving area for freelances, some specializing in certain areas of showbusiness, and for the input of pictures into newspaper offices. It is also an area of some of the most banal and forgettable writing in British journalism.

Much of this is probably due to the 'stereotypes' with which the industry is bugged. Showbusiness is projected, and believed in, as a world of glamour which, though often illusory, perhaps compensates for the absence of it from many ordinary lives. Likewise, the well-loved television actor or 'pop' star enjoys a hero-figure status which is hard to discount except in the most serious forms of analysis.

To some extent the world of showbusiness itself is responsible for the unreality of these concepts since it is from actors' agents and managers that the information flows.

News management

With political journalism and showbusiness writing we encounter the dangerous shoals of news management, a hazard that also awaits a number of other specialist writers.

The management of news, and this also includes features material, strictly means the controlling or specifying of newspaper content from, and by, sources outside newspapers, often for ends in which the public good is not a consideration. The rapid growth of publicity and public relations techniques has increased the danger of news management cropping up in subjects where the newspaper is the catalyst between the news sources and the public.

Former Fleet Street editor Charles Wintour observes: 'The most difficult of all pressures for an editor to withstand is that of news management by practised hands who understand the media and want the paper to give a favourable slant to their activities.'[2]

People in showbusiness depend on publicity. The popular press finds their material attractive, accessible and in keeping with the market image of readers' tastes. Managers and agents, for their part, are happy to funnel stories and free pictures to showbusiness writers to give their clients an advantage. The process is oiled by free 'facility' trips where film-making is in progress, free tickets for shows and previews and often close personal friendships between agents and showbusiness writers.

All this does not necessarily mean that newspaper readers are being given managed news all the time but it does mean that some of the stories and pictures appearing in the popular dailies, for instance, have probably been planted. News management could be a factor in the lack of even minimal analysis which characterizes a good deal of popular showbusiness writing and the perpetuation of boring stereotypes in interviews: the 'comedy is fine but my ambition is to play Hamlet' theme, or 'now I've kicked drugs and have never felt better', or 'this really is going to be my big comeback.'

Press officers need to be watched in some fields. They can ease the job of news-gathering by providing an avenue between their client or company and the press. But avenues which can be opened can also be closed if a press officer feels it is not in his client's interests to talk to the press. Industry and town halls are areas which can hide behind a press officer whose job is to put their image in a beneficial light to the public. The chance of managed news in these circumstances is high.

There is a danger in accepting facility trips, not only in showbusiness but in the case of airlines, the motor car industry and even of foreign governments anxious to improve their image. There is a chance of writing a favourable account under the influence of the selective impressions that have been put before a correspondent by hosts.

It is Government, however, which as developed the most sophisticated responses to the Press. Lobby correspondents who terrorized Cabinets with their disclosures in the 19th century might find themselves today being used by politicians to plant a controlled 'leak' of information as a sounding board to the public for some Government policy idea.

The timing of speeches and press releases is carefully prepared by Whitehall Press officers to secure the best advantage, and some well known politicians have shown a skill little short of genius for manipulating the media for image-building purposes. Tunstall[3] says that 'journalists themselves sometimes point out that senior politicians spend much time and energy trying to get things into (or keep things out of) the newspapers and TV bulletins,' although he says too, that 'deliberate news management, while it may be successful on specific occasions, is subject to rapidly diminishing returns.' The assumption is that, in the end, a Lobby correspondent will suspend belief in a Minister's utterances.

Yet a Lobby journalist cannot afford to ignore what senior Ministers say, nor be sure at the time, without preternatural intuition, what is information 'on the level' and what is managed news. This was particularly so under the

Harold Wilson Governments when, as contemporary writers pointed out, the Prime Minister personally dominated Government Press relations. This did not mean that Lobby correspondents necessarily benefited. In 1965, for instance, the *Sunday Times* announced that it would be running a 'Whitehall Column' by Anthony Howard in which the activities of the various Government departments would be examined. After one column had appeared the *Sunday Times* was told that on Mr Wilson's instructions Howard would be given no further information. 'I'm not going to have Howard writing about my civil servants,' the Prime Minister was reported to have told an astonished Lord Thomson at a *Sunday Times* lunch.[4] The column ended abruptly.

Managed news is not necessarily harmful to readers. Much of it probably is useful information, yet there is a danger that where journalists lend themselves, wittingly or unwittingly, to manipulation, perhaps in return for favours granted, the public interest might not be being adequately considered. Great vigilance is needed, for instance, to keep news management from such sensitive areas as the City pages where planted stores about companies could have serious as well as beneficial consequences for investors.

One must beware of exaggerating the problem. News management is possible only in certain areas, and astute editors are aware of the dangers. Moreover, news and features stories go through much scrutiny before they are printed, and newsworthiness and the public interest are the yardsticks by which they are assessed for publication. Yet the danger will continue to exist in the writings of some of the specialists upon whose judgement a newspaper has to lean.

The critics

At the opposite pole to popular showbusiness writing comes the work of the arts reviewers, the critics, writing under their own names, who are concerned with the evaluation of new books, theatrical and musical performances, films, records, television and radio programmes and art exhibitions.

Arts reviewing is a highly specialized branch of journalism, more akin to the old technique of essay writing, with its own value concepts and frequently its own special terminology. Since most live performances are in the evening it has also, for morning papers, its own stringent deadlines.

The critics, many of them freelances, can be found, in one guise or another, in most newspapers, popular and quality, local and national. The arts in general usually get more space and more varied coverage in the quality press, and a review of a chamber music concert in *The Times* might seem a long way in writing style from an analysis of a new 'rock' record in the *Daily Mirror*. Yet there are factors common to both which enable us to examine the function of the reviewer.

Both these reviewers are concerned with:

1 The intentions of the composer/lyricist.
2 The texture and character of the music.
3 The interpretation given by the performers.

This breakdown can, with some adjustment, be applied to a number of art forms. Take a new play and the factors would be:

1 The intentions and message of the playwright.
2 The texture of the dialogue and construction of the play.
3 The interpretation given by the performers.

Or a film:

1 The intention and style of the director.
2 The camera work, dialogue and development.
3 The interpretation given by the actors.

The same formula can be applied to a TV or radio programme or a new record, whether classical, jazz or popular. With books and art exhibitions the formula would need to be adjusted but the reviewer would still employ a similar approach. For instance, he would be concerned with:

1 The intention, or message, of the writer (or the aim of the exhibition).
2 The style and texture of the writing (or the choice and aptness of the exhibits).

Thus, while the style of writing by critics varies considerably for the different reader/audiences, the basic things with which the reviewer would be concerned would have a good deal in common.

There are other factors that could be taken into account, where relevant, such as audience reaction and (though less likely) value for money. The latter would be important in gift-buying reviews.

The reviewer is providing a reader service; he or she is assessing the success or recommendability of the various performances and art forms. The reviewer has also an additional role – though this is not the prime intention of the editor – of being a sounding board for the various productions and publications for the benefit of the promoters. What a reviewer says is of great significance to publishers and theatrical managements where their investment is at stake.

First night tickets and copies of books and records are sent to reviewers with the hope that a 'good crit' will result. Reviewers thus find themselves in the position of a mediator between publisher and management on the one hand, and the public on the other. Yet no reviewer who wants to retain credibility dare recommend to the readers (and one must never lose sight of readership), anything that is patently unsuccessful or unsatisfactory, or is unsuitable for them, though there are cases of waspish theatre critics being denied tickets because they have stuck to their standards. There is really little likelihood of reviewers who value their job being in a promoter's pocket.

Women's pages

The women's pages in any newspaper accommodate a wide range of features material. The main story might be an interview or a human interest account, or a fashion-based consumer piece with perhaps a big picture. Consumer journalism – the assessing of products and services on behalf of the reader – provides the 'bread and butter' for these pages.

Special pages for women have been criticized by sociological writers for perpetuating an old-fashioned concept of women as a mother and housewife, and the modern tendency is to widen their scope so that women are not seen as perpetually presiding in the kitchen and looking after the children. Fashion is broadened to include clothes for the older women and even clothes for men (who do not normally have pages of their own). Marriage, morals, home economics and women's place in society are being dealt with in a more penetrating way.

Yet the popularity of women's pages of traditional style with readers, including men, as shown by polls and letters, and with advertisers, make editors shy away from a more 'lib' content.

An examination will show these pages to contain a wide practically-based service element covering such things as cookery, home decorating, medical advice, slimming, bringing up children, furnishing, wine-buying, hobbies and various forms of advice (see Chapter 4) which newspapers adapt to their particular readership needs. A more accurate name for them would be family pages.

Style and vocabulary in such writing can vary almost as much as the content, depending on the readership market of the newspaper.

Worlds apart

Two important areas of specialization which come neither under the orbit of the newsroom or the features department are those of sport and financial journalism. They have a good deal in common. Both usually have an autonomous head – the sports editor and the city editor. Both forms of writing contain a high proportion of comment and speculation, both present news items in their field in an interpretative rather than an objective fashion and both rely on special vocabularies and an assumption of special knowledge by the reader.

Sport usually has its own specialist staff for each type of sport, though on local papers, the newsroom and local stringers and freelances are recruited to help with a variety of match coverage on Saturdays. The sports editor controls page planning, sub-editing and production.

Sport is usually given a bigger proportion of total editorial space in national dailies and Sundays than in local papers, due mainly to its greater catchment area and the use of sports coverage to promote circulation in edition areas. Soccer, rugby, cricket, racing, golf and athletics can take up to a sixth of the space in a national daily and a quarter of the space in a popular national Sunday paper. Here, teams of casual sub-editors are employed to deal with the heavy editionizing of sport arising out of Saturday fixtures. The vocabulary and interpretive style of sports reporting is shown in the following examples:

> Clive Rees cut inside from Dacey's pass with Scotland in turmoil. The ball switched magically between Dacey again, then David Richards, Eddie Butler and then to Robert Ackerman. He completed the break, Mark Wyatt surged through on the over-lap and gave the final transfer to Elgan Rees . . .
>
> *(rugby)*

> Kevin Reeves had one solid 20-yarder touched wide by Mick Leonard and centre-back Caton found the net with a seventh-minute header only to be ruled offside.
> The tricks and illusions misfired, and when Hartford and Bodak combined at speed, centre-forward David Cross hit his close-range return embarrassingly 10 feet over Bodak's head . . .
>
> *(soccer)*

> Soon afterwards, Brewgawn raced clear and it became a Dickinson monopoly as the chestnut's four stable companions followed on.
> Captain John looked a big danger but made a mistake at the third last and had to settle for second. David Goulding said: 'He was very unlucky – nearly on the floor – and it took the stuffing out of him.'
> Jonjo O'Neill produced Wayward Lad to perfection to have every chance at the last, but the eight-year-old could do no more, finishing third . . .
>
> *(racing)*

'It is easy enough to report sport adequately; it requires inspiration and great care to report it really well,' write Geoffrey Harris and David Spark in *Practical Newspaper Reporting.*[5] Sport is an area where the pressure of deadlines and comparatively restricted content of each sporting activity make really first-class writing difficult to achieve. Yet modern journalism is noted for its great sports writing stylists.

Financial journalism is even more removed from the centre of a newspaper than sport. A national paper's City office is frequently housed in a separate building in the City. Many provincial papers take a group City service or, in some cases, a syndicated one from a City agency.

Financial journalists, many with economics degrees, have a tight specialization that normally has no overlap into other parts of the paper, although the City Editor might contribute a special feature to the general pages at times of economic problems or a big financial story. A City journalist's role is similar to that of a lobby correspondent. They work through contacts, briefings and inside information. Much of the writing, as with sport – and to some extent politics – is assessment and speculation. In this case it might be concerned with company plans, the money and commodity markets or the state of the economy.

The interpretative approach to financial news stories and the reliance on a special vocabulary and the reader's special knowledge is seen in the following examples:

> All in all, the outlook for A & GI looks brighter than for some time. Yet the share price is languishing at 245p, a hefty 95p down from its high of the year. The yield is a modest 2 per cent (covered 2.2 times), but for those seeking growth, now could be the time to move in.
>
> *(investment)*

> Sir Robert Clark, the merchant banker who now chairs UDS, was distinctly cool and in mid-February Ronson improved his terms to 14p cash. Two days later Sir James came in offering five of his own shares for every eight of UDS.
>
> Hanson have picked up around 7% of UDS since the tussle began. Acquiring the stores group would much strengthen their financial position and help them maintain their spectacular growth. So Sir James will not give up easily. The existing bid is already an ambitious move. But to raise it further would be stretching his paper to the limit.
>
> *(a take-over bid)*

> Uncertainty of outlook and the problems of borrowing customers dictate a period of consolidation. But balance sheet and turnover should continue to grow in real terms. In the UK Lloyds will improve productivity to meet impact of lower interest rates, and use service and innovation to counter competition for deposits from building societies and public sector.
>
> *(profit prospects in banking)*

The pundits

Opinion columnists are one of the most enduring survivals in British newspapers. The idea goes back to the earliest period of journalism when literary figures such as Swift, Steele, Addison, Defoe and their successors, sometimes under their own names or under pseudonyms which became famous, aired their views and prejudices on issues of the day (Figure 5).

Figure 5 The pundits: by-line columnists are projected on their name. They are encouraged to be controversial and give views which sometimes do not coincide with the paper's

Staff columnists today, some still writing under house by-lines, but generally with names well known to their readers, are given their head to write personalized and slightly barbed pieces about talking points from the news that happen to take their fancy.

The aim is to be readable and controversial and the result is often to cause violent agreement or disagreement among the readers, thus generating reader reaction. Feedback in the form of letters is one of the signs of the success of such a column.

Columnists are usually given scope to develop their own style and to express views which do not necessarily coincide with those expressed in the paper's 'leader' or editorial opinion. Successful columnists can operate their own opinion forum within the columns of the paper. In other papers such a column allows the editor an opportunity to air matters which are outside the normal pattern of editorial opinion.

The style can vary from the matey/personal to a terse epigrammatical delivery suited to the oracle-like wisdom in which some columnists specialize. This style of journalism, however, has never reached in Britain the status enjoyed by American special columnists whose authority is based on nationwide syndication.

Aspects of feature writing

The question, 'What makes a good feature?', is almost impossible to answer. If it depends on readership then horoscopes usually come out high in editorial surveys in popular national papers. So do women's page features which have been found in some papers to be read by an unexpectedly high percentage of men.

The reasons behind the use of certain features vary. Broadly they reflect the spectrum of interests of the modern newspaper which, as we have seen, are wide. On many national dailies and Sunday papers for instance, it is usual, from time to time, to invite well known public figures such as politicians, trade unions leaders and even churchmen to give their views on leading issues of the day. There is, in some offices, a tariff or 'going rate', in descending order of fees for ex-Prime Ministers, junior Ministers and MPs, and a similar one for archbishops, bishops and lower clergy, who might be invited to submit articles.

It is no secret that for various reasons, including the short time available, or gestation problems, the words of personalities in a few cases might be discreetly 'ghosted', following an interview, and then read, modified and finally signed by the contributor to indicate that he or she is satisfied that their style and views are faithfully represented. The practice differs little, perhaps, from the drafting of speeches for politicians by their advisers or the answers for Ministers at Parliamentary question time being prepared by Civil Service researchers.

There are some public figures, in fact, whose views are important and whose names are attractive but who are not brilliant performers with the pen or who are too busy. Such contributions, nevertheless, can give the public important opinions and ideas and lend a newspaper exclusiveness. They may also get the paper talked about, which has remained one of the aims of editors since Lord Northcliffe propounded the idea as a marketing factor.

The use of ghost-writers to present regular sports columns under the name of well known sportsmen who may not actually write the material, however, has caused concern for some years to the National Union of Journalists (to which most British journalists belong) on the ground that the employment of ex-sportsmen for this purpose threatens journalists' livelihoods. A union instruction is that columns by non-journalist sports writers should be used with an 'interview' credit to the reporter who 'ghosts' them.

Humour has a too infrequent part in newspaper features pages but some quality papers – the *Daily Telegraph*'s Peter Simple column is an example – publish it regularly. The idiosyncratic humorist does seem to belong to a declining newspaper race, though cartoons and comic strips retain their place, with a few such as Andy Capp and Peanuts becoming household names round the world. Humorous writing can be found in the work of political sketch writers in some papers.

Chequebook journalism

An aspect of the competition among national papers, particularly Sunday papers, has been the spending of money to secure serial rights of notable books, or 'confessions' of the famous, to run as circulation boosters. Over the years this has put before readers works including Churchill's War Memoirs, a selection of political diaries and a great number of showbusiness life stories. Even fiction has been bought up from time to time. The *Sunday Dispatch* created a record just after the war by running *Forever Amber*, a bawdy period novel, for nearly 60 weeks.

It was in the field of criminal 'confessions', however, that big money payments for circulation boosters became tainted with the description of 'chequebook journalism'. A series of notable court cases, starting with the William Vassall spy case in 1962 and culminating in the Christine Keeler–Stephen Ward scandal the following year, provided some vintage 'confessions' which brought the press into conflict both with Parliament and the law.

After the jailing of Vassall, an Admiralty clerk and a homosexual, for 18 years for passing secrets to the Russians, the *Sunday Pictorial* (now *Sunday Mirror*) appeared with a series of articles under the traitor's name headed, 'Why I Betrayed My Country.'

In the debate on the findings of the Radcliffe Tribunal, which inquired into the Vassall affair, the then Leader of the Opposition, Mr Harold Wilson, condemned the Press for 'this odious practice of buying for large sums of money the memoirs of convicted criminals'.

In reply to a Parliamentary question a few weeks later, Lord Hailsham, Lord President of the Council, said he would welcome any consideration the Press Council (see Chapter 10) felt able to give to the matter.

Later in 1963 the War Minister, Mr John Profumo, resigned from the Government following a scandal involving call-girl Christine Keeler. The *News of the World* afterwards ran for several weeks 'The Confessions of Christine Keeler', for which they were said to have paid her £23,000. Mr Stafford Somerfield, editor of the *News of the World*, defended his action in publishing the Keeler 'Confessions' on the grounds that the story was news, the facts were authentic and 'in order to provide the facts the newspaper had to pay'.

In an interim statement on the Keeler affair, the Press Council, which said it had received complaints, deplored the 'excessive prominence given to . . . people concerned in the prostitution and vice revealed in this case,' and the 'publication of personal stories and feature articles of an unsavoury nature'.

At this stage the Press Council was undergoing reconstitution following the recommendations of the 1962 Royal Commission and did not resume formal meetings until January, 1964. Finally in 1965 the Council issued a special statement which contained the words: 'The Council unhesitatingly condemns as immoral the practice of financially rewarding criminals for disclosure of their nefarious practices by way of public entertainment. Crime is antisocial and it cannot be other than wrong that an evildoer should benefit

– often times substantially – by offences against the community. These payments for revelations by the notorious might also be held to constitute and encourage others.'

The Council reinforced this adjudication a year later by issuing a 'Declaration of Principle' following the discovery that a newspaper had signed a contract with the principal Crown witness in the Moors Murder trial, in which Ian Brady and Myra Hindley were accused of the particularly gruesome murder of several children.

The *News of the World* issued a statement saying that it was the paper involved. After being pressed in Parliament to bring proceedings against 'such newspapers' the Attorney General, Sir Elwyn Jones, said the possibility of making changes in the law to this end was being examined, but he added: 'I hope that, even before any Government action is taken, Fleet Street will now put its house in order.'

It was thought later that direct Government action against the press was averted by an undertaking from the new chairman of the Press Council, Lord Devlin, to issue assurances in the form of a Declaration of Principle to which would be given the support and consent of all editors of national and provincial newspapers.

The Declaration, issued in November 1966, took into account the comments and suggestions made by the editors and it spelt out three principles:

'1. No payment or offer of payment should be made by a newspaper to any person known, or reasonably expected, to be a witness in criminal proceedings already begun, in exchange for any story or information in connection with the proceedings until they have been concluded;
2. No witness in committal proceedings should be questioned on behalf of any newspaper about the subject matter of his evidence until the trial has been concluded;
3. No payment should be made for feature articles to persons engaged in crime or other notorious misbehaviour where the public interest does not warrant it; as the Council has previously declared, it deplores the publication of personal articles of an unsavoury nature by persons who have been concerned in criminal acts or vicious conduct.'

Though the Declaration was invoked several times in the years following 1966, including an occasion in 1969 when the *News of the World* was censured for publishing extracts from a further book by Christine Keeler, the Press Council was able to claim to the Royal Commission in 1976 that as a result of its actions standards had improved. In its evidence the Council said that 'there had been a decline in certain kinds of complaint (to the Council) and in the degrees of gravity within complaints relating, for example, to chequebook journalism.'

The National Union of Journalists, which had condemned the practice of chequebook journalism as long ago as 1962, was less satisfied that voluntary control administered by the Press Council was sufficient. At the 1982 Annual Delegate Meeting, when the subject again came up for discussion, it passed a resolution that . . . 'This ADM believes that recent examples of chequebook journalism have demonstrated the futility of relying on self-imposed disciplines by the media industry to curb this abuse, and calls for the introduction of legislation which would require publishers to disclose full details of any contracts they have entered into in order to procure information for publication where such information derives from, or is connected with, any recent, current or pending criminal proceedings.'

The resolution added that the ADM 'believes that such legislation should incorporate also the principles enunciated in the Press Council Declaration of November 1966.'

The Press Council's 60,000-word report into newspaper coverage of the Yorkshire Ripper murder case, published in February 1983, added further fuel to the controversy with a serious criticism of the Press for its harassment of Peter Sutcliffe's (the Ripper's) family and the family of his last victim, and its attempts to buy up stories from them and from colleagues of Sutcliffe. Some of these people, the report pointed out, were at the time likely to be witnesses at the trial.

After censuring a number of Fleet Street papers, and also the *Yorkshire Post*, for their behaviour, the Council announced that it has extended the Declaration of Principle barring payments for articles to persons engaged in crime so that in future it would also be wrong 'that persons associated with the criminal should derive financial benefits from trading on that association'.

The revised Declaration went on:

'What gives value to such stories and pictures is the link with criminal activity. In effect the stories and pictures are sold on the back of crime. Associates include family, friends, neighbours and colleagues. Newspapers should not pay them, either directly or indirectly through agents, for such material and should not be party to publishing it if there is reason to believe payment has been made for it.

'The practice is ·particularly abhorrent where the crime is one of violence and payment involves callous disregard for the feelings of victims and their families.'

In a long article in *The Journalist*, organ of the NUJ, a few weeks later, Ken Morgan, the Director of the Press Council and former General Secretary of the NUJ, underlined the dangers to the Press. The Press Council's findings, he said, 'offers newspapers a final warning: put your house in order, toe the line with a voluntary non-statutory Press Council that is consistent with Press freedom, and demonstrate your responsibility

– or face the likely consequence of statutory legislation covering newspapers' payments and contents and journalists' conduct'.

The message appeared to strike home with editors. After the furore about the Ripper murder case in 1983 and the Press Council's toughened-up Declaration of Principle (to which editors subscribed) complaints about the excesses of chequebook journalism ceased to be one of the charges levelled against the press. When the Calcutt Report came out in 1990 (see page 167) Parliamentary agitation was concerned entirely with the issues of intrusion and privacy and the right of reply by complainants.

Upon the demise of the Press Council following the report's recommendations, the new Press Complaints Commission, however, included in its code of practice for the press a section entitled, Payment For Articles. It said:

(i)   Payments or offers of payment for stories, pictures or information should not be made to witnesses or potential witnesses in current criminal proceedings or to people engaged in crime or to their associates except where the material concerned ought to be published in the public interest and the payment is necessary for this to be done.

The public interest would include:
(a)   Detecting or exposing crime or serious misdemeanour.
(b)   Detecting or exposing anti-social conduct.
(c)   Protecting public health and safety.
(d)   Preventing the public from being misled by some statement or action of that individual or organisation.

(ii) "Associates" include family, friends, neighbours and colleagues.
(iii) Payments should not be made either directly or indirectly through agents.

Further reading

The work of specialist correspondents is researched and discussed in Jeremy Tunstall's important book, *Journalists at Work: Special Correspondents* (Constable, London, 1971) pp. 74–249. His book *The Westminster Lobby Correspondents* (Routledge and Kegan Paul, London, 1971) also has useful insights. The early days of Insight investigations is related in *The Pearl of Days, a memoir of 150 years of the Sunday Times* by Harold Hobson and others (Hamish Hamilton, London, 1972) pp. 374–88. Brendan Hennessy's *Writing Feature Articles* (Focal Press, 3rd Edition, 1995) has sections on reviewing and other feature specialisms, particularly for freelances. There are some useful notes on amateur theatre reviewing in G. Harris and D. Spark's *Practical Newspaper Reporting* (Focal Press, 2nd Edition, 1993) pp. 192–5.

A more general analysis of feature writing in provincial papers is given in Ian Jackson's *The Provincial Press and the Community* (Manchester University Press, Manchester, 1971) pp. 176–200.

Two American textbooks offer useful advice to the freelance: A. C. Schoenfeld and K. S. Diegmueller's *Effective Feature Writing* (Holt, Rinehart & Winston, New York, 1982 Edn), and Betsy Graham's *Magazine Article Writing* (Holt Rinehart & Winston, New York, 1980).

Style is dealt with in Nicholas Bagnall's *Newspaper Language* (Focal Press, 1993). There is also an excellent exposition on style in Ted Bottomley and Anthony Loftus's *A Journalist's Guide to the Use of English* (Express and Star Publications, Wolverhampton, 1971) pp. 3–12. William Strunk Jnr and E. B. White's *The Elements of Style* (Collier Macmillan, London and New York, 3rd Edition, 1979), pp. 66–85, remains useful. See also Hennessy, above, on style and structure.

References

1 TUNSTALL, J., *The Westminster Lobby Correspondents* (Routledge & Kegan Paul, London, 1970), p. 44.
2 WINTOUR, Charles, *Pressures on the Press* (Andre Deutsch, London, 1972), p. 44.
3 *The Westminster Lobby Correspondents*, p. 15.
4 HOBSON, Harold (and others): *The Pearl of Days, an intimate memoir of the Sunday Times, 1822 to 1972* (Hamish Hamilton, London, 1972), pp. 417–21.
5 HARRIS, G. and SPARK, D., *Practical Newspaper Reporting* (Focal Press, 2nd Edition, 1993) p. 161.

4 The reader

The phrase 'reader participation' is applied by editors to a variety of activities which generally mean getting the reader to help produce the sort of newspaper he or she will want to buy.

Up to the late 19th century, national newspapers were primarily intended as journals of influence (except for some of the Sunday papers). It was popular mass circulations, starting with Northcliffe's *Daily Mail* in 1896, that first made readership size an area of concern to editors and proprietors. Under the Northcliffe formula you maximized readership in order to provide lucrative mass advertising. The resulting income enabled the owner to sell the newspaper at a cover charge below the cost of production, which stimulated still higher sales and made the paper even more attractive to advertisers.

Northcliffe wooed readers deliberately and extravagantly and he achieved the world's first one million circulation with the *Daily Mail* to prove the success of his ideas. He is credited with inventing newspaper canvassing, which came to have such a damaging effect on the image of the Press during the circulation war of the 1930s, and also give-away prizes to persuade readers to commit themselves to regular purchase. The Northcliffe hat and phials of Jordan water were among the more bizarre gimmicks that helped to get his newspapers talked about.

Northcliffe, however, also realized the value of readers' letters and advice columns as ways to readership loyalty. He had seen them used for the first time on a national scale in Sir George Newnes's pioneering family magazine *Titbits*, to which he contributed as a young journalist in the 1880s. His passion for giving his readers advice and instruction reached its peak in the publication of the *Harmsworth Encyclopaedia* (he was at first Alfred Harmsworth), with which he helped to advance self-education.

The modern newspaper has come a long way from the emergent consumer society of the early 1900s. The new popular press then undoubtedly saw itself as the torchbearer of instruction for the literate proletariat produced by the late 19th century schools reform.

Today, concern about readership is just as great but the parameters have changed. Society is more complex and mature, and more varied, in its taste and needs. New subtleties of method mean that wooing readers is no longer getting someone to sign on the dotted line in return for a set of Dickens or a Box Brownie camera. What sort of readers are newspapers selling to; how much do they earn; what are their jobs, and what do they spend their money on? These are the sort of things that have come to be important.

National papers, in particular, have become market conscious. In response to this development they have divided more sharply into popular and quality newspapers and within these areas divided again so that there are significant variations in the profile of readership between, say, the *Financial Times* and *The Guardian*, or between the *Daily Mail* (as it now is) and *The Sun*.

Behind this is the need, from a purely commercial point of view, to achieve a market identity as a weapon in the quest for advertising, which has remained the principal source of newspaper income since the adoption of Northcliffian economics.

The adman's view of the reader

Market research is the basis of modern advertising practice. The sample survey, developed by American agencies between the two world wars, became the means of relating people's taste and spending power to the marketing side of the manufacturing and service industries. The process was stimulated in Britain by the launching of commercial television in 1955.

John Goulden[1] in his book *Newspaper Management*, wrote:

'The vigour and ruthlessness with which British television companies tackled the selling of television advertising time shocked many in the newspaper world ... Audience measurement, studied psychology in advertising marketing areas and market techniques, had arrived.'

Today, newspaper advertising is a complex and technical business in which readership is analysed in detail to assess its market potential for every conceivable type of product. The basis of this assessment is the National Readership Survey formerly carried out by the Joint Industry Committee for National Readership Surveys (JICNARS) and taken over in 1992 by National Readership Surveys Ltd, a company set up on behalf of the various sides of the newspaper, magazine and advertising industries.

The method used is the random, or interval, sample in which people in each location are selected at arithmetical intervals from a list of names and addresses such as an electoral roll, and are then interviewed. This 'every nth name' principle is considered to give a more accurate cross-section of the population than any other method of sampling.

The National Readership Survey[2] reflects social grades, which are considered important in advertising. These place readers of national and the bigger provincial papers in six classifications based chiefly on the occupation of the head of the household or chief wage earner:

A   *Upper middle class* (3 per cent): higher managerial, administrative or professional.
B   *Middle class* (15 per cent): intermediate managerial, administrative or professional.
C1 *Lower middle class* (24.7 per cent): supervisory or clerical, and junior managerial, administrative or professional.
C2 *Skilled working class* (27.1 per cent): skilled manual workers.
D   *Working class* (17.3 per cent): semi and unskilled manual workers.
E   Those at lowest levels of subsistence (12.9 per cent): state pensioners or widows (no other earner), casual or lowest grade worker, the unemployed.

The questions asked in the survey are based on the occupation and spending patterns of the population of Great Britain aged 15 and older. To advertising people, they indicate the likely spending habits of people when confronted with various advertisements.

Other surveys in advertising measure the 'take up' of goods and services and reader response to given campaigns. The effect of newspaper advertising is analysed area by area. Newspapers are tested for the strengths and weaknesses of their readership, or the size of their readership age groups. Specific placings of advertisements – front half of paper, outside edges of pages, right-hand side, spread, solus positions – are tested and are reflected in rate cards in an elaborate system of premiums or 'loadings', with discounts for certain days.

The reader is thus seen as a unit of consumption, a marketing statistic, a percentage figure on a wall chart, which information can express volumes to the advertising agency and its clients.

During the 1990s, however, readership profiles of newspapers based on the National Readership Survey (NRS) were having to be adjusted to take account of the fact that unemployment had affected all social grades.

The editor's view of the reader

There is a gap in sympathy and values between the advertising man's view of the reader and the editor's. Nevertheless, the editor is influenced, to some extent, by the statistical information that is available in the National Readership Survey. The fact that a newspaper is shown to have a predominantly A and B class readership profile, or has the highest percentage of D class readers, or even that an up-market paper may turn out to have a higher than expected percentage of C2 readers, is important. The editor would be unwise if editorial planning were allowed to fly in the face of strong statistical information suggesting a certain social structure in a paper's readership.

Under the influence of the NRS classifications, editorial attitudes harden against wild experiments in reader appeal that could take a newspaper away from its social stance and it tends to become more firmly committed to its readership market, or to specialize further in the direction in which it was already tending.

It is uncommon for a newspaper to undertake a radical change in its readership appeal except as a desperate measure if it is suffering a disastrous drop in circulation. It is interesting to note that as early as 1949 the Royal Commission on the Press[3] of that year gave the opinion that it was the personality of a paper that made people buy it:

> 'A newspaper can act as the vehicle of another personality, whether that of editor or proprietor, only within the limits set by its own. It cannot radically alter its character without destroying itself.'

There have been cases where a subtle shift in appeal within the general pattern has helped. The *Sunday Times*, under the Thomson ownership, in the 1960s and 1970s, broadened its readership spectrum successfully and gained circulation. *The Times*, under the Murdoch management, moved in the same direction during the price 'war' of the mid-90s and lifted its sales. The *Daily Express*, on the other hand, was unsuccessful when, in the 1970s, it moved first towards the *Telegraph*'s market and later towards the *Mirror*'s market in attempts to bolster its declining sales.

In recent decades, of the British national dailies, only *The Sun* has changed its whole character successfully. After it was bought by Rupert Murdoch from the International Publishing Corporation (IPC) in 1969 it moved perceptibly down market and into a younger age group and was able to reverse dramatically the circulation losses it had suffered under its previous market image.

Having acknowledged the influence of the NRS classifications in the concept of readership groups it has to be said that the editor's view of the reader is in other respects quite different from that of the advertising interest. It is a more caring, anxious relationship. At the editor's daily conference the reader emerges not as a unit of consumption but as a being of flesh and blood who has the freedom to choose which paper he or she wants to read or to read none at all.

The advertising agency does not have to persuade people to read any given newspaper. It merely has to identify where the readers are, what their tastes and likely spending habits are and to take the clients' business to them. In this case the statistical approach makes sense. For the editor, the reader is an individual who needs to be persuaded, helped, informed, advised and entertained, and who may, if the contents of the paper fail to attract, be lost. Here, reader participation becomes a meaningful phrase in the daily business of making a newspaper. And it is here that one of the crucial worries of an editor lies. For under the modern market-conscious ownership of newspapers editors who fail to attract or hold readers may be relieved of their job, particularly in the competitive national field (see Chapter 5, pages 69–72 on editorial independence).

The following sections describe some of the ways in which an editor may try to secure and hold readers' interest and loyalty.

Service columns

Consumer journalism is the name sometimes given to the area of a newspaper in which specialist writers advise readers on what to wear, eat, drink, drive, make, spend their money on or do in their leisure time. These are the service columns, so called because the specialist writer, either retained as staff or hired as a freelance, gives advice and instruction to the readers, thus offering a service.

The concept behind a service column is that the expert is familiar with the latest, most useful, most effective, best value etc., of the products, services or methods being considered and can therefore save the reader time, disappointment or even money. The writers must have a thorough knowledge of the field so that the writing can be seen to be authoritative and relevant to the readers' needs and – most of all – reliable. A reader wanting to buy a pet, a motor car, take a holiday or invest some money must be able to ask for information in the full confidence of being soundly advised.

There is no doubt that those service columns which deal in merchandise, or that are likely to lead to its purchase, are an attraction for advertisers. To a media space buyer they are an essential part of a paper's profile. Yet the job of the service columnist is to serve the reader, not the advertiser. Where actual products are mentioned – fashion garments, cars, any goods that can be bought – it is important for the writer not to favour repeatedly any one manufacturer or source. Such partiality is quickly spotted by readers and editors and the writer's intentions become suspect (see Chapter 5, pages 80–1 on advertising supplements).

The style of writing in service columns should be simple and informative since the column is often brief. It should contain information relative to the moment. The gardening writer cannot afford to neglect pruning time or the fashion writer the onset of spring.

It was considered at one time that such columns were more necessary in popular national papers whose readers were less resourceful or less educated and therefore more in need of help. Nothing is further from the truth. They cut across the board, though the subjects may change from paper to paper as they have changed with taste and circumstance over this century.

Among national dailies, the *Financial Times*, for example, devotes much of its Saturday issues to columns of advice for its readers on tax, investment, the running of small businesses and answering a variety of inquiries about money. The *Daily Mail* has a weekly section on similar topics. The quality dailies and Sunday papers devote space to book, theatre, film and music reviews.

Spring marks the seasonal appearance of home maintenance columns in the popular Sundays. 'Agony' columns – the perennial advice to the young in love or those with sex or compatibility problems – are a feature of the popular tabloids, as also are horoscopes, while holiday, gardening and motoring columns appear in all manner of newspapers. So, also, do articles on fashion, food and drink.

Provincial evenings, mornings and weeklies likewise add their quota to the torrent of advice to readers.

The writers of service columns need to have qualifications or special experience in their subjects. They can be journalists primarily, as in the case of most motoring and travel writers and writers on fashion, home and beauty. Or they can be experts primarily who have found a market for their knowledge through a facility with the pen. In this category come most writers on cookery, gardening, medical and legal advice and the more esoteric areas covered by some papers such as wine-making, bridge and coin collecting.

The more important of the service columnists, the fashion, motoring and travel writers for example, might also be expected to provide news stories in their field during their week's work – a new motor car being launched, a human interest story of holiday mishap or a new fashion trend exemplified by an exclusive picture. Almost invariably they stick to their own field in which the contacts they build up, and the reader rapport, are of value to their paper.

The more specialist and less newsworthy areas are often covered by outside or freelance contributors on a fee per column basis usually with a contract or retainer as well. Such specialists, depending on the terms of their contracts, may write for other publications such as magazines, local papers or even give radio or television programmes, though they may not, as a rule, work for newspapers in direct competition. Some may even syndicate their work through an agency and perhaps sell it abroad.

A newspaper's choice of service columns depends upon the model of the reader implicit in the editor's planning, and it is possible to learn a lot about a newspaper by observing what service columns it carries.

The characteristics of nearly all such columns are their regularity, their standard typographical presentation and often their position in the paper and the page. They need to be found and recognized instantly by those they seek as regular readers. Most of them deal with readers' inquiries which, in turn, generate correspondence, and a consideration in the fee to an outside contributor is the need for secretarial help in dealing with mail.

Whether the writer pegs a column on to readers' letters or whether the columnist deals with these separately they must not be neglected. This form of participation is vital to the editor's view of the reader.

Readers' letters

Letters from readers (Figure 6) flood into newspaper offices in their thousands each week. A single topical subject on which views are invited in a national daily can bring in 3,000 in a few days. The sheer administrative problem of opening, sorting and answering them all has resulted in most national papers having a correspondence department, or central registry, staffed by journalists, clerks, secretaries and even a typing pool, working all day. In addition the more popular columnists might have one or two secretaries dealing solely with their own mail.

The Mirror group of newspapers, embracing the *Daily* and *Sunday Mirror, The People* and *Sporting Life*, for example, has a department staffed by full-time experts who answer readers' queries on a wide range of things such as divorce, compensation claims, tenancies and wills. The department also carries out research for the columnists on the group's papers.

The quality national papers are not exempt from this flood of correspondence. Each has its correspondence department staffed by two or three journalists, together with secretaries and typists. That at *The Times*, whose famous letters column is the attraction, deals with more than 50,000 letters a year, and the number is growing. (It would seem that a letter to *The Times* has about a one in twenty chance of publication.) The editor of *The Times* takes

Figure 6 Involving the reader: letters columns are a well read part of any newspaper. They also help editors to 'listen in' to their readers

a close personal interest in the column and each letter published is carefully checked. The same system applies at the *Daily Telegraph*, which also receives more than 50,000 a year and where the editor takes an interest in the selection of those to be published.

Generally, letters are acknowledged whether they are addressed to the editor, to a columnist or to various features in a newspaper. Thus, in one way or another, a reader who seeks a reply or a piece of advice or information will get it. This is regarded as most important.

Most papers run a regular 'letters to the editor' column. This is apart from any special letters features such as advice columns or showbusiness 'viewpoints' that might be used. Such a column is a selection of the general letters addressed to the editor on a variety of subjects, some personal, some on topics of the day, some criticizing or blaming the paper, some offering what the writer believes is interesting information, others just pieces of chat from lonely people whose newspaper is their contact with the world beyond the end of the street. Popular national dailies get around 500 to 1,000 such letters a week.

Obviously not every letter addressed to the editor is read by the editor. The volume of the daily post would make this impossible but it is the job of the editor's secretary to sort through the mail and draw attention to those the editor should read. The editor will personally sign a good number of the replies and leave a secretary to sign the less important ones. Letters seeking advice will be passed to special writers dealing in this field with perhaps a note sent first to the writer.

Some newspapers count and list letters under subjects in a daily or weekly report filed for reference. This shows what matters and what aspects of the paper have occupied the readers' minds. It can be a useful source of statistical information in editorial planning.

An important stage is the short-listing of letters for the 'letters to the editor' column. This job is done by an experienced journalist sometimes in conjunction with the editor. It can be time-consuming but it can uncover letters which may have in them the germ of a news story, about which the newsroom is then alerted.

The column may have a regular slot or a title such as Your Opinion or Readers' View, and the space available will be known in advance. The aim is to have a balanced selection with a variety of topics, though 'runs' of letters may be used on a subject that may have taken the readers' fancy or have stemmed from a letter in an earlier column. Such vigorous correspondence sometimes has to be formally closed with an editor's note.

Few readers realize that most newspapers do not have the space to print letters at great length. Reducing them to their essential points (and keeping the style) has to be carried out with great care so as not to distort or misrepresent the writer's view. *The Times*, for instance, cuts letters only with the consent of the writer.

The Press Council (and Press Complaints Commission) have had many complaints over the years about readers' letters. The Press Council declared that while an editor has discretion to select letters for publication, that discretion must be properly exercised. There is no right for anyone to have a letter published. A person who has been subjected to an attack in a newspaper's columns, however, has a moral right to space for a reasonable reply.

Adjudicating on one complaint about deletions from a letter, the Press Council said it was 'desirable, where practical, to obtain consent from a correspondent to any substantial alterations to his letter'. The Council also ruled that editing should be done solely to qualify a letter for publication, and it should never be allowed to defeat or obscure the point or points which the correspondent wanted to make.'

In fact, letters published in national papers are usually checked back with the writer not only to verify their contents but to ensure that some, which may give personal details, are not fakes. Fake letters to newspapers are not uncommon and a telephone call or a check call by a local reporter can save a lot of trouble.

Some newspapers and many magazines pay a small fee for each letter published but it is doubtful if this significantly 'improves' the number of letters which lend themselves to use in the column. An exception would be a letters 'stunt' in which correspondence on a certain subject is solicited to make a feature in which each letter published is paid for.

A fee can attract cranks and 'professional' letter writers who are sometimes blacklisted as 'not to be used.' Such correspondence is not much use as a guide to readers' tastes and views.

Apart from the reader participation aspect, letters columns have proved by in-house surveys to be among the most popular parts of both the national and the provincial press. In a survey of local paper letters columns, Ian Jackson[4] found them of value to editors and guidelines to local opinion and a means of 'listening in to some of the leading themes of local conversation,' in which readers could express exasperation and join in controversies.

Publicity

In the effort to win and retain readers, the editor of the modern newspaper can use a number of methods which might vary from paper to paper and which are conveniently summarized under the heading of publicity.

The most notable example is the actual front page of a newspaper as it confronts the potential buyer on the news-stands. In a competitive publishing centre like London with its ten national dailies and nine national Sunday papers,[5] the visual character of the paper is as much its brand image as is the design in the case of a car.

The 'pull' of page one is particularly important to the competing popular tabloids who rely more than other national papers or local on the proportion of bookstall and newsvendor sales compared to home deliveries. Strenuous efforts are therefore made to get an exclusive picture and an eye-catching headline, or some compelling indication of the contents on the inside pages if one will only buy the paper and look. This is vital in building up sales among casual readers who may buy one newspaper one day and be tempted to buy a different one the next.

Among other ways an editor might use to publicise a newspaper are these:

Advertising. Television advertising is handy for projecting the image of a newspaper in an evocative fashion and publicising editorial contents. Information, however, has to take second place to image-creating by the camera. This method is also expensive, though it is valuable as part of a combined promotional drive along with other methods when a national Sunday paper is heavily plugging a big series.

Press advertising has a wider application and can convey more detailed information over a longer visual life. For instance, a national daily advertising itself in its Sunday stablemate has the advantage that Sunday papers are read over a longer leisure period.

Such advertising is usually devised, planned and placed by an agency on a contract basis, working in conjunction with a newspaper's own publicity department, where there is one, and operating in phase with editorial planning. Expenditure is usually from the promotional budget and not the editorial.

Bills. A bill is the name given to a newspaper poster displayed outside a newsagent's shop and at street sale sites telling passers-by of an important story in the paper or of a story with a local connection; i.e. BRITISH FLEET SENSATION or HALIFAX GIRL IN DEATH DRAMA. The traditional aim is not to give away too much of the story so that the potential reader's curiosity is aroused. Writing news bills is usually the work of a special sub-editor, while their distribution is the job of the circulation department, who also display stock bills advertising racing cards, football fixtures or TV programmes.

Blurbs. A blurb – sometimes called a puff – is a piece of self-advertisement, often on the front page which refers the reader to items inside or to be published the next day or week. It consists of a headline or 'selling line', text and illustration embodied in special artwork. The idea is to catch the reader's eye. In this, a blurb shares the same function as an advertisement, though it is usually written and devised by the editorial department.

Competitions. Small-scale competitions for readers may be run as part of normal editorial planning and the cost, which is low, comes from the editorial budget. They might involve an invitation from the women's page editor to readers to submit descriptions of a holiday mishap or a favourite wedding story, in return for a prize and some consolation prizes and the publication of the best letters. Service columns, or even the readers' letters feature might be linked from time to time with similar competitions to stimulate reader interest. Sometimes a crossword puzzle has a prize.

At the other extreme are the big, well advertised promotional competitions for prizes such as cars, holidays, a bingo prize or a money jackpot. The aim here is to win sales by making people buy the paper and fill in a coupon. Sometimes the prizes are given in a joint promotional venture with a manufacturer and are accompanied by lavish publicity, TV spots and stock bills at points of sale. This sort of competition is usually devised by a separate competitions or promotions department within the newspaper company, often working with agencies, and promotional copy is submitted by the department for placing in editorial space.

The incidence and duration of such competitions depends on the state of the newspaper market at the time. Where there are long running copycat promotions among rival newspapers, such as bingo competitions, the effect can be self-cancelling in the end. Also, an upturn in sales might be partly due to other factors in the paper. The loss of editorial space taken for a prolonged publicity back-up also has to be considered.

Bargain offers. A useful and profitable way of attracting readers and at the same time giving them a service is to offer merchandising bargains such as fashion garments, jewellery or even knitting and dressmaking patterns in return for filling in a coupon, or extra coupons for several items, and enclosing a cheque. Again, this is not just in the popular field. The wine-buying club run by the *Sunday Times* is in the same category. Such offers fit usefully into magazine and service features.

Sponsorship. A very old-established method of publicity is that of sponsoring newsworthy undertakings such as explorations, feats of endurance and adventure or exhibitions, in return for exclusive information or news and feature rights. The idea dates back to 1871 when the *New York Herald* sent Henry Stanley up the Congo to look for Dr Livingstone. The *Daily Telegraph* sponsored Harry Johnston's expedition to Africa's Mountains of the Moon in 1884 and was a leader in this field.

In recent years most national papers have been involved in sponsorship at one time or another, examples being the *Daily Mail*'s Ideal Home Exhibition, and the *Sunday Times* sponsorship of the exhibitions at the British Museum, the Royal Academy and elsewhere.

A worthwhile aspect of sponsorship is that the public usually derives some benefit from the money put up by newspapers, and projects are carried out which might otherwise not have been possible.

Canvassing. Door-to-door signing up of newspaper readers, in return for give-away prizes or concessional subscriptions, is not now in favour among national papers, although it has been used in recent years in the launch of provincial evening papers.

Editorial surveys

Ad hoc and in-house surveys to assess readership tastes are being used more than they used to be. These are the work of the newspaper marketing-orientated managements introduced by the new type of newspaper ownership (see Chapter 5). The aim is to build up a more detailed advertising and circulation profile for the paper, with an obvious spin-off in information for editorial planning.

In the past, there has been little faith among Fleet Street editors in such methods. Given the accepted slot or market within which a newspaper sells, editors' tendency has been to rely on a combination of 'gut instinct' and a study of telephone and letter reaction to given items, or the sales figures in response to editorial promotions. Such promotions are invariably in the context of the proved and accepted formula of the newspaper. For example, if the sale is based on strong crime coverage then promotion would aim at offering bigger and better crime stories. If sport is the selling point then the best and most exclusive sports stories would be sought coupled with the most personable and informed sports writers.

The history of readership surveys for editorial purposes has not commended itself to editors. Dr W. A. Belson, who carried out a readership survey for the London Press Exchange in 1960, showed that most readers who were questioned deplored what was described as 'the sex, violence, scandal and gossip' in popular papers and wanted more 'real news'. Yet the papers which might be accused of specializing in the things they complained about were the ones most sought by readers.

The Sun, as launched by the International Publishing Corporation in 1963, based its market image on a specially commissioned survey carried out by Dr Mark Abrams.[6] The replies to questions were interpreted as suggesting that success for popular papers in the future lay in moving up-market. The IPC *Sun* as thus conceived was a failure in readership terms and had lost nearly half its circulation by the time it was sold six years later.

Two interesting points arise. How many readers of popular national papers, who might enjoy the girlie pictures and the titillating items they contain, tell the truth about their newspaper reading preferences? Secondly, is the change in social attitude between the 1960s, when the above well-known examples occurred, and the present day such that readers are now more likely to tell the truth?

Further reading

The advertising man's view of readership and the working of readership surveys are covered in Simon Broadbent's *Spending Advertising Money* (Business Books, London, 2nd Edn, 1975), and W. A. Evans's *Advertising Today and Tomorrow* (Allen and Unwin, London, 1974). A good general picture of advertising is given in A. H. Hart and J. O'Connor's *The Practice of Advertising* (Heinemann, London, 1978). James R. Adams's *Media Planning* (Business Books, 2nd Edn, 1977) is much used by those in advertising.

Readers' letters are looked at in A. C. H. Smith's *Paper Voices: The Popular Press and Social Change* (Chatto and Windus, London, 1975), and in Ian Jackson's *The Provincial Press and the Community* (Manchester University Press, Manchester, 1971).

References

1 GOULDEN, J.: *Newspaper Management* (Heinemann, London, 1967), p. 48.
2 National Readership Survey, 1992.
3 Report 1947–49 Royal Commission on the Press (HMSO, London, 1949).
4 JACKSON, Ian: *The Provincial Press and the Community* (Manchester University Press, Manchester, 1971), pp. 152–75.
5 Dailies: *The Times, The Guardian, Daily Telegraph, Financial Times, Daily Mail, Daily Express, Daily Mirror, The Sun, Daily Star and The Independent.*
  Sundays: *Sunday Times, The Observer, Sunday Telegraph, Sunday Express, Mail on Sunday, News of the World, Sunday Mirror, The People* and *Independent on Sunday.*
6 ABRAMS, Mark: *The Newspaper Reading Public of Tomorrow* (Odhams, 1964).

5 The editor

There are probably more variations in style to be found in editing than in any other area of modern newspaper practice. Some editors are writing editors. They have risen perhaps through reporting, political journalism or feature writing and in day-to-day editing they are concerned more with what the words say than how they are presented. They tend to write their own leaders, or editorial opinions.

Such editors are the scourge of reporters and sub-editors. They are inveterate revisers of stories and markers of proofs and they focus attention on the news writing and feature writing side.

Other editors are production people. They have probably been promoted from the 'back bench' – the executives who control the putting together, or production of the paper. Their concern is particularly with pictures, headlines and projection. They see editing primarily as a job of presentation. They are fussy over the wording and fit of headlines, the amount of white space between items on a page, the way a picture is likely to print and the visual balance between the top of one page and another as the paper is opened.

Such editors lean heavily on the back bench and they have been known to rearrange the layout of a page at a late hour, leaving the production staff the almost impossible task of 'getting it right' in time to meet the printing deadline.

A third species of editor is the 'political figure'. Here politics often means politicizing. Such editors are primarily concerned with the overall opinion and image of the paper. They frequently sit on the board and are publicly identified with the paper's political and social stance. They are out of the office a lot, representing the paper at public functions, perhaps being interviewed on TV. They sit on committees and get involved in special causes. They are fussy about the attitude taken over certain issues and about what the editorial opinion says, although they are too busy to write leaders themselves except on Very Special Occasions.

Such editors are the scourge of leader writers.

There exist a number of variations of the above. There is the editor who tries to do it all himself or herself: formulate the policies, decide what goes into the paper, sub-edit the main items and write the headlines, rough out the page 'schemes', read and mark up the page proofs, write the leaders and conduct the publicity of the paper.

Such editors usually become ill in the end. They are difficult to work for.

Then there is the editor who delegates everything through an elaborate network of titles and duties which are so confusing that executives finish up quarrelling over who does what.

Such editors divide to rule, usually take all the credit, and stay healthy.

Finally there is the 'caretaker' editor, the one who has been appointed as a stop-gap to keep the seat warm while the board thinks the matter over, or because there is no-one else immediately in view, particularly if the last editor has departed precipitately. Such an editor is frequently an old servant who knows the ropes, is familiar with the people he or she is dealing with and gets on with the job. They have been known to be more successful than other sorts of editors but seldom get the credit.

Titles and functions

The Editor is the title that matters on a newspaper (though Northcliffe did cause chaos once by appointing two editors for the *Daily Mail*). Whatever other titles exist, the editor, as thus designated, is the person physically responsible for what goes into the paper, how it is edited, how it is presented to the public, and for getting the paper out on time. If serious legal trouble arises out of the contents, and anyone has to go to jail, it is the editor. Unless they are on holiday or away ill at the time they are presumed to have seen everything and to have authorized everything that goes into the newspaper (though this has been challenged in court). For this responsibility an editor has to work long hours but is paid well.

The next most important title is that of the *Deputy Editor*, who assumes all the editor's duties and responsibilities when the editor is on holiday, ill or not able to be physically present to edit. At these times the deputy editor is, in fact and in law, the editor.

What the deputy editor does while the editor is actually editing varies according to the editor's style. With a writing editor the deputy might keep an eye on production. With a production-orientated editor the deputy might concern himself more with the words. In general the deputy will take from the editor the weight of administrative duties such as interviewing new staff, checking and signing expenses and authorizing special editorial expenditure. The deputy editor will usually be the editor's first counsel in any matter to do with the paper.

The *Night Editor*, on national dailies and some provincial morning papers, is often next in seniority. To him or her is delegated charge of the production of the paper once the main decisions about content have been taken. The night editor is head of a production team which might include a deputy night editor, perhaps a couple of assistant night editors, and also the chief sub-editor and the art editor, among whom the general duties of editing and presentation are carried out. On evening and weekly papers the night editor's role can be taken by a 'production editor' or even the chief sub-editor.

Assistant Editors, where there are any, occupy the area between the deputy editor and the various department executives such as the *News Editor* and the *Features Editor*. They are usually given 'overlord' responsibilities for areas of the paper with such titles as assistant editor (news), assistant editor (features) or assistant editor (special projects). Their job is usually not to run the department but to initiate ideas and co-ordinate departmental activities and to serve in the editor's 'inner cabinet'. Sometimes the title assistant editor is given to long-serving executives to make way for new younger departmental heads, and some national papers have been known to have as many as six or seven of them.

Below the examples given there can be found on a newspaper a great variety of titles, depending on the readership market. Some have a *City Editor*, a *Political Editor*, or a *Foreign Editor*. All papers (except the *Financial Times*) have a *Sports Editor*. Special titles crop up where a newspaper has a body of specialist writers who need supervising. On some papers, the office lawyer, often a staff barrister or solicitor, is called the *Legal Editor* or the *Legal Manager*.

At the highest level, a group with several newspapers might have an *Editorial Director*, who provides a boardroom and policy link with the various editors, lays down matters of group practice and is responsible for appointing editors and deputy editors.

A *Managing Editor* is a less precise title. He or she might, on the one hand, be a sort of editorial director with overlord functions, or may be concerned with day-to-day editing or even with matters of editorial administration or management.

Titles containing the words 'associate' or 'executive' mean different things on different papers. They can involve a promotion, maybe with shared responsibility, or a sideways movement to make way for someone else.

Editorial independence

Editors are freer from proprietorial interference than they were fifty, or even twenty-five years ago. Lord Northcliffe, who took newspapers into the world of big business in 1896, set a pattern in which the proprietor not only had financial control through his shares but was an all-powerful editorial figure, laying down policy, mapping out editorial campaigns, re-shaping the content, intervening at every level, and choosing an editor who was expected to produce the sort of paper the proprietor wanted.

Northcliffe's style was adopted by Lord Beaverbrook, with his *Daily* and *Sunday Express*; the first and second Lord Rothermere, with the *Daily Mail*; Lord Camrose with the *Daily Telegraph*, and to some extent Lord Kemsley with his great empire of national and provincial papers. This style of ownership, which lasted into the early 1960s, gave rise to the legend of the Fleet Street Press Barons – a sinister club wielding life and death influence over millions.

It was not sinister in the way the critics claimed, or collusive at all, but it did produce a Press that reflected power and influence and produced high circulations. Yet the industry developed a reputation for weak management and bad union relations and profits were poor on the capital invested.

A change in ownership and control began to appear from 1959 which resulted in the old founding families, both in Fleet Street and in the provinces, giving way to new industrial companies.

By the late 1980s most of the eleven national dailies and nine Sunday papers published in London, and also segments of the provincial press, were owned either by big industrial groups with diversified interests, or by specialist newspaper companies run on an 'industrial' basis. Of the old-style dynastic families there remained only the third Lord Rothermere, at the *Daily Mail* and *Mail on Sunday*. Of the new companies, News International, which owned *The Sun*, the *News of the World, The Times, The Sunday Times* and *Today*, dominated by Rupert Murdoch; and Mirror Group Newspapers, dominated (until 1992) by Robert Maxwell, were part of global communications groups with a multiplicity of interests.

This shift in ownership has not totally freed editors from company control. It has left them, however, freer than they were in formulating day-to-day policy on a wide range of public issues without fear of a proprietorial phone call at 2 a.m. telling them what the editorial opinion should be saying. Editors today more frequently become directors of their operating company, and the political and social attitudes of the paper are left to develop more variably within the loose limits of a paper's traditional stance.

The first of the new style proprietors, Lord Thomson, who took over the Kemsley newspapers, including the *Sunday Times*, in 1959, and *The Times* in 1966, said frequently that he believed editors should be left to express their own opinions without interference and gave an undertaking that this would apply when he bought *The Times*. He believed a newspaper should identify with its readers and with the community which it served.

Victor Matthews, later Lord Matthews, chairman of the company set up to run the *Daily* and *Sunday Express* after they were taken over by Trafalgar House Investments in 1977, disclaimed interest in the political scene[1] and when the group started the *Daily Star* morning paper in November 1978, the

Right-wing *Express* papers found themselves with a broadly Left-wing stablemate under the same ownership.

The Observer, when control passed from the Astor Trust to the Atlantic Richfield Oil Company in 1976, asked for and secured guarantees of editorial freedom which were reinforced when control passed to Lonrho in 1981. Rupert Murdoch gave similar guarantees when his company, News International, took over *The Times* and *Sunday Times* from the Thomson group in 1981. The editors of the Mirror Group Newspapers' publications, the *Daily Mirror, Sunday Mirror* and *The People*, had editorial freedom written into their contracts under their conglomerate owners, Reed International, which Robert Maxwell, their next proprietor, assured them would still apply.

Yet the new style of ownership has brought with it different problems for editors. The old incubus of proprietorial whim has been replaced by the commercial pressures of more aggressive marketing in sales and advertising and by managements who expect all their subsidiary companies, including the newspapers, to make a profit. Financial and marketing directors have taken the place in the counsels of chairmen once occupied by editors. Editorial costs have come under close scrutiny in companies' forward planning strategy.

Under the new style management a toughness in tackling the industry's production problems resulted in the leap into new technology in the 1980s and a freeing from the dominance of the print unions. There became a new emphasis on efficiency and accountability.

Jeremy Tunstall, the media sociologist, writing in 1971, noted an increased interaction between editors and the business side of the newspaper – the executives in charge of finance, advertising, circulation and promotion. In a questionnaire to 15 national newspaper editors and top executives, he recorded, 'a number of editors explicitly stated that certain kinds of editorial content had a primary purpose of attracting advertising revenue'. And again: 'Several editors stated that the great expansion of financial coverage during the 1960s was primarily due to advertising and revenue considerations.'[2]

Charles Wintour, then editor of the *Evening Standard*, London, noted in 1972 an increase in advertising supplements with editorial backing in *The Times* and the *Financial Times*.[3]

The Thomson management brought to its newspapers American marketing techniques – sectional newspapers, the colour magazine and a rash of supplements. Editors, by the early 1970s, were being urged to broaden the spectrum of readership, and advertising staffs were adopting more positive space-selling techniques. While still insisting that his editors had full freedom, Thomson in his later utterances rated managers higher than editors.

The greatest impact of Rupert Murdoch's News International on the *News of the World* and *The Sun* in the 1970s was on the advertising and circulation side where staff changes were made and more aggressive selling methods introduced. TV advertising and competitions helped to boost *The Sun*'s circulation, and union problems were tackled with vigour, paving the way for a wholesale move by national papers into hi-tech sites outside Fleet Street and the computerization of production.

At the same time it would be wrong to say that the tail is wagging the dog and that advertising men and marketing men are running newspapers. The editor's post and telephone calls, the contacts made by reporters, and the weekly and monthly reports of district circulation reps can be closer to the grassroots of readership than the in-house readership surveys beloved of marketing directors. All surveys are placed before the editor – who would be wrong to ignore them – but in the end the decision of what goes in the paper is the result of the editor's feeling for what is right for the readers. The editor's view of the readership, based as it is on a compound of factors, is one of the most important elements in a paper's marketing strategy and it would be a foolish marketing director who ignored it.

Nevertheless in the end it is success or failure that counts and the number of ex-editors on Fleet Street and in the provinces whose ideas have been tried and found wanting is a growing reminder of this fact.

Former *Times* editor Simon Jenkins,[4] writing in 1979, applauded the new stress on viability and accountability, but made an interesting point. 'It is seldom realized,' he wrote, 'how close the old proprietors were to their papers. Since they derived most of their satisfaction and prestige from them they took a deep interest in their content and quality. This did not just mean directives and meddling suggestions ... It could also mean protection from advertising pressure, insistence on certain standards, preservation of editorial budgets and support in the inevitable battles within the organization. By contrast the new proprietors find editorial costs are easiest to cut and more revenues can be raised by increasing a paper's advertising ratio ...'

A steady reduction in the number of British newspaper correspondents working overseas has been one consequence of this policy.

Policy making

There are two sorts of policy in a newspaper: its traditional political and social stance by which it is known to its readers, what one might call its colour; and its day-to-day policy on such things as legal decisions, municipal affairs, and the doings of personalities.

Its traditional stance usually determines its attitude to fundamental things: racism, unions, sexual equality, the European Union and divorce, for example. Thus, on such perennial issues we know what views we are likely to find when we open the paper. As we have seen, it is not often that a paper changes its basic political or social stance, though its attitude to a government in power can vary on day-to-day issues cropping up in Parliament or in the light of the Government's performance.

In the case of a wide number of day-to-day issues, however, the editor will generally formulate an attitude in which the chief ingredient is what he or she believes is good for the paper and its readers. In the case of provincial papers, policies are constantly being formulated on issues of concern to the community as a glance at local editorial opinion columns will show.

We have seen that editors under modern ownership are more free to formulate attitudes than used to be the case. Yet it would be simplistic to say that all policy begins with the editor. It is truer to say that sources of policy vary from paper to paper, with the following being the principal ones:

1 Tradition: This is probably the strongest element where the social and political stance is concerned. National papers such as *The Guardian* and the *Daily Mirror*, which both stand to the left of centre, have long-standing political and social attitudes which are visible immediately on opening the paper. Changes of editor in recent decades – and of ownership in the case of the *Mirror* – have made little difference to this pattern. The personality of the two papers hinges upon the editor's acceptance of this fact. Tradition is also strong in the leading provincial morning papers.

2 Proprietor: A strong element of proprietor control over editorial policy, sometimes extending into day-to-day matters, remains at the *Daily Mail* and *Mail on Sunday*. With dominant shareholder figures such as Rupert Murdoch, and Conrad Black at the *Daily* and *Sunday Telegraph*, control is aimed more at commercial viability, though this can involve corporate decisions over staffing and carrying in editorial space circulation boosters such as bingo and other competitions and the use of colour, and can also entail the removal of editors for failing to bring the paper commercial success.

3 Editor: *The Times*, the *Sunday Times* and *The Observer* have a tradition of strong editor control over all aspects of policy which has survived several changes of ownership, though social caste remains an element in the attitudes of *The Times*. Financial and marketing pressures have to some extent affected editor control in recent years.

4 Company: Shareholding pressure is a hidden but potential influence over the content and readership market of newspapers in large industrial groupings of which some newspapers now form subsidiaries. Simon Jenkins notes the boardroom pressure of shareholding interests concerned about a newspaper's performance in some of the conglomerate companies.[5] It is also a strong influence in the bigger provincial groups.

5 Political party: The *Morning Star* is the only nationally circulating daily in Britain which propagates a party political viewpoint, in this case a Communist one.
6 Reader opinion: The feedback of reader reaction through in-house surveys and readers' letters (see Chapter 4) is a growing influence on editorial policy in most newspapers, particularly in day-to-day and social issues.

There is also a tendency among both serious and popular newspapers, though less so in the provincial press, to throw open space to opinion-forming articles by independent experts whose views might be at variance with the paper's editorial policy. This frequently happens in articles on political events, industrial relations and the economy.

One could say, in summing up, that the shift in newspaper ownership has made for more pragmatic and varied policy making and has given greater independence to editors but that this is tempered by new commercial pressures from managements.

Leader writing

A newspaper's opinion on what it considers to be the important issues on the day of publication can be found in the leader, or editorial opinion column. This is usually located in a fixed position on a left-hand page, sometimes page two, or the left-hand page of the centre spread. It is set in larger-than-normal type, often inside panel rules, so that it stands out from the rest of the page and can be found easily.

Regular reading of the leaders in a newspaper over a period will give a vivid insight into where it stands on the main current issues.

Leaders vary in number from one to maybe three or four but they usually occupy the same total space. Ian Jackson, in an examination of the leaders in 16 provincial evening papers,[6] has remarked upon the uniformity of length – what he calls their 'predetermined spatial mould'. There is, in fact, no reason why this should vary any more than the City column or women's page should vary. Small variations in total length do happen due to the position of advertisements.

National dailies employ two or more leader writers and Sunday papers and the bigger provincials usually one, though some editors also write leaders on subjects about which they feel strongly and specialist writers might contribute leaders on foreign or economic issues. The job demands a clear head, an informed background and an ability to mould a few words into a piece of incisive, persuasive prose. The writer must feel strongly about a subject, to cast special light upon it, to see a complex issue in terms of the ordinary reader, and to have a way of getting to the root of a matter. Every word counts in this tightest of all journalistic techniques.

A subject on which a paper can express strong feelings on behalf of its readers is a natural. Take the *Daily Mirror* on employment during the Thatcher administration:

'But the cries for help are ignored by Mrs Thatcher.
    She doesn't even listen to appeals from employers and members of her own party.
    She will not change. So the jobless figures go up and up and up.
    It is a waste of lives, a waste of people's skills, talents and hopes, a waste of resources.
    It is a waste of a nation.'

Or the *News of the World* taking up the cudgels on behalf of working-class travellers:

'Nothing exposes bureaucratic muddle more quickly and effectively than to take a ride by public transport.
    The dreary waiting, poor services, dirt and disorder are enough to drive a saint up the wall.
    Even worse is the horrendous cost of moving about the country, which has denied the train to a large section of the working class.
    BR's standard London–Glasgow second class return, for instance, costs £57. You can do the same journey in a private luxury coach for £17.'

A little bite can enter the leader writer's soul in a subject near to a newspaper's heart, as in *Today*:

Sir David Calcutt is as vacuous with the spoken word as he was with the written ones in his report on the Press.
    Twice yesterday when he appeared before a Commons committee he was asked if particular news stories were the sort which might be referred to the censorship tribunal he wants established.
    Both times he replied with the contemptuous phrase, 'Why not?'
    Here is another question: Should Sir David Calcutt be seen as an Establishment dogsbody who gives the impression of caring nothing for democratic freedoms and treating all except his masters with cold disdain?
    The answer, of course, is, 'Why not?'

Having dealt with the world's problems, there is still room for a good down-column chortle, *Sun* style:

'Customs men in York have launched a swoop that recalls the old Prohibition days in Chicago.
    Their target? Not bootleggers, but the nuns in a Poor Clares' Convent.

Their "sin" is that they made rhubarb wine as a nightcap and sold 200
bottles they had left over.

Now the revenue men are seeking unpaid duty.

Holy flypaper!

Is the country really that hard up?'

Subjects on which a national newspaper chooses to express its views are
discussed at a daily or twice-daily leader writer's conference, attended
perhaps by the editor, deputy editor, leader writer and often the political or
industrial specialists. The leader writer is expected to put up a number of
ideas. Jeremy Tunstall[7] sees the leader writer as one of the policy makers in
the national press. The editor, on the other hand, may be certain what he or
she wants in the leader column; other days an idea might arise obliquely
through comments from one of the specialist writers. 'Boardroom' leaders
are not common under today's newspaper ownership, but they can happen.

The aim of the leader writer's conference (which is usually very informal)
is to arrive at policy through consensus. From the point discussion ends and
consensus is achieved the leader writer then provides the words. The page on
which the leader appears is usually one that is easy to 'get at' for revision
should new developments during production hours require a change of
subject or of angle.

Editorial planning

The amount of consensus that goes into the editing of a newspaper varies
according to the editor's style, but one thing that is essential in a well-ordered
office is delegation. This is the method by which the editor, with many and
varied functions, is able to get the sort of paper he or she wants by
apportioning the work to trusted executives.

The choice of staff and appointments are the editor's in whose interests it
is to have the right person doing the job as the editor wants it done. It is usual
for newly appointed editors to make key changes in the executives in order
to secure personal editorial control. It is in an editor's interest equally to show
favour to talented younger members of the staff. Good editors quickly
earmark tomorrow's executives.

The day-to-day work, as we have seen, is departmentalized under
executives such as the news editor, the features editor and the picture editor.
The editor usually exerts control over the departments through an 'inner
Cabinet' consisting of the deputy editor, the night editor and the various
assistant editors with overlord functions. The most important decisions in
editorial planning are taken at this level as the issues arise. It is rare for an
editor to take such decisions without discussion with senior colleagues, or
with the executive concerned.

In order to formalize daily editorial planning and initiate the contents and plan of the paper, a twice-daily conference is usually held on morning and evening papers, or when needed on Sunday and weekly papers, at which subjects are discussed and directives given. These conferences are attended by the 'inner Cabinet' and by the various departmental executives. In the case of daily papers the early conference is concerned mainly with news gathering and features ideas, the later one with production.

At the early conference the editor might draw certain policy matters to the attention of executives, report on the circulation, and conduct an inquest on the previous day's paper, comparing it with rival papers. Praise or blame is handed out and the news and features programme for the day is then considered. The news editor, features editor, sports editor and pictures editor

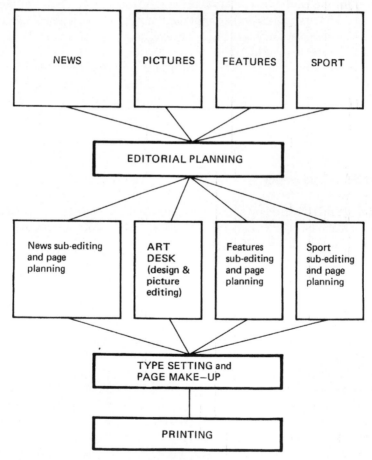

Figure 7 The planning and production sequences from copy input to printing in a national or big provincial newspaper

present their schedule of work and the likely balance of the paper is discussed. It might be decided to drop certain stories or increase coverage of others.

An important function of the conference is that the executives can find out in detail what each other is doing. It also allows ideas to be tested by discussion. Part of the paper will, in fact, be already in hand, since pages containing women's page features, service columns and TV programmes are usually set up the day before. The conference then breaks up, the departments embark on the jobs for the day and the editing of the paper begins.

As production work on the main news pages draws near, the second editor's conference, the production conference, is held. This is a smaller meeting involving mainly executives concerned with news and production, and its function is to 'sell' to the editor the worth of the main news stories and pictures for the later pages and to receive guidance on the choice of the Page One 'splash' story and any other important stories. Once these are agreed and a balance established the job of producing and 'bringing out' the paper is delegated to the night editor and the production team and the main editing, layout, type-setting and make-up of the pages are carried through. Each page is slotted into a time schedule, page one and the main sports page being the last to be completed, leading up to edition time when the paper is ready to go to press (see Figure 7).

Advertising and policy

The charge that advertising exercises an undue influence over editorial policy has been made frequently over the years. The 1947–49 Royal Commission on the Press reported: 'We have some evidence that individual advertisers occasionally seek to influence the policy of a newspaper or to obtain the omission or insertion of particular news items . . . We are glad to record that such attempts appear to be infrequent and unsuccessful. We have no evidence of concerted pressure by advertisers to induce newspapers to adopt a particular policy.'

The Commission did make one important point, however:

'As far as is consistent with its general character, a newspaper which is not very strong financially will . . . probably avoid taking a line detrimental to advertisers' interests unless by so doing it can increase its interest to the public.' On the other hand, 'a newspaper which is strong financially or able to command a market which advertisers are anxious to reach is under no necessity to have regard to the interests of the advertisers where those interests conflict with its own policy. If it does have regard to those interests it is in comparatively trivial matters.'

The Report added pointedly:

'The Advertising Association put the point succinctly: "An editor who thinks more of his advertisers than of his readers will soon have neither advertisers or readers to think of".'

Thirteen years later the Royal Commission of 1961–62 again examined the charge and recalled the evidence and findings of the previous Royal Commission. It concluded: 'We ourselves canvassed this matter as widely as we could; our own conclusions correspond broadly with those of the 1949 Commission.'

When the 1976–77 Royal Commission looked at advertising it was entirely to do with revenue and the viability of the press. The question of influence was not referred to in either the Interim or the Final Reports.

In his work on specialist correspondents, written in 1971, Tunstall recorded that of 193 correspondents who were asked: 'Are you aware of any advertising pressure on yourself at present?' a figure equal to 84 per cent replied 'No.' Of the remaining 16 per cent who said they were aware of at least 'a little' advertising pressure, the highest proportion were those whose work impinged on the advertising field, such as fashion and motoring writers.[8]

Fleet Street editor Charles Wintour, writing a year later, observed: 'More nonsense is talked about the influence of advertising than about any other area of newspaper activity . . . Indeed it would be ridiculous to pretend that if a newspaper draws up to eighty per cent of its revenue from advertising, the source of all this money has no influence on editorial policies. But a clear distinction must be drawn between the various types of influence. Certainly I have never known of an attempt whatsoever to affect the politics of a newspaper.'[9]

Certain sections, such as travel, he agreed, were 'clearly influenced by the advertisers whose appeals surround the editorial content. . . . However, it is my opinion that in general advertising influence is negligible and even where it is not, that it is harmless.'

Day-to-day examples of 'harmless' influence occur when editors avoid needless clashes of editorial material with advertising on a page so as not to damage either the editorial or the advertiser's interests. For instance, a feature criticising car insurance in general would be kept away from a page on which a car insurance company was advertising. Criminal cases involving servicemen would be kept off any page containing a service recruiting advertisement. A motor column might be kept away from a car company's advertisement in case other car companies complained of favouritism. Any form of investigative exposé would be kept off pages where advertisers could complain that its proximity implied a criticism of them. If advertisers ask for special positions near editorial matter, the editor has the last word.

Such examples of tactical placing of material make sense when advertising income is vital to a paper's survival. It does not involve an undesirable advertising influence on editorial policy or overall content.

Special supplements

The reference to travel sections, however, brings us to an area of the paper where critics might have good grounds for complaining about advertising influence in some newspapers. Features of this sort have grown under the more market-conscious managements in recent years and reflect management decisions which editors have to learn to live with. *The Times* has run supplements on wine and food; the *Evening Standard*, the London evening paper, has run a Pub of the Year Contest which promotes reader interest and is aimed at advertising support. The *Financial Times*, in particular, has massive multi-page supplements on development, technology, banking and other matters relating to its field. All manner of papers run holiday and gift supplements.

Yet such enterprises could be said to be attempts to use the editorial side of papers to influence advertisers rather than the reverse, since a forward plan for an editorial survey of a given field is used to attract advertisers who might not otherwise buy space.

When attempts are being made by newspaper companies to achieve viability there is unlikely to be much disagreement between editors and management over this development, particularly since there is growing scope for editors to make such supplements better written and informative. Even so, this sort of content worries editorial staffs, and also the National Union of Journalists and (until its demise in 1990) the Press Council, all of whom have been anxious to maintain a clear division between editorial and advertising content, however usefully they might merge in certain types of supplements.

The NUJ at its Annual Delegate Meeting in 1978 called for the drawing up of an agreement with the Newspaper Society and other employers on a code of practice for the handling of 'advertising support material,' which would allow individual journalists the right to refuse to work on such material, and to provide bonus payments for those who did. Such work is often given to junior staff on provincial papers.

The Code did not materialise, but the union returned to the subject at its ADM in 1982, which agreed an instruction for a working party of the union to collate 'at a national level all information on advertiser pressure on editorial content' to present to the next ADM.

The main guideline that emerged from the Press Council was that 'editorial and advertising matter should be clearly distinguishable. (This is also in accord with the view of the Advertising Standards Authority.) Readers should not be misled, and the propaganda of an advertiser should not be construed as the considered opinion of a newspaper. An article written to publicise a named product and to support accompanying advertising display should be identified as an advertising feature.'[10]

Since the text of supplements frequently is not tied to specific 'named products' but is of a general background nature, the Council's guideline, in most cases, would seem to leave discretion to editors on how to handle them. Where matter accompanying a number of advertisements is clearly advertising copy, and occupying space which has not been designated as editorial, an editor can, and usually does insist on it being labelled 'advertisement' at the top.

Further reading

Charles Wintour's *Pressures on the Press* (Andre Deutsch, London, 1972), though its references are becoming dated, remains the most useful work on editorship. Simon Jenkins's *Newspapers: The Power and the Money* (Faber and Faber, London, 1979) gives aspects of ownership and pressures. Jeremy Tunstall's *Journalists at Work* (Constable, London, 1971) contributes from its mine of research.

Biographies such as Arthur Christiansen's *Headlines All My Life* (Heinemann, London, 1961); Hugh Cudlipp's *Walking on the Water* (Bodley Head, London, 1976) and Stafford Somerfield's *Banner Headlines* (Scan Books, Shoreham, Sussex, 1979) are mostly personal and anecdotal but give insights into styles of editing. Editorship in the quality field is well served by Donald McLachlan's *Barrington Ward of The Times* (Weidenfeld, London, 1971) and David Ayerst's *The Guardian, a Biography* (Collins, London, 1971).

References

1 JENKINS, Simon: *Newspapers: The Power and the Money* (Faber and Faber, London, 1979) p. 100.
2 TUNSTALL, J.: *Journalists at Work* (Constable, London, 1971) pp. 44–45.
3 WINTOUR, C.: *Pressures on the Press* (Andre Deutsch, London, 1972) Chapter 3.
4 JENKINS, S., *Ibid.*
5 *Ibid.*
6 JACKSON, I.: *The Provincial Press and the Community*, p. 122.
7 TUNSTALL, J., *Ibid.*
8 TUNSTALL, J., *Ibid.*
9 WINTOUR, C., *Ibid.*
10 ROPER, MEAD: *The Press Council* (Media Guide Series, 1978) p. 23.

6 Layout and design

Newspapers are published in two main sizes: broadsheet or text-size as, for instance, the *Daily Telegraph* and *Financial Times*; and tabloid or half size like *The Sun* and the *Daily Mirror*. There can be slight variations of this. The exact depth of a tabloid paper can vary from one to another to a small degree. Provincial broadsheet morning papers vary in size. The tabloid page area is approximately half that of broadsheet.

Generally, all papers are of these two sorts, whether national or provincial, popular or quality. There is no historical significance in the sizes. Most early newspapers were half size; later broadsheet became popular. In recent decades the tabloid size has come to be associated with the popular national papers, perhaps because it is easier to hold for people hurrying to work using public transport, or with little reading time. Other reasons can be adduced. The tabloid size lends itself to the sort of bold poster-style layout pioneered by the *Daily Mirror*, which has strongly influenced the layout of other tabloids. It also lends itself to cheaper full page advertising and more regular solus (single) positions, which are thought by the marketing side of newspapers to please advertisers and therefore to help maximize advertising income. Two national papers which might be termed 'middle of the road', the *Daily Express* and *Daily Mail* (with strong B and C readership) have also changed to tabloid size in recent decades, while *Today*, launched in 1986 as a colour daily, and closed in 1995, adopted a deeper tabloid format.

Conversely, quality papers in Britain, *The Times*, the *Financial Times*, *The Guardian*, the *Daily Telegraph*, *The Independent* and the quality Sunday papers have retained the traditional broadsheet format, although there is no evidence that a change to tabloid shape would have necessarily injured their character. *Le Monde*, in France, is a quality tabloid. On the whole the longer text of news and features in quality papers is perhaps better accommodated in larger pages.

In the case of provincial evening and weekly papers the use of the tabloid size has increased in recent years but there are still plenty of examples of both, and there are also cases where tabloid size papers have changed up to broadsheet as well as the other way round.

Planning a newspaper

There is a method in the way newspapers are put together. Stories and features are not just dropped into the pages as they are written, starting with page one and finishing up with the back page. There is an overall plan or model in the editor's mind of the sort of contents the paper must have. Newspapers, in fact, usually stick to a basic contents format that suits them. This is refined by the various executives to whom the task is delegated so that there is a balance of editorial contents (i.e. news and features) and a balance between the editorial content and the advertising, which occupies a percentage of the space on each page.

There is also an order in the placing of the ingredients. The reader knows where to look for things. He or she knows that the leading news story of the day, or week, will occupy the biggest space on page one, where to find the sports pages, or the editorial opinion, where the City, or business section is placed, and where the showbiz gossip is. In the quality nationals, the reader even knows where to look for the foreign and political news; in *The Sun*, that Page Three has the big glamour girl picture of the day.

Most editors put their women's pages in a regular part of the paper, depending on the number of pages in the paper (which varies) and they are particularly careful to see that much-read features such as the horoscopes, the television programmes and racing cards can be instantly found. The aim is to help the reader.

Familiarity is an important principle in newspaper layout and design. It not only concerns where things are located but the form in which they appear. Thus a fixed typographical format will be given to the television programmes and the racing cards to make checking easy. A distinctive typeface will be used for the headlines on the women's pages so that they cannot be mistaken for news pages. The editorial opinion will appear regularly in a box or panel, set in a special type of its own, usually on the same side of its chosen page. The business news, the regular columnists, and even the horoscopes will be marked out by a distinctive heading or label by which they can be recognized. Yet, allowing for these practices, a considerable variation in page pattern is still possible.

The purpose of design

Once the plan of a newspaper is agreed, the presentation of the contents becomes an exercise in design by which the contents are commended to the reader. It is a process akin to packaging and, as with most forms of packaging, the visual display is rooted in psychology.

Under the influence of competitive selling, most of Britain's national papers, popular and quality, have created a separate design department, or art desk, where the pages are drawn in detail, the types chosen and the pictures edited by newspaper artists or journalists trained in layout and typography, working under an art editor, or art director. He (or she) supervises the projection of all editorial contents once the shape of the pages has been roughed out and the main items placed by the executive in charge of them – i.e. usually the night editor or chief sub-editor (see Chapter 7; Editorial production).

The bigger provincial papers are moving towards this system and it is common with magazines. The governing elements are cost and the degree of sophistication needed in presentation. In most local papers the executive in charge of the page, or a specialist sub-editor, will do the required work.

Page design, we can say, has three aims:

1 To attract the eye of a potential reader.
2 To signpost the various items and signal their relative importance.
3 To give a newspaper a recognizable visual character.

On each page, headlines, text and pictures are used to form an eye-catching shape to command attention. As readers turn the pages, the various sizes of type denote the relative importance of each story, while special type motifs help them to recognize regular features. Overall the balanced and repeated use of certain typefaces helps to give the page a visual character instantly recognizable by readers as being different from other newspapers.

The page design, or 'scheme', is achieved by placing the elements in relation to each other so that the eye is persuaded to move round the page to inspect the various items. The main headline mass and the dominant picture become focal points separated from each other by the intervening grey areas of text. These highlights are themselves placed in relation to the advertising content so that a boldly displayed advert does not damage the eye appeal of the editorial items. The location of the main headline and the picture, or pictures, thus perform not only an editorial function but also a design function by being part of a deliberate composition. Without the relief provided by pictures and variations in type size the design would revert to a grey columnar mass as in 18th and 19th century papers before visual appeal came to matter.

The use to which the various ingredients is put varies from paper to paper, though the basic aim of design remains the same. *The Times* has a more words-orientated presentation than *The Sun* and the *Daily Mirror*, for instance. The latter have shorter items and bolder headlines producing what has been described as the poster technique (see Figures 8–11). The quality Sundays have introduced imaginative methods in the use of typography and rules, or borders (Figure 13), particularly on their features pages. An examination of those newspapers will demonstrate these points. Distinctive variations can likewise be seen in the provincial press.

Above all, boldness, where it is used, must serve an end. It should not degenerate into garishness or a typographical mish-mash. It must afford the reader what newspaper designer Alan Hutt calls 'eye comfort'.[1] It achieves this by the balance of 'colour' – not just colour in the chromatic sense but in the juxtaposition of blacks, greys and white space, though full colour might be available on some pages.

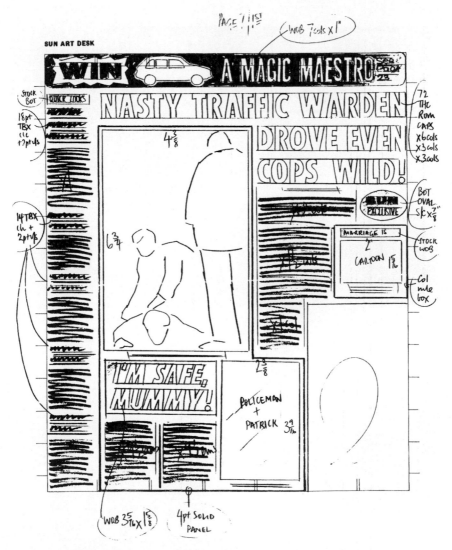

Figure 8 Layout tabloid style: a page 7 plan for *The Sun*

Planning a page

It is usual on national papers for page layouts (especially features pages), even with electronic make-up, to be drawn up in some detail on full-size or half-size blank layout sheets so that precise measurements can be taken and instructions written down. These sheets are printed to show the column widths.

A newspaper page is divided into a fixed number of columns – usually eight or nine in a broadsheet, seven in a tabloid. These columns establish the

Figure 9 *The Sun* as it appeared

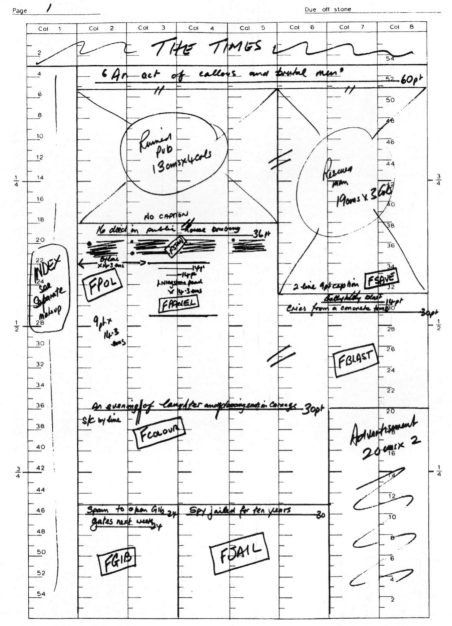

Figure 10 Layout quality paper style: a Page One plan for *The Times*

Figure 11 How *The Times* Page One appeared

standard typesetting width to be used in each paper for headlines and text. Headlines, and occasionally text, can also appear across multiples of a column: i.e. double column, across three or four columns or, in the case of important headlines across all the columns.

It is also possible, for display purposes, for headlines and text to be at an arbitrary width, thus breaking the general rule. This is called *bastard setting*. The practice is used more in the popular tabloid for certain display ideas.

A page consists of four elements: text, headlines, pictures and advertisements.

Advertisements, in terms of layout, is the element over which the editor normally has no control. At the start of each day (or week in the case of Sunday or weekly papers) a *flat-plan* of the paper (Figure 12) is produced by the advertising department, containing the number of pages and showing which spaces on each page have been sold to advertisers. From this a more detailed *dummy* of the paper is put together for production purposes. The shape and design of these advertisements have already been decided between the advertisers and their agents and the space allocated to them by the newspaper's advertising department. The aim of the latter is to give a balanced proportion of advertisements through the paper and also a balanced pattern of products (i.e. no clashes or excessive similarity of product on each page). In some cases precise placing in pages has been guaranteed.

The editorial layout has to accommodate these shapes. The type and contents of an advertisement cannot be altered and only in the case of a serious clash with editorial content is an advertising position changed, or if an important story needs a special placing.

It is important, though not always possible, for the art editor or page executive to get an early glimpse of an advertising proof so that any glaring clash of type or picture with editorial material alongside can be avoided. For instance it would be bad design to have a head and shoulders picture of a couple next to a similar picture in an advertisement, or to have a picture of a sinking ship next to a picture of a cruise liner in a holiday advertisement, or even a headline in the same type used in an advertising slogan alongside it in the page.

Headlines. Newspaper pages have headlines of different sizes and widths, most of them in a matching type, but with the odd one or two in a different type to give variety.

The biggest headline on a page is usually at the top of the page and mostly on the longest story. If it crosses the top of the page it is called a *banner* headline, or *streamer*, and its size and prominence indicate that this is the most important story. We call this the *lead* story. The streamer might have above it a smaller line of heading containing a separate statement. This is called a *strap-line*, a subsidiary or introductory headline which comes first and qualifies the main headline.

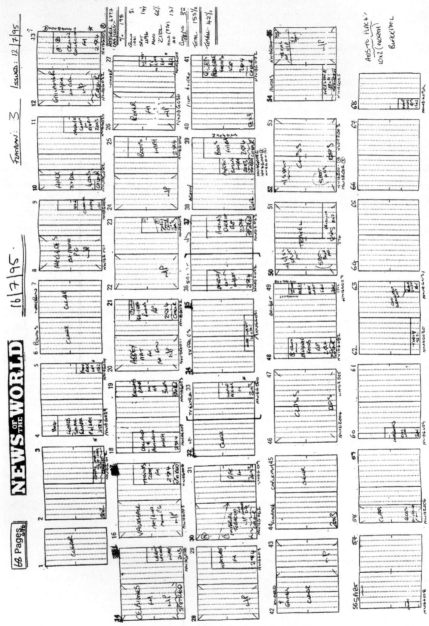

Figure 12 Planning the edition: a 68-page flat plan before being consigned to the screen. Note the advert placings in this *News of the World* example

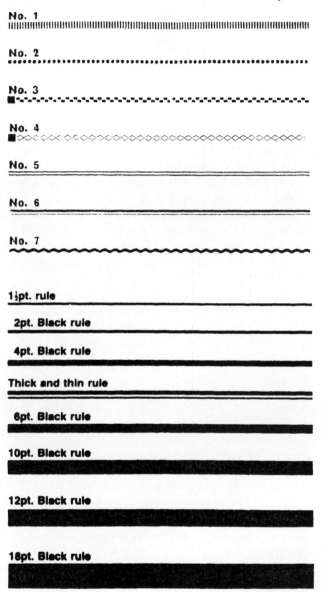

No. 1

No. 2

No. 3

No. 4

No. 5

No. 6

No. 7

1½pt. rule

2pt. Black rule

4pt. Black rule

Thick and thin rule

6pt. Black rule

10pt. Black rule

12pt. Black rule

18pt. Black rule

Figure 13 On both news and features pages panelled-in stories and the use of print rules can give a lift to design. Here are some examples of plain and decorative rules or borders

The second biggest, or second most prominent headline indicates the second most important story. We call this the *half lead*. The remaining stories with headlines at the top half of the page are called *tops*. These are usually single column, but can be double column or more depending on the shape of the page left available by the advertisements.

The lead story, the half lead and the various tops fill the main area of the page. There will still be left a few small places to fill, mostly in the bottom half. Here the stories of least importance are placed. They are usually called *fillers* and may consist of one, two or three paragraphs with a headline of maybe one or two lines in small type.

The use of the term 'tops' dates back to the period when design was non-existent and all stories started at the top of the page, often with only a single column headline, and ran down on to fillers. The evolution from this 'vertical layout' to 'horizontal layout' marked the start of modern newspaper design in which stories with sizeable headlines were allowed to cross the page in several 'legs', thus making 'strength below the fold' possible.

Text is the body matter or body setting of the various stories. It is usually set in a regular column-width, and in a standard size reading type which is increased in size only to give the first few paragraphs, or *intro*, of a story prominence.

Pictures, the final ingredient in the page, are there, as we have seen, not only to illustrate the stories, but also to help in the design by giving visual balance.

News v. features. Generally news and features are kept separate, though there can be an overlap, and there is a difference in design approach as examples in this chapter show. A news page shape has to be flexible to allow for the late story so its design is simple with generally single-column setting, making stories easy to replace. There are also more headlines and shorter items and, as well as the one or two main pictures, there might be the odd single column picture illustrating a story.

The projection of news is simpler than features with the main variation being in the length of the stories and the size of the headlines. There are usually short identification *captions* under each picture, and some of the stories might carry *by-lines* – the name or title of the writer at the start of the story. The longer stories might have *cross-heads*, which are lines of type, usually of one word, used to break up the text of a story to prevent it appearing in grey slabs.

Features pages usually have their own special headline type and a more deliberate projection of the items, which are fewer in number. Intros tend to be wider with more bastard setting and the use of variant body type to highlight points. There is sometimes some special setting above the intro displaying the circumstances out of which the feature arose, or giving the background of the writer. This piece of setting is called a *stand first* because it stands first above the intro. See Figure 14.

A features page is more likely to have various forms of type decoration such as *drop letters* (see Figure 20, page 117), in which the letter starting the story is in a larger decorative type, or of black blobs, squares or stars to highlight part of the text. Quotations might be taken from a long feature and set in bigger type, or with *drop quotes* (i.e. large-size quotation marks) and displayed among the body type as *breakers*, a device to prevent a page with long items from appearing too grey to the eye, but it must be done with discretion. The various devices must not be over-used or their effectiveness is ruined.

Panel rules can be used to enclose part of the main feature or the whole of a secondary one. This idea is also used on news pages (see Figure 13 on page 91). The items on the page might be separated by white space instead of column rules.

The *Today* leader page reproduced in Figure 14 on page 94, shows the features approach in action. A combination of pictures, panels, an art motif logo and a deliberately wordy headline are used to project a special feature, VIOLENT '93. White-on-black labels tab the same-size pictures effectively, and the black-on-tint headline is tied into them by a piece of 8 pt black rule across the top of the display.

Notice the emotive effect of the wording of the main headline and the lift given to it by setting the number 12 in large type; without this device the number would have looked lost. The text under each picture is used to build up the menace posed by a string of murders. The main text rams home to the reader the dangers to women in violent Britain. It is a story with a message.

By comparison, the panelled-in leader column with its two items is low key. With its *Today* logo and its consistent shape, position and style, unvarying from one day to another, it demonstrates that here, no matter what, is the paper's opinion on the important issues of the day. It is an example of projection by familiarity.

The pages from *The Sun* and *The Times*, reproduced on pages 85 to 88 show differences in the approach to news between a popular tabloid and a quality daily. *The Sun* uses a Tempo Heavy sans face mainly in capitals for its headlines with the occasional use of a Ludlow Black serifed variant of small size. The items are short – seven stories plus a blurb and a cartoon and two pictures – with the single advert having to fight for attention against the heavy news display. The panelled-in action pictures of siege victims makes an eye-catching focal point. At the same time the five stories in column one give an impression of busyness to the page. The effect is one of movement and controlled emphasis.

Today

What a way to run a country

STRANGLED

STABBED

BURNED

STRANGLED

12
women have been murdered since Rachel Nickell died in a hail of knife blows

VIOLENT '93

CHRISTIAN GYSIN

Words apart

BEATEN

ABDUCTED

STABBED

COSHED

Figure 14 Techniques in projecting features: a main feature page from *Today*. Note the effective use of a centre-page logo and the clusters of matching tabbed pictures. The wordy free-style headline is given emphasis by being type on tint, or BOT (see glossary for terms)

By comparison *The Times* goes for plenty of words with wholly lowercase headlines in Times Roman used horizontally across the columns to break the page up into reading segments. The column of briefs enables the page, despite its relatively long reads, to carry nineteen stories. The picture display on the public house bombing is a bold eye-catcher, although the lower part of the page could have done with a small picture to offset the greyness, particularly since the single advert also consists of type. The general impression, with the restrained type use, is one of authority, which throws into unusual emphasis the boldness of the picture treatment.

The ingredients themselves on pages can vary. Pictures can be supplemented by line drawings and graphics, as in the *Today* page logo. Headline type can be reversed so that it prints as white type on a black background (a white-on-black or WOB) or as black type on a grey background (a black-on-tone or BOT), as can be seen in the *Today* example. Headlines can also be overprinted on to pictures or can become part of a composite of picture, type and WOB. The term *compo* is applied to this device.

The changes in page make-up, first to paste-up and latterly to electronic pagination, have enhanced the speed and flexibility with which these various typographical devices can be used on pages.

If paste-up opened up a new world in display techniques after the strictures of hot metal, the breakthrough in computer-generated graphics has put even more exciting tools in the hands of those involved in page design and make-up. For instance graphics can be drawn straight on to the screen, either for one-off use or to store as stock to pull down for future use.

Typography

The type character of a newspaper is achieved by the consistent use of a limited number of typefaces, one main choice on the news pages and perhaps another as the main choice on the features pages, with a regular variant in use in each case.

Much has been written about the philosophy of type, yet a feeling for it remains intensely personal to those who work with it. To some extent its use in newspapers has a traditional basis. The quality, and generally older established, papers in Britain favour the older serif ranges, while popular tabloids of more modern growth, favour the sanserif which are the more recently introduced faces.

These two terms, serif and sanserif, denote the two basic type families by which Western alphabets are rendered and from which have sprung the thousands of typefaces in use in printing today.

Serif type is type in which the letters possess a serif, a characteristic crossline finishing off each stroke – i.e. in the form of a decoration (see Figure 16).

Figure 15 How to balance opposing pages: illustrations and all-lowercase headline type are used effectively in this example from London's *Evening Standard*. Note the central role of the Woody Woodpecker picture and the offsetting of the illustrated car advert against legs of body type

EVENING STANDARD   ****   WEDNESDAY, 12 JULY, 1995 7

Nicholas de Jongh's
FIRST NIGHT REVIEW

Erotic icon Julie triumphs in the sex war

Celebrating: Julie Christie at the first-night party

Old Times   *Wyndham's Theatre*

JULIE CHRISTIE, who positively oozes inscrutability, might have been born to slip into the ambiguous world of Harold Pinter. And her West End stage debut last night at the greatish age of 55 turns out to be a triumph in miniature — her role's not that dramatically testing. So there she sits, aloof and dreamily smiling, marooned in Pinter's elusive drama of memory and desire. She takes and altogether makes the role of Kate, a forty-something wife for whose forbidd favours her husband, Deeley, and long-lost female friend, Anna, tensely canapére. Miss Christie's Kate, behaving as all the best erotic icons should, preserves an air of elegant detachment: like some prize cat, which is reluctant to bite the hand that feels it compliments, she rests curled up, watchful, on a red sofa, as though glad to be so savoured.

What exactly is going on? Well exactness is the enemy of the best of Pinter. And Old Times does not rank with his best. It begins, in typical Pinter style, with an outsider who attempts to disrupt the home territory.

Leigh Lawson's Deeley and Kate, in their country farmhouse, which designer Julian McGowan turns into a sinister, stone-walled office, are talking one autumn evening about an expected guest: Anna is the friend whom Kate has not seen since they were best friends and arty girls about town in Fifties London.

But, as if to scotch the thought that any Pinter play could settle down in solid, realistic terrain, Harriet Walter's Anna, who has been standing unacknowledged, by the window, abruptly begins her reminiscence of life with Kate. Is this then a dream play? Does the fact that Kate complains "You talk of me as if I were dead" suggest Pinter is conjuring a backstairs piece — straight from limboland? Or is it more simply a Proustian scavenging of memories from scraps pesigd?

The director Lindy Davies, with a set which towers in the direction of dreamland,

rightly provides no firm answers. She keeps ambiguity going. The one certainty is that Leigh Lawson's rambling, nervy Deeley and Harriet Walter's winsome Anna are locked in a cold war of words. Each wants to prove the other matters less to Kate.

Both sing anarchic old songs while Miss Christie, in her white shirt and grey trousers, remains sweetly dispassionate. Both insist that they just hot at a film show of Odd Man Out.

But then the women suddenly slip heading into the past, speaking as if back in the Fifties. And there's no missing Anna's smitten ardour, nicely implied in Miss Walter's otherwise arch performance, or Deeley's sense of jealousy and exclusion.

AND WHEN Miss Christie's Kate tartly recalls what sounds like a long-past sexual rejection of both husband and best friend, she again confirms her detachment from their sexual competing.

Old Times may ingeniously move between planes of dream and memory, and it raises spectres of trade and jealousy and exclusion. But even with Miss Christie trevalising as a femme fatale who gives next to nothing away, there's something irritatingly repetitive and dramatically reductive about the duel of words between Deeley and Anna. And as a view of the double pull of bisexuality it seems rather old hat.

Christie's the thing.

5,000 cheers for Placido's singalong

PLACIDO DOMINGO sent a crowd of around 5,000 into ecstasies last night with an impromptu singalong in Covent Garden Piazza, *writes Robin Stringer.* He emerged from the Opera House to greet his fans after singing the lead role in Verdi's *Stiffelio,* part of the Royal Opera's current Verdi Festival. As he took his place under the Big Screen he led co-star Catherine Malfitano and the rest of the cast in The Drinking Song from Verdi's La Traviata.

Shock rise in train knifepoint muggings

by BARBARA McMAHON
Crime Reporter

NEW YORK-STYLE train robbers are plaguing London's suburban rail services, with muggings soaring 10 per cent to 1,648 in the past year.

Knife-wielding thugs, in gangs of two and three, threaten passengers and steal cash, jewellery and even designer clothes.

Most of the robberies, known as "taxing," have taken place around the Streatham, Tulse Hill and Clapham Junction areas of south London and in parts of east London, with danger routes the late night local suburban services operating from Victoria or London Bridge.

The problem has been steadily escalating and crime figures due to be released this month by British Transport Police confirm the trend.

British Transport Police would not confirm the ethnic origin of the robbers, but while many are known to be black, while gangs also stalk the train system.

In the Stratford area, a gang of predominantly white youths was identified as being responsible for 87 knife attacks and 14 gun robberies. And a gang of Afro-Caribbeans is being hunted for at least four robberies on mainline Thames trains. The robbers buy a

one-day travel pass to enable them to roam the system at will and tend to strike at off-peak times.

They usually travel in threes, getting in and out of evening trains until they find a potential victim and steal cash and valuables before jumping off at the next station, leaving their victim in a state of shock. In some cases passengers have pulled the communication cord and the robbers have fled across electrified tracks to escape.

Supt Ted Lightfoot said: "London is experiencing a rise in street robberies and what happens on the streets is mirrored on trains.

Special police squads are targeting known railway blackspots.

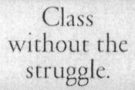

Class without the struggle.

The Saab 900 2.0i – £14,583* on the road

For the same price as an ordinary saloon, you could be driving the class-leading Saab 900i. With its 16 valve twin force performance, combined with a host of safety features including a driver's airbag, ABS brakes, unique Saab Safeseat,

safe impact protection and power steering is often compromised value for money – something most ordinary saloons struggle to compete with.

Call us today to arrange your own personal test drive.

BEXLEYHEATH	CHISWICK	WEST END
Lex Saab	AFN Chiswick	Saab City Ltd
75 Broadway, Bexleyheath, Kent	Chiswick Garage, Great West Road	77 Piccadilly, London W1Y
Tel: (0181) 304 3804	Chiswick, London W4	Tel: (0171) 493 4730
	Tel: 0181 747 7000	
BRENTWOOD	**THE CITY**	**WIMBLEDON**
Grange Saab	Saab City Ltd	Currie Motors
Brook St, Brentwood, Essex	60 The Highway, London E1	Wimbledon Saab
Tel: (0277) 210161	Tel: (0171) 480 7740	24 Merton Road, Wimbledon, London
		Tel: (0181) 543 4032

 SAAB

PURE DRIVING PLEASURE

Price correct at press date will include a choice of £400 free VAT 18 months service and service plan base charge £90. All new Saabs come with a Saab Care 3 year/60,000 mile warranty.

This characteristic dates back to the carved Latin inscriptions of the Romans. Types based on this pattern replaced the black letter text, which had been developed from monastic manuscripts, soon after the printing press came into use, though black letter continued to be the standard for some years in parts of Europe. Over the centuries many distinguished type designers such as Sir William Caslon (1692–1766), John Baskerville (1706–75) and Giambattista Bodoni (1740–1813) evolved and gave their name to versions of the original Roman serifed type. Its development has continued into the present century with Stanley Morison's (1899–1967) Times New Roman and others.

Sanserif type is the generic name for a range of typefaces characterized by the absence of the serif or decorative cross line on the strokes of its letters (see Figure 17). Early examples were considered unattractive but the work of Eric Gill (1882–1940) and other imaginative designers this century has resulted in a varied range of sanserif types which have boldness and elegance.

Factors in use. Serif type is more readable in small sizes (because it is less uniform than sans) and has remained the standard book text in its various ranges, and also the standard body setting in newspapers, even in those which use mainly sans serif types for their headlines. In its more modern designs it has remained popular in advertising typography. Special versions such as Playbill and Rockwell Condensed dominate theatre poster advertising. The larger sans serif ranges such as Placard and the various forms of Gothic Titling give great boldness to headlines in tabloid papers, and some elegant sans serif ranges such as Record Gothic and the various condensed Gothics make useful variants in papers that have chosen a predominantly serif format.

Within both the main type families each typeface has been further developed into condensed and expanded versions, and often into bold and italic versions, as well as the standard or roman. The bold has a fatter stroke and the italic a sloping configuration. There is also sometimes a light version in which the stroke is thinner than the standard, or roman. In all these variants, the dominant design characteristic is kept. In a popular serif face such as Century (Figure 16), which is used by many newspapers as a standard news type, the expanded, or wider version is still unmistakably Century, as is the light and the italic versions. (See Figure 15, pages 96–7.)

It is thus possible for a newspaper to take a type such as Century and, by the use of the expanded, light and italic versions, achieve a varied and attractive format without departing from the type characteristic – i.e. the format is still a Century type format. The *Daily Mail* is an example.

Other variations can be obtained within a fixed typeface through having some headlines in capital letters, or caps, and others in small or lowercase letters, or lc. More and more newspapers, in their search for homeogeneity,

abcdefghijklmnopqrstuvwxyz ß
ABCDEFGHIJKLMNOPQRSTUVWXYZ
1234567890

abcdefghijklmnopqrstuvwxyz
ABCDEFGHIJKLMNOPQRSTUVWXYZ 1234567890

Figure 16 Ludlow Black, with squat serifs, here in its italic form, is sometimes used for caption headings and panels. The other serifed type is the more elegant Century Schoolbook, much used as a stock news type

abcdefghijklmnopqrstuvwxyz
ABCDEFGHIJKLMNOPQRSTUVWXYZ 1234567890

Figure 17 This example of sanserif type is one of the variations of Univers, which is used frequently in modern page design

give all headlines in lowercase versions, in bold, light or italic, of a particular typeface. Examples of this are *The Observer* and the *Sunday Times*, *The Times*, *Financial Times* and *The Independent*. On features pages more variety of type appears, with the choice of a variant occasionally extending into an entirely different or opposed typeface.

Some of the lighter and more decorative faces are used in some papers for special contents such as the women's pages and an entirely alien bold face might be introduced to project a special serialization.

In a predominantly serif format such as the tabloid *Daily Mail*, which favours Century type, a condensed sans face may be used for a *kicker* or special item in the middle of a news page. For this purpose the text is set in a bold body type. Equally, in the sanserif format *Sun* a special item on a news page might have a headline in Ludlow Black (Figure 16) which is a serif type with very fat serifs.

The correct and consistent use of white space between the words in headlines and text and also between the lines is important in projecting type balance. A fault with some photo-set papers is a failure to allow adequate white space when pasting up type and text on to the page.

Whatever variations are introduced, and for whatever purpose, the main aim in page design is to choose a stock type for the main part of the paper and to use this consistently. It is thus that the type character of the paper is achieved. An examination of successive issues of any newspaper, national or provincial, will demonstrate this. A total change of type format is extremely rare in British newspapers, and is usually coupled with a re-launch or a merger of papers.

The newspaper pages reproduced in this chapter and described above, show this consistency of type character. *The Sun* inside news page on page 86 is typical of the tabloid style based on up to 72-point heavy sans headline type. In this case the variant is the small Ludlow Black italics on the cartoon. Each page and each edition conforms to the same broad type principles. *The Times* page one on page 88 has a basically serif (Times Roman) lowercase type dress in traditional broadsheet style.

Type measurement. The principal variation in type use, and the one which indicates the relative importance of various items, is the size of the headlines. This is worked out according to the depth of the letter. Here we encounter one of the oddities of typography, for sizes are measured not in inches or in metric but in a 250-year-old system of points of which there are, as a guide, approximately 72 to the inch. Thus, in theory, a 36-point letter would be half an inch deep, an 18-point letter a quarter of an inch deep, and so on. A word of warning here, however – the points size of type is the measurement of the original metal base upon which the shape of the letter rose. It has to be remembered that with lowercase letters, some, like a 'k', have ascenders, which stick above. Others, like a 'g', have descenders which hang below.

Some, like an 'f' and a 'j', have both ascenders and descenders which were accommodated on the metal base of the type in its traditional form.

The size of the type is thus the height from the bottom of the descender to the top of the ascender. The constant depth of the letter, assuming there is neither ascender nor descender, is called the 'x' height (see Figure 18). This can vary according to whether or not the particular typeface is designed with long ascenders and descenders. As a result a 36-point line with a big 'x' height looks bigger than a 36-point line with a small 'x' height. The non-printing part of the body is called the beard.

This explanation is necessary to show why, despite the fact that there are approximately 72 points to the inch, the actual measurable depth of the type that prints is often less than that, and can vary in its 'x' height from type to type, depending on the design. Thus type is referred to as being big or small on its body. In certain headline types which exist in capital letters only, called *titling*, the type depth can fill the full depth of the body.

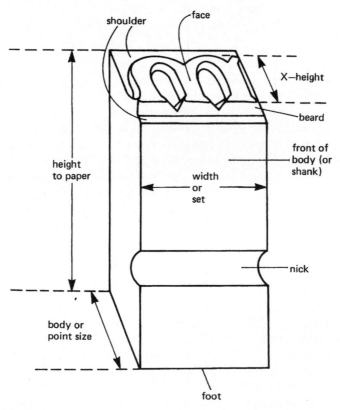

Figure 18 This perspective drawing shows how type letters were traditionally designed and produced by a type founder. Note the 'x' height of the letter

In practice it is best to forget the connection with inches, since type is used in a series of standard point sizes which journalists involved in sub-editing and production quickly learn to use and recognize. These sizes ascend in regular order starting with the smallest body type and rising, in headline sizes, to a normal maximum (used only in the popular tabloids) of 144 point.

Body type (in points): 5½, 6, 7, 8, 9, 10, 12, 14.
Headline type (in points): 14, 18, 24, 30, 36, 42, 48, 60, 72, 84, 96, 120, 144.

The smaller sizes are sometimes referred to by their old names which are:

5½ pt = ruby
6 pt = nonpareil (pronounced nonprul)
7 pt = minion (usually min)
8 pt = brevier (brev)
9 pt = bourgeois (burjoyce or bjs)
10 pt = long primer (primer, or LP)
12 pt = pica.

As a rule there is only a limited number of typefaces in use in the small body sizes and they seldom exceed 14 point. A newspaper will adopt one of these as its stock body (i.e. reading) type and will vary it only occasionally. In headline sizes, from 14 pt upwards, there are a great many faces available in both the serif and the sanserif families. As we have said, a newspaper will adopt one or two such faces as its stock headline type with suitable variants, and will not normally range across the type book in its page design.

With computer-generated type, which is now universal as a result of the adoption of new printing systems, the facility exists to vary type sizes in the computer to within half a point of each, and even to italicize and condense or expand faces in response to commands, since the type 'master' will deliver what it is asked to do. Nevertheless, in order to have controlled and balanced page design which will produce pages that look as they have been visualized – and indeed to help in the visualizing – it is the custom to programme type to the traditionally accepted series of type sizes as described above. Type books continue to be prepared in these sizes, showing specimen column and multi-column widths appropriate to the paper for which they are used.

It is beneficial for sub-editors to use type books to familiarize themselves with the types normally used in their papers, as well as to try out the letter count of a headline, so that they are not blindly pressing keys. This does not mean that the programmed type instruction cannot be overridden in special cases, such as to create a bastard size to accommodate an editor's much loved headline that would not otherwise have fitted, or to take a wanted legalled headline. But beware – to use variable type sizing excessively endangers the type balance of the page and can make it look out of character.

Experienced typographers and newspaper designers are aware, too, that italicizing or expanding or condensing typefaces arbitrarily within the computer by overriding programmes can produce undesirable effects. Italic faces within a type range are usually specially designed to counter problems of shape and character with some of the letters, and it is better to stock the system with type masters of specific italic faces that are likely to be used.

Type measure is still calculated in ems, or what hot-metal printers used to refer to as muttons. An em is the width of a standard 12-point roman letter 'm' which, in fact, is 12 points wide as well as 12 points deep. Since an em equals 12 points there are six ems approximately to the inch. In typesetting systems today, however, the em has been replaced by its American term, the pica (which is 12 points, of course) and setting widths are called up in picas and points (across 12p6 means across 12 picas and 6 points) unless single and double column measures are programmed as such. Likewise in measuring the standard column widths of newspapers we say that a broadsheet has a 9½-pica column rather than a 9½-em column and a tabloid an 8-pica or 8½-pica column.

The common form in sub-editing is to key in the type and setting instructions as a command at the beginning of a story and at each point thereafter where type size or setting width changes. Thus a story might start off as 9rom,8p6 and later change to 8rom,8p6, finishing up as 7rom,8p6. Where single column setting is the norm it is the practice in some systems to simply key in 8romsc, 10romdc. With electronic make-up the setting is usually automatic.

Indented setting can be commanded, and also extra letter, word or line space, although it is not a good idea to vary space where this has been correctly formatted to suit the style of the paper except where the spacing requirements on a page demand it. Likewise reverse, or hanging indent is usually formatted on to a simple setting command. In this setting the first line sticks out in front of the paragraph.

Picture editing

The final aspect of layout and design which must be examined is that of picture editing. As with page design, the process is partly imaginative and partly technical. Imagination (and a good deal of experience) is needed to look at a photograph and decide that this will make the right picture that will print well and enhance the page.

Factors in the choice include its relevance to a story and the position of the figures in the picture in relation to the space available on the page. For instance, figures must not look out of the page or away from the story which the photograph illustrates. In certain cases, in 'head' shots for instance, it is sometimes the practice to reverse the print so that the face or eyes look in the required direction, provided that this does not harm the image in any way or make a nonsense of detail, such as coat buttons or lettering.

Also important are the picture's general composition and its tonal qualities. A mono photograph of predominantly grey tones will not print well on newsprint, which is unkind to fine detail.

The photograph may have to be chosen out of a large number of the same person or incident and is arrived at by a process of sorting and rejection. The person who actually chooses the photograph (these days often by viewing screen – see page 28) is usually the executive in charge of the page who might be the night editor or the chief sub-editor, though the picture editor's advice is valued. Once the photograph has been chosen and its position on the page decided, its actual editing falls to the art editor or to the artist or journalist who is originating the page.

Picture editing is not usually carried out by the picture editor, who is really the chief photographer, and whose job is to brief photographers, gather and provide pictures and run the picture desk. On small papers where there is less division of labour the job of picture editing can fall to quite junior staff involved in editing a page. (For editing transparencies see below.)

Once the photograph is chosen, the next thing is to decide how much of it to use – in other words, to decide what irrelevant parts should be excluded, such as people or detail not essential to the story, so as to give the best picture. In some cases people may have to be excluded from a photograph for legal reasons.

The process is carried out by *cropping* or marking off with pencil lines on the back of the photograph the area to be used. To do this, the photographic print, either mono or colour, is placed face downwards on to a light source such as a 'light box' in which the bulbs shine up through a ground glass screen, outlining the detail. The area thus indicated by cropping becomes the image and shape which appear in the final picture as printed. Generally, the more that can be excluded the bigger and better is the image that is left, though composition is still a vital factor.

After the photograph has been cropped to an agreed image the size needed for the page has to be worked out by a process known as *sizing* or *scaling*. This consists in drawing a diagonal in pencil from the top right of the cropped rectangle to the bottom left (see Figure 19), while holding the picture face downwards on the light source. If the width is known, the measurement (single column, double column or whatever is needed) is taken across from the left side of the cropped area until the line intersects the diagonal. To find the depth corresponding to this width, the measurement is taken downwards from the point of intersection to the bottom of the picture. Alternatively, if the depth is fixed a line is taken upwards to the diagonal for the depth required and the measurement from the side to the diagonal indicates the width that needs to be allowed on the page.

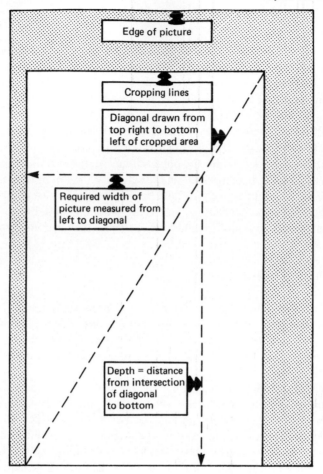

Edge of picture

Cropping lines

Diagonal drawn from top right to bottom left of cropped area

Required width of picture measured from left to diagonal

Depth = distance from intersection of diagonal to bottom

Figure 19 Pictures are cropped and scaled (measured) in the traditional way by placing them face downwards on a light source. This diagram shows how the pencil lines on the back of the picture will look

Scaling can also be done with a slide rule calculation based upon the width needed, or with the use of a 'wheel', which is two calibrated wheels revolving on a common centre and giving readings in similar fashion to a slide rule.

The required size is marked on the back of the print in pencil (so that any marks can be rubbed off should it be needed to be re-cropped and scaled) and the photograph is then ready to be processed into the page.

Transparencies

While the above method is adequate for mono or colour prints, colour in newspapers often means editing from transparencies (trannies). Here the practice is to use a special enlarger called a **Grant projector**, or the newer **Canon or Konica colour copier**, by means of which the detail on the tiny piece of film can be enlarged sufficiently to be worked on.

With the Grant, which many art desks are still using, you place the film on the light box below the lens and bellows of the projector and focus up the machine to the size needed for the page. Then you trace off the required image on a sheet of tracing paper placed on the screen at the top of the machine, and thereafter use the same cropping and scaling technique as with a print. Be certain that the transparency is the right way up, and be sure to place identifying marks on both film and tracing in case they become separated.

Picture improvement

The editing work thus complete, prints and transparencies are sent to the **scanners** where they are electronically retouched if need be, colour-corrected as appropriate, and then imaged onwards into the page-making terminals (see Figure 4, page 28). It is also now possible to crop and scale electronically on screen.

Unlike with manual retouching with an airbrush carried out in the old days, alterations to an electronic image by moving pixels about are invisible if competently done. The work should, however, be confined to improving detail and getting rid of marks and unwanted background, and must be carried out under editorial supervision. Responsibility for the finished product rests with the editor in the same way as does responsibility for the printed word. Pictures that have been tampered with have been known to lead to expensive lawsuits.

Where **cut-and-paste** make-up is still being used (see page 131), pictures are laser printed to the size and quality needed for the page card. The quality control built into the printer enables pictures to be reshot for improvement. In offices using hybrid page-making systems that lack complete graphics generation partly made-up pages are printed out as bromides with blanks for laser-shot pictures and adverts to be pasted on. The completed pages are then photographed to produce the negative required for plate-making.

Remembering principles

While technology has put control of page-making firmly into editorial hands, it should be remembered that the basic purpose of layout and design remains the same. In fact to get the best out of the new systems the need for typographical and visualizing skills is greater than before, and can easily be neglected.

Even in the extreme case of paperless systems, in which the pages are actually designed on screen, types still have to be chosen and juxtaposed to give balance and a consistent overall character. Pictures still have to be selected, cropped, scaled and retouched, and the text, headlines, illustrations and advertisements placed in relation to each other to achieve an attractive design that will draw the reader to the page and its contents. (See Chapter 7 for page production.)

Further reading

V. Giles and F. W. Hodgson's *Creative Newspaper Design* (Focal Press, 2nd Edition, 1996) is comprehensive in this field. Alan Hutt's *Newspaper Design* (Oxford University Press, London, 2nd Edn, 1967) remains a pioneering classic, as does Edmund C. Arnold's *Modern Newspaper Design* (Harper and Row, New York, 1969) in the American field.

Reference

1 HUTT, Alan: *Newspaper Design* (Oxford University Press, 1967).

7 Editorial production

One of the most important decisions a young journalist has to make is whether to remain a writer – that is to say a reporter, feature writer, reviewer, etc. – or to move to the production side of newspapers and become involved in sub-editing and presentation. The choice is often dictated by temperament. The variety and creativity in writing are things that attract many young people into journalism in the first place. Yet sub-editing and presentation have their own satisfactions and the production cycle generates a special sort of excitement.

An advantage of training on a small or medium-size provincial paper is that it offers a many-sided experience upon which to base the decision. Responsibility for handling a big story, both as a reporter and as a sub-editor, can descend at an early stage on young shoulders. Reporting work, as we have seen, is often laced with feature writing. Early experience of sub-editing and page layout, too, is usually available for those who want to make use of it.

The staffing and simple structure of a small paper do not permit the division of labour found in national papers. There are times when it is 'all hands to the pumps' to get the paper out, and young journalists of either sex can sample a variety of work and responsibilities. It is here that a taste for production journalism is born.

The editorial staff of a newspaper can generally be divided into those who find and write the material and those who edit and project it. Sociological writers on the press have evolved useful terms for the two sorts; the gatherers and the processors. National dailies employ between 200 and 350 journalists of all types, including executives. The average of this is about four times the number of journalists employed by a typical provincial evening paper. More than half those on national papers are processors. The 1976–77 Royal Commission found that of 2,720 full-time journalists employed on national newspapers in London, 1,151 came under the headings of reporters, feature writers and photographers, while the remainder were senior editors and 'other editorial'. This is about twice the proportion of processors to gatherers found on provincial paper staffs.

The disproportion has arisen because of a greater striving after polish and originality of processing in national papers as a result of competition. On a town evening paper speed is of greater importance as a result of tighter distribution schedules and complex editionizing and the processing is simpler.

We will now examine editorial production, by which we mean this processing of news and features. The model taken will be that of a national daily paper, but the procedures apply to all newspapers. The only difference is in the titles and numbers of those involved and the division of the work.

The back bench

The main production effort on a daily paper, whether national or provincial, concerns the news and sports pages. It is here that the sub-editors put the pages together under the control of the chief sub-editor and the 'back bench', or of the sports editor, as edition times draw near. These are the pages that carry the bulk of a newspaper's content and the ones at which the main body of incoming copy is aimed.

In the case of certain quality papers such as *The Times* and the *Daily Telegraph* the sub-editing is divided into home and foreign pages, each under a separate chief sub-editor, but the procedure and the deadlines are the same, and the back bench control is common to both. Only with sport is there a separate production system under the sports editor – an autonomy common to nearly all papers.

The sub-editing of features is carried out separately with pages containing women's features and the television guide, as we have said, being prepared the day before, and specially ordered material edited and planned in advance of the news pages. By comparison, the main input of news copy increases in volume towards edition time and a continuous process of reading, selection and editing goes on through the production period.

The term 'back bench' is a loose one and its composition varies from paper to paper, but in general it is where the night editor sits, together with his (or her) deputy, and maybe one or two assistants. This is the control centre once the detailed editing and presentation begin. The assistant editor (news), where there is one, and sometimes the editor, might also sit in on the back bench at the critical moments when the paper begins to take shape.

The night editor is the title usually borne by the executive who takes charge of a morning paper once the production cycle begins, which is from about 4 p.m. On an evening paper, where production can begin as early as 10 a.m., the role is carried out by the deputy or managing editor or in some cases by the chief sub-editor. Subject to decisions already taken at the editor's conference, the night editor, or senior executive in charge, decides which are the more important stories and where they should be placed. He (or she) is particularly responsible for choosing the contents of page one, including the *splash*, or *lead story*, if this has not already been decided.

The night editor and deputy choose the main pictures to be used and draw rough designs for page one and the more important inside pages including, in a popular tabloid, the *centre spread*, on which pictures are usually dominant. The features pages and remaining news pages might be roughed out by the features editor or the chief sub-editor in consultation with the night editor, whose supervision extends to all pages until the edition has been completed.

The rough page plans are passed to the art desk, where there is one, or to a page editor so that the layouts, or schemes, can be drawn in detail, the types chosen, spaces measured and the pictures cropped and scaled. On smaller papers specialist sub-editors sometimes do this work. A copy of the completed page is passed to the chief sub-editor who by this time has discussed the treatment of the main stories with the night editor and is ready to give detailed briefings to the sub-editors on individual stories and the length, placing and headline required.

The art editor, who is in charge of the art desk, discusses with the night editor any special projection needed for stories, commissions graphics such as line drawings and maps, as needed, organizes the editing of pictures and the detailed scheming of the pages, and sees that finished copies of each layout are given to the back bench, the chief sub-editor, and to the composing rooms where pages are being made by paste-up. Where pages are being made up wholly or partly on screen the sub-editor operating the screen terminal is given layouts.

The copy taster is the vital link between the 'gatherers' and the 'processors', and is usually a senior sub-editor whose job is to read every story that is submitted from the news room (nowadays on screen) or from any other copy source. The aim is to select, by a process of rejection, a short list of the stories which are likely to be used. The copy tester works closely with the night editor and chief sub-editor. The more important stories are shown first to the night editor, and the rest of the likeliest ones put into an electronic queue for use by the chief sub-editor as each page is put together.

There is usually a mountain of text to read, with far more stories being rejected than are accepted (there is an electronic 'spike' for stories that are regarded as non-starters), and a constant check being kept on agency copy being routed in on various services. The job is thus responsible and the copy taster needs to have a strongly developed news sense and mental stamina. The job is one of a newspaper's 'hot seats'. There can be a serious inquest on a story that has been given a good space in a rival paper and which did not get used because the copy taster 'spiked' it.

The sub-editors

The detailed editing is carried out by the sub-editors of whom there might be up to twenty or more on a national daily, and ten or twelve on an evening paper, working under a chief sub-editor, though the shift system and holidays reduce the number at any time. Their job, in the case of news stories, is to:

- Check the facts, names and places in a story.
- Check and put right errors of grammar and spelling.
- Cut the text, if necessary, to fit a given space on a page.
- Alternatively, combine material from several sources to make a composite story of the required length.
- Reword all or part of the material, if need be, to attain the required balance and length.
- Check that the story is legally safe, consulting the office lawyer if necessary.
- Key in the appropriate command instructions so that the story is set in the right type size and measure, with correct 'header' instructions indicating catch line, page, column and edition.
- Revise the story as needed for editions in the light of later information or edition area requirements.
- Provide any captions needed for pictures.
- Write a headline on the story in the required type to fit the space available.
- Most important, see that the above procedures are carried out so that the story is ready on time for its page and edition.

Accuracy. The sub-editor rather than the reporter is responsible for the accuracy of what is printed. The best attitude is to be suspicious of everything, especially the spelling of names and places and so check, check, check. There are shelves of reference books, directories and gazetteers in every newspaper office, plus a *cuttings library.* There, stores from national and many local papers, going back perhaps three decades or more, are cut and filed under names and subjects, sometimes electronically. It is a wise precaution, even if the reporter has already done so, for the sub-editor to check a story back through the cuttings. Checking will sometimes reveal if the story the reporter has written is old – and therefore not news.

Failing all else, if you as a sub-editor are still not happy about what has been written, go back to the reporter and check. There may be a vital fact the reporter has forgotten to put in the story.

Be particularly aware of well-known names with hyphenated or unusual spellings (check them in *Who's Who, Crockford's Clerical Directory, Kelly's Handbook to the Titled and Landed Classes* etc.), and of place names where boundaries have changed. Always check literary quotations – they are often wrong and some smart alec will write in and tell you so. Stay close to *Whitaker's Almanack* and the *Municipal Year Book*. They are a mine of information. Don't leave anything to chance.

Grammar and structure. Grammatical mistakes look worse in the paper than in reporter's copy. Some good reporters, you will discover, cannot spell (some famous writers can't).

The general grammar guide in Chapter 1 (The Language of Communication) should be followed, but beware of sub-editing faults that can arise in condensing material or in livening it up. If the meaning is dubious due to grammatical errors, check with the reporter rather than risk the danger of attaching the wrong meaning.

Simplify the grammar where necessary, but in breaking up a long sentence avoid the temptation of starting with 'And', 'But' and 'For' in order to turn it into a string of short sentences. Sentences beginning with conjunctions are allowed in modern newswriting style but should be used sparingly, and for special effect. Resist using dashes in places of commas under the impression that they jolly up a story. Dashes should be kept for genuine parentheses, and these should be few in number.

In shortening or rearranging paragraphs beware of breaking up sequential statements or attaching two non-sequential sentences together in one uneasy paragraph.

See that the story is correctly dated 'yesterday' or 'today' as the paper appears on the streets.

Avoid excessive use of shortened forms such as can't, don't, won't, isn't and hadn't in attempts to colloquialize a story.

A few sub-editorial faults to watch:

- No-one and none are singular.
- Different from, not different to.
- Fewer than, not less than (of numbers).

If you have solved the problem of whether to treat a subject as singular or plural, be consistent; do not use 'it' and 'their' for the same thing in the same sentence.

House style. Use your house style book as a guide for permitted abbreviations and variable spellings, and stick to them. It will tell you whether to say Lt-General or Lieut-Gen.; Flt-Lt or Flt-Lieut., etc., and give standard short forms for countries, political parties and the abbreviations for trade unions and other organizations. If the date style is 6 May, do not say May 6th. Follow the style where it spells: jail not gaol, inquiry not enquiry, dispatch not despatch, organise not organize (or if it recommends vice versa); also whether to say Jugoslavia or Yugoslavia, Tokio or Tokyo. The variants are not necessarily wrong. It is simply a question of being consistent. You will soon find that you know exactly what the style is without referring to the style book, and consistency will be achieved.

In keyboarding copy for setting avoid all abbreviations of words such as: aftn for afternoon, btwn for between, ct for court or chm for chairman or they will turn up in the page like that.

Trade names. There are legal pitfalls for the unwary if trade names are not given initial capitals, even though the name might have come into general use. Manufacturers have a right to insist on initial caps in such names as:

Fibreglass	Hoover
Coke (Coca-Cola)	Photostat
Coalite	Sellotape
Thermos	Elastoplast
Biro	Terylene

It is best to use the non-copyright equivalent: glass fibre, vacuum cleaner, cola, photo-copy, smokeless fuel, sticky tape, vacuum flask, sticking plaster, ball-pen, artificial fibre.

The house style book will list some of these, but there are many more that need to be learned and remembered.

Casting off is the name given to the process of editing a story to fit exactly a given space. It comes from a printing term meaning to cast a line of metal type to an exact fit. Stories have to be cut to fit.

The first essential is to ensure that a story starts in such a way that it takes the reader's attention. The salient point must, as a rule, appear in the introductory paragraph, or *intro* (for guidance on intro writing see Chapter 2: News Writing). Once you, as a sub-editor, are happy that you have an intro which sells the story properly you will find that most stories can be reduced in length, if they have to be, by two methods:

1 Word pruning: take out all expendable words and phrasing so that every remaining word counts. Be severe on adjectives. Leave in long quoted passages only where they are doing a job.
2 Fact pruning: take out facts, starting with the least important, working back until what you have left fills the space. It is useful if a reporter writes a story so that it cuts easily from the bottom upwards. Many are not so obliging, so do not cut it blindly in this way. The reporter might (quite wrongly) have buried the main news point at the end of the story and you will have to rearrange the facts in sequence until your length is achieved.

To cast off accurately you have to know the precise column space which a given number of words will fill. It is a good idea to cut out and keep some specimen column inches from your newspaper, in the various body types in use, so that you have examples of the number of words to an inch. Lengths of stories are usually asked for by chief sub-editors in column inches of the appropriate body type. Thus if 7pt Jubilee 1.c. takes 40 words to the column-inch you will know that a 5-inch story for Page Five in this type will take approximately 200 words – i.e. five times 40. However, most systems will give a word and line count in the 'header' while a story is being subbed.

The technique is the same if your material is from several sources – i.e. maybe from two reporters, a news agency and a few 'ends' from local correspondents. The story has still, in the end, to be cast off to fit a space, though in the case of some *running stories* – stories that last over a period of time – it might be worth while asking for more space if you think the material is better than was expected.

A clear mind is of the essence in dealing with stories of this complexity. It is at this point that you may find it easier to rewrite your material to achieve a coherent narrative of the required length. This can be done on 'split-screen' alongside the original text.

Rewriting is usually done for speed as well as for coherence where a story is poorly written, with the facts in the wrong sequence, or where a story is being collated from several sources. In some cases it may have to be partly re-written, usually the intro and first part. In other cases the sub-editor might decide that a complete rewrite is easiest. Stories that are clearly re-write candidates at the outset are usually given to experienced sub-editors who specialize in this sort of work.

Legal checks. Beware of copy that appears to need only 'tick marking'. Apart from accuracy and grammar, every story has also to be checked by the sub-editor for legal safety, a factor which a reporter might confidently leave to the sub-editor's all-seeing eye. Skill and concentration is just as necessary to watch for the traps in a story that may basically seem simple and well written. There is no story on which a sub-editor can relax vigilance.

A journalist is taught aspects of law that relate to his job – libel, contempt of court, privilege, the effects of the Official Secrets Act, etc. (see Chapter 10) – and a sub-editor, in particular, is expected to beware of the pitfalls that lurk. If an aspect of a story requires extra legal expertise then it is the sub-editor's job to draw it to the attention of the office lawyer. He or she can be a barrister who is a staff journalist as well, or a practising barrister who sits in by arrangement during production hours, or a senior journalist with special legal experience. The office lawyer's role is to read all copy likely to be used in the edition and also all proofs of edited matter.

If a story is legally unsafe the office lawyer will *kill* it – i.e. throw it away. If only part of it is legally unsafe the sub-editor, on the lawyer's advice, will alter the story to put it right, or go back to the reporter for further checks and information so that the story can be made safe. If a story has already been put into type then the lawyer issues a *must kill*, or a *must legal alteration* on a proof or print out, and the story has to be thrown away or put right before the page can be completed.

Instructions. It is the job of the sub-editor to key in command instructions on each story so that it can be put into the right type and measure for its place in the page. In the header area of the monitor screen on to which the story has been recalled for sub-editing should be marked the catch-line of the story, and the page, column and edition. These are printed out with the story so that it can be identified for page make-up, whether on screen or by paste-up. A story that has insufficient information in its header can cause delay in page make-up.

The procedure is exactly the same as it was in 'hard copy' subbing. The header on screen is, in effect, the top of the first sheet. Thus a single column top might be marked, 1st edn, page 1, col 1, with perhaps the catch-line GEM. Then in the story come the command instructions on type and setting which tell the computer what to do. These are not printed out with the story.

Thus the first paragraph of GEM might be given the keyboarded instruction 'uf8rom,8p6', meaning: use format for 8-point bold body type across a width of 8 picas and 6 points. The second paragraph might be marked 'uf7rom,8p6', meaning: use format for 7-point roman body type across the same width. If there is no further instruction the rest of GEM will be set this way. The computer is programmed to continue setting to the last instruction until it encounters a fresh command. It is important, therefore, to see that all instructions are correctly placed before sending copy to the page.

A catch-line, as we have said, should, to be memorable, consist of a word or syllable that relates to the story. Since catch-lines originate in reporters' and feature writers' copy it is a good idea for the subbed versions to have a letter such as 'z' or 'y' appended before being sent for typesetting. This helps to differentiate between the original and the subbed version of stories, both of which remain inside the system since either might need to be called up for some purpose. The old danger of catch-line duplicating and causing confusion during typesetting and make-up no longer applies since the computer will reject a nominated catch-line if it is already in use in the system. Directories of catch-lines are held in modern systems so that the stories can be traced.

Revision. A revision of a story after editing is completed and the story put into type is called a *rejig*. This can come about either because facts have arrived which alter or improve the story for a later edition, or because the position of the story has been altered for a later edition and it has to be shortened or lengthened, or because of matters of taste or legality in the light of second thoughts by the back bench. In all such cases the story, after alteration, is given a catch-line such as 'rap jig' and fed back into the system after being marked for its new position. Some newspapers use the term 'redress' or 'dress' for rejig.

Caption-writing. The job of a caption is to explain the subject of a picture. There are two sorts:

1 Self-contained stories built around the subject of the picture and often carrying a small headline;
2 Simple line captions to explain pictures used to illustrate a story.

Writing a self-contained caption story is a skilled job usually given to a sub-editor who specializes in it. It gives scope for whimsy and imagination since it often has to establish a justification for using a picture which, in itself, may be decorative or visually attractive rather than newsworthy.

A line caption, on the other hand, is simply for identification, although a quotation or a news point should be used where possible, as, for instance:

AFTER the ordeal: Jane Smith yesterday
   or
JANE SMITH: 'I am lucky to be alive'

It is a general rule in newspapers that no picture, however closely it is identified with a story, should be without a caption. A reader is almost certain to see the picture first and is entitled to know who or what it is about.

Proof marks. Where proofs are being marked for contract printers, standard proof correction marks, as authorized by the British Standards Institution, should be used. These cover insertions, deletions, transpositions and marks correcting a wide range of typographical errors.

Typography and text. The style in various newspapers allows some scope for the sub-editor for typographical variation in text (see Figure 20). Apart from the width and size of intro and body setting specified in the page layout, the actual text might need highlighting, especially in the case of long stories. Assuming the body setting is the standard (or roman) body type, some paragraphs can be marked 'bold' or 'italic' as the style allows. This should not be done more than about every four inches, and not at all in short 'legs' where a story crosses several columns.

In the case of lists of items in a story, blobs or black or open (usually pica size) squares can be attached to the start of each paragraph, or even *drop figures* (i.e. figures bigger than the body type). Lengthy quotations can be shown by big *drop quotes* at the beginning and end of the quotation. The essential point with these and any other devices is not to overdo them. A page full of blobs, squares and drop quotes can look very bitty.

Another method is to underscore the lines of type in certain paragraphs for emphasis, although this is done more on feature pages where the items are longer as a rule, and more in need of highlights and breakers.

A more frequent method is to break up long sections by *cross-heads*, sometimes called shoulders, which are a line of type, of perhaps 12pt or 14pt, consisting of one or two words taken from the story and, which in effect, divide it into sections. Some stories might have the *by-line* (the writer's name) set in a panel, or box, and placed in the middle or near the intro of a

Figure 20 Typographical variation. *Left*: feature display showing a standfirst with by-line and a three-line intro drop letter; drop quotation used as a text breaker. *Centre*: a stand-up drop letter; news briefs with a BOT logo; stock motif from sport. *Right*: page one blurb cross-referring to inside items

story. In other cases the by-line might come at the end in the form of a *sign-off* giving simply the writer's name.

Some variation is achieved by setting stories narrower than column measure – i.e. *indented* – or in panels made up of print *rules* or *borders* or in a different body type to the standard one used. Such variations, however, are normally specified on the page layout and should not be introduced by the sub-editor unless instructed to do so. Special setting, as with cross-heads, drop letters and other devices, can be programmed on to special keys. They are referred to as setting formats.

Speed. If deadlines lend drama to a reporter's assignment they count for even more to sub-editor of an evening or morning paper. Not only is the final press time fixed and inescapable; every few minutes bring intervening page and edition deadlines which have to be watched and kept as the sub-editor grapples with the flow of copy, maybe subbing several stories at the same time. A long running story, such as an election or a disaster story, can last all day and into the next day as well while, in intervals of coping with it, the sub-editor might also be handling other stories.

The schedule of copy times for the pages in a big six-edition evening paper, with a page due for completion every few minutes, is a daunting sight for a new sub-editor. He or she is quickly made aware that speed and a clear head are necessary as well as the other talents needed for the job.

On a national morning paper the pressure of speed is less, and the number of hands to do the work greater, but there is an added pressure of polish, word perfection and headline aptness in its place . . . and the deadlines are still there to be met.

Headline writing

A headline performs two functions. First, it draws the attention of the reader to a story and, second, it forms an element in the typographical pattern of the page. While the second function governs the first by nominating a type size and width, which limits the choice of letters and therefore of words that the sub-editor can use, it has to be said that the first function is the most important.

There have been headlines thought up by sub-editors that have been so good that the night editor and chief sub-editor have relented and changed the type on the page to accommodate them. They do not reckon to do this often. The visualizing that goes into a page is considered to be important in itself and to have been arrived at to suit the stories it contains.

In the main stories, the headlines might already have been decided and written as part of the page strategy. The type and space allowed for the remaining ones are regarded as fixed points and a challenge to the sub-editor's headline-writing ability.

The Rules. There are various commonsense do's and don'ts about the headline but what it must do, above all, is make the reader want to read the story. It can do this, broadly, in one of two ways:

1 It can give the important factual point in the story, based upon what the intro says. Such a headline would be:

TEN DIE IN
MIDNIGHT
RAIL CRASH

2 It can take an oblique approach such as:

TOO MUCH FOR
THAT DOGGY
IN THE WINDOW

– which would immediately suggest a fun story about pets. Such oblique headlines often exploit the reader's familiarity with song titles and popular catch phrases.

A variation of the oblique approach is the style immortalized by the *News of the World*:

AFTER HE CALLED TO
MEND THE FUSE

– which can arouse curiosity, even though the reader has a good idea of the sort of details likely to follow.

For most purposes a story with strong factual elements deserves a factual headline. It is annoying for readers to be presented with a headline of such obscure whimsy that they are put off reading an important news story. Equally, a page with too many headlines employing the oblique approach can look trivial even when the contents are not. Like all other elements to do with sub-editing it comes down to a question of balance. The sub-editor must use the headline approach that best suits the contents of the story.

There is no fixed way to write a headline. Some sub-editors are better at it than others. Sometimes the heading suggests itself when you, as a sub-editor, first read the copy; other times it requires much cogitation and the writing down and juggling of key words on your note pad until something comes up. Sometimes the chief sub-editor will present you with the headline idea when handing you the copy and thus rob you of the chance of making your name with a brilliant effort.

Here are a few points that should be kept in mind, whatever sort of heading you are trying to write.

● Keep punctuation out of headlines as far as possible. Commas, dashes, exclamation marks and quotes look messy.
● Avoid stale jargon words where you can (see page 124: Journalese).

- Try to use an active verb, especially in factual headlines.
- Do not cram in too much information – you have only a few words to play with.
- Avoid abbreviations. They look messy, too, apart from being incomprehensible to some people.
- Try to avoid, he, she, or they. Personalize where you can.
- Do not ask questions of the reader.
- Avoid using the past tense in hard news headlines. It dates the story.
- Avoid place names unless they are a vital news elements in themselves – as they sometimes are in local papers.

Some newspapers have house rules such as never writing a headline in which the lines end in 'a', 'the', or 'in'. Such rules are hard to justify and many a good headline has been spoilt in an attempt to conform to them. A more justifiable rule is never to use a headline that needs a *tag-line* (i.e. a secondary line) to explain or justify it:

PARISH IS

A SINK

OF INIQUITY

– says Vicar

In such a case include the Vicar in the headline.

Headline typography. If the count of words is important in casting off a story to fit a space, the count of letters is even more important in headlines, for here the sub-editor is dealing with anything from 12 letters down to about six in headlines of between 18-point and 36-point across single column. In streamers or other multi-column headlines there is more space for letters, but the type is larger. Thus the overall count of a headline across six columns into three columns may be no more than the count for four smaller lines across single column. Either way the headline might have to be accommodated in six or seven words.

On popular tabloids, with their bigger, bolder sans headlines, the problem of letter count is acute, leading at times to strangely distorted phrases and jargon words such as *The Sun*'s GAG BY PRINT MEN RAPPED: i.e. print workers' censorship of editorial material is condemned!

In the quality national press such as *The Times*, *Daily Telegraph* and *The Guardian*, there is more scope through the use of generally smaller, and mostly lowercase, headlines. The extra words available, however, are not always put to the best use. An excessively wordy headline can be limp and weak, or alternatively tell the whole story, leaving nothing for the first few paragraphs.

Whatever the problems, the sub-editor has to be guided by the office *type book* in which the types in use are shown with standard counts, in capitals and in lowercase, across single column and usually double column and three column. The type book remains a useful piece of the headline writer's equipment even in the computer age.

A headline must not only read right and command attention by its message, it must also look typographically right. Since the size and width of the type has been chosen to fulfil a design element – i.e. to match other types and contribute to the character of the page – the sub-editor must compose the headline so that it has an intrinsic balance of its own. The lines must be of the right width within the permitted measure. They must not be too narrow, for lack of letters, or too wide and lacking in word space because of too many letters. The lines must match and not distort.

They must not, for instance, be pyramid shaped:

TEN

DIE IN

MIDNIGHT

RAIL CRASH

or be of too many, variable widths:

TOO

MUCH FOR

THAT DOGGY

IN

THE

WINDOW

If you are new to sub-editing, clip out and file specimen headlines from the paper for reference, and study types used in the paper against examples of word counts given in the type book.

Effect of the computer

The principal effect of the computer for writers and sub-editors has been the disappearance of paper from editorial departments. Not only do text and editing instructions arrive on screen; so also do staff lists and telephone numbers, internal memos, duty and holiday rosters, calls to conference and notes of style changes. Databases and dictionaries are consulted from the keyboard. In some offices even the cuttings library can be called up on line, a search for particular items instituted and the results displayed on split screen alongside a story while checks are made.

Yet in the broad area of writing and sub-editing traditional principles are still important. You are the person in charge of editing the text. The computer is the tool that enables you to carry out your tasks. You have to tell it exactly what you want it to process and in what way, and to be precise in your instructions. Sloppiness in editing and typing that could have been put right in the old days by a discerning linotype operator can cause chaos inside a computer. Failure to define the setting of an intro can result in the entire first paragraph being set in the 42pt type of the headline. Failure to tell the computer where to start new paragraphs will result in an entire story being set as one paragraph.

There is no particular handicap for writers or sub-editors through the use of electronic copy entry; in fact there is a gain in speed if the keyboard and its commands are used correctly. By the use of split screen, rewriting from original sources can be accomplished; the facility of retaining in the system the original and edited versions of each story is useful in cases of queries or rejigs. The hyphenating and justifying of text ready for the page shows exactly how the paragraphs will fall in the paper; the line and word count for text and headlines should ensure an accurate fit in the page.

Stories on the sub-editor's screen instantly rearrange themselves as cuts and adjustments are made, and the days when heavily subbed pieces of paper were misread by linotype operators are looked back upon as a curiosity.

Proof-reading. The old idea of a proof-reading department to which galley proofs of everything were sent for setting errors, or literals, to be spotted and marked has long since gone. The facility of reading back edited and justified text on screen means that keyboarding errors can be seen and put right before the text is consigned to the page. The usual safeguard is for edited text to be passed through the chief-sub or revise sub on screen before being released so that any uncorrected mistakes, including spellings, can be put right or late changes made in length or setting.

Electronic pagination

The duties and roles of sub-editors might remain the same but the change to electronic pagination has brought with it new responsibilities. The total system, in which everything before plate-making happens inside the computer, has meant the final demise of the composing room in most newspapers, thrusting responsibility for making up and preparing pages for the press upon the journalists.

On Britain's national and bigger provincial papers today pages are built up wholly on screen in the editorial department by means of clusters of PCs such as the Apple-Macintosh which uses a program called QuarkXpress to input page materials from the mainframe copy and editing system being used (see Figure 21, page 136). Some newspapers have moved on from mainframes and have networks of Apple-Macs and other PCs serving writers, sub-editors and designers.

To ensure that the pages, now under total editorial control, meet their deadline to the plate room, editors have set up page production teams manned by sub-editors under the overall control of the senior production editor or night editor. The pages, having been drawn and approved, are blocked out on screen by the make-up person and the stories, pictures and graphics identified to the sub-editors and the art desk by on-screen instructions so that editing can be carried out to make them fit.

Stories and headlines, having been checked and cleared by the chief sub-editor, are sent electronically to the page to slot into their space. Pictures and graphics, after cropping and scaling by the art desk, are electronically scanned, colour-corrected if necessary, and imaged into the page via the scanners.

An added factor is that the adverts, too, have to be input from advertising production on to the screens in the editorial production department so that the pages can be completed. Page copies are printed out in mono or colour to be read by the page executive, the legal reader, the editor and the advertising department, and any necessary alterations made. Colour quality is checked on screen.

A final keystroke sends each page forme (one broadsheet page or a pair of tabloid pages) electronically to the pre-plate department or **RIPS** (raster image processor) to be turned into a high resolution negative from which the printing plate is made.

Effects of the change

Page times. A consequence in offices using electronic pagination is that the journalist in charge (by whatever title) of page production has taken over the responsibility formerly held by the head of the composing room for making ready, timing and, in the case of tabloid size, pairing page formes in correct sequence for the plate room and thence to the presses where a prompt start-up is essential to transportation and distribution. Added to this is editorial responsibility for meeting edition change times or for any pages that need to be 'slipped' between editions.

A detailed on-screen 'book' is prepared for each edition notifying plate room and machine room of the times and (for tabloids) the pairing of the pages that are to be expected.

Copy-fitting. Since text cannot be cut and re-edited in the page at make-up stage as under cut-and-paste (see page 131), sub-editors must cast off their stories accurately to fit the setting width and depth. Any small left-over line space resulting from changes in body setting should be evenly 'lost' between paragraphs to fill to depth. Spacing on the whole, both in headlines and text, is more consistent and often tighter in electronically made-up pages.

Because of the need for precise fitting, rejigs and edition changes require stories to be sent back to the sub-editor's screen for reworking and H and J-ing. Every story space is precisely nominated to its 'box' on the page.

Type style. The worry of editors that the computer might somehow alter the look of a successful paper and damage it has long since been resolved. In the early days of the computer it was important to have editorial involvement in the fitting-out stage to ensure that the right type masters were installed to maintain the paper's typographical character.

Some early systems had poor quality type and lacked such thing as stars and blobs and forms of type decoration. Later systems had very extensive ranges of type available and also useful computer graphics. Today, companies produce custom-built type programme packages to suit any newspaper and any requirement, and a number of editors have taken the opportunity to discreetly upgrade their type range out of choice and opportunity.

Likewise in programming at the outset it is essential to put such things as line and word spacing, drop letters, measures and regular forms of special setting on to programmed keys so that speed and consistency of setting can be assured. Bad setting formats, line spacing and kerning is the fault of the programming, although all systems have the facility to override default spacing and kerning.

A regular programming check is a good idea.

Journalese

Headline English, or the use, in the text, of certain words and phrases that stem from the strictures of headline writing, is at the root of journalese, a debasement of the language sometimes found in newspapers. Journalese creeps into stories when sub-editors are not vigilant. It involves the use, in stories, of headline words such as quit for depart, probe for investigate, quiz for question, rap for criticism, axed for dismissed, row for discussion or argument, and drama for almost any sequence of events that you care to name. All are short words which save headline writers time and trouble when they are faced with a single column count of six and a half letters and two minutes to press time.

Letting them spill over into the text can lead to such felicities as:

'Police last night quizzed two men following a probe into a cash grab drama at a West.End bank.'

A good headline writer tries to do without such tired words, although the limitations of space might sometimes make use of one or two inevitable. In the text there is no excuse for them. Editors assiduously avoid all civil service and business jargon only to be threatened by this home-produced jargon creeping in from the editorial shop-floor. Such language can turn stories into stereotypes in which circumstances are in danger of being simplified to serve a set of labels. A new play has to be hit or a flop. A Parliamentary debate is inevitably a row. All actors, singers and soccer players are stars or superstars.

Clear, unambiguous English does not need such tired verbal shorthand. The best journalism the world over is rooted in the demotic language of the people. The test when such jargon words threaten is to ask yourself: do people talk like this? Would a suburban wife really say:

'My Jack's been axed because he quit after his boss slammed him over a cash row.'?

The answer is she would not, and nor should a sub-editor introduce such language into the text.

Here are some more headline words which the text can do without even though they may be justified in a headline:

boss	– chairman, editor, leader etc.
slashed	– reduced
hit	– affected
curb	– restriction
snub	– ignore or overlook
move	– preparation, plan, idea, etc.
clash	– disagreement or meeting
ace	– good at something
shocked	– surprised
sensation	– event
rushed	– taken
boob	– mistake
blasted	– criticized
chopped	– ended.

The distortion factor

Commenting on the practices of some journalists, the most perceptive of all Royal Commission on the Press reports, the one published in 1949, drew attention to headline angling to catch the readers' attention and to the distortion that could arise out of sub-editing.

'Some of our witnesses,' it said, 'suggested that with the popular papers journalistic technique was becoming an end in itself, and that the staff of these papers were concerned to impress their rivals in Fleet Street rather than to serve the public. This is a tendency which needs to be watched because smart journalism carried to extremes may produce a result as far from the truth as carelessness and inefficiency.'

It warned against the drift towards the point when '... liveliness of presentation becomes sensationalism ... to pursue eye appeal to the point where form becomes more important than content is to make the newspaper the slave of its own typography.'

The criticism arose not in the course of a damning attack on the press but in a report that was, on the whole, favourable to the press. The words thus require some consideration, for there are signs, more particularly, but not entirely, in the popular tabloids that the offence is still uncured today.

Keith Waterhouse draws attention to the glut of puns and facetiousness, both in text and headlines, used to jolly up stories, in some of which the facts are sufficiently lively already. He criticizes popular papers' obsession with knickers and underwear, puns on people's names and lavatorial headlines. Of the use of puns and wordplay in the rewriting of stories he says: '. . . this probably stems from a deep-seated fear of a once-insecure profession that its readers would probably rather be playing darts than reading their newspapers. The object is to be entertaining at all costs.'[1]

Waterhouse, a one-time *Daily Mirror* man, has an interesting explanation for what he calls 'silly writing': 'Deadline fever encourages taut, crisp writing with a maximum of facts and a minimum of frills . . . The truly awfully-written story, of the kind that ought to be hung on the walls of schools of journalism as an example of how not to do it, demands time. The puns have to be sweated over, the laborious intro has to be reworked again and again until it cannot possibly be any more forced.'[2]

There is no doubt that the sub-editor, in the search for the telling phrase, a lively style, and words of the right length to give a headline, can be in as much danger of doing an injury to the facts as any reporter, however rushed by events. The demands for a compelling headline within the limits of a word-count can cause the sub-editor to push the meaning of a story to its limit, and distortion in headlines has become one of the more frequent causes of complaint to the Press Complaints Commission along with inaccuracy through 'abridgement'.

There is also the insidious distortion, or slanting, that can arise from using a photograph in which a grimace or gesture, caught in an unguarded moment by a cameraman, acts against the interests of a subject such as a politician or a trade union leader. Such pictures, sometimes taken from stock to use with a news story, can help condition the readers' response.

There can be a danger of distortion even in the typographical display given to a story. The supply of news and features to a newspaper each day is not constant in quality or quantity, whereas the amount of display tends to remain about the same. It can happen that an item that one day merits a modest amount of attention might on a different day, when the supply of news and features is not so strong, be given a disproportionate amount of display. The daily unpredictability of content can thus result in the treatment of two comparable news or feature items varying so much on different days that there would be reason for a complaint of distortion of treatment. This situation is almost insoluble for editors who have to bring out a paper of more or less similar size and character day after day. It is the explanation that lies behind what Stanley Morison, in the *History of The Times*, calls 'the curse of invented news' – the dilemma of sub-editors on the days when, no matter how little news there is about, the paper has somehow got to be filled, and made to look interesting.

As the Royal Commission says, it is a situation that needs to be watched.

Features editing

The processing of news and features follows the same basic procedures whether there is a total or partial separation of the two departments. As explained in Chapter 3, there are some newspaper features which relate very closely to news stories and are, in effect, extensions of them, while others – women's and show-business pages, for example – are usually quite separate. The material has still to be written, assessed, fitted on a page layout, headlined and projected typographically. A features sub-editor has pressures and deadlines the same as a news sub-editor.

There is a difference, nevertheless, in the degree of editing. Features are unlikely to be a composite of a number of copy sources in need of rewriting. In fact, rewriting should not normally be necessary. Features are ordered for a purpose from a writer qualified in his or her field, often to a specified length and for a pre-planned page. The writing is programmatic and revolves around a point of view supported with premises, whether it is a simple pets column or an explanation of defence policy. Features also tend to express more than any other element the paper's special character.

The sub-editing is therefore gentler and more sympathetic, both of style and content, than with news sub-editing. Features are edited for accuracy, grammar and legal safety. Any rewriting is subtly done to keep the material within the writer's style and there is much less cutting of text than in news. In the case of some writers, cutting is forbidden except in special circumstances, and the layout is 'bent' to suit the text.

There is also generally a more deliberate typographical and visual projection than in news stories, based upon the length of the feature.

Further reading

F. W. Hodgson, *Subediting: A handbook of modern newspaper editing and production* (Focal Press, 2nd Edition, 1993) updates sub-editing practice. Leslie Seller's *The Simple Sub's Book* (Pergamon Press, London, 1968) has useful information. Keith Waterhouse's *On Newspaper Style* (Viking, 1989) has some cautionary words on sub-editing styles. Vic Giles and F. W. Hodgson's *Creative Newspaper Design* (Focal Press, 2nd Edition, 1996) is essential for coverage of page production techniques.

8 Printing

Nearly all British newspapers or groups of newspapers own their own printing facilities. Some early newspapers were founded and owned by printers. Contract printing was common during the 19th century, but newspaper companies from the time of Northcliffe found that they had better control over their product by having their own print works. Today this has been rationalized so that many weekly papers and some evenings are printed from centralized plants, either under the same ownership, or as a result of sharing arrangements. At the same time some companies that have replanted with sophisticated modern presses have been able to offer such reasonable terms to other less well provided newspapers that there has been a movement back into contract printing since the 1980s both by small newspapers and some new titles that have appeared.

As a result of these developments the printing of regional and local papers has come to be concentrated at fewer but better equipped sites, with printing plates being made centrally by electronic transfer of pages from several editorial offices.

A reverse situation has occurred with national newspapers which, during 1980s and 1990s have moved some, and in a few cases all, of their printing to a number of sites around the country and even abroad. This has been made possible by the electronic transmission of made-up pages in facsimile (see pages 135–7) which enables printing plates to be made locally.

The aim, in the case of the national newspapers, is to shorten delivery times to wholesalers and bring later news to edition areas formerly dependent on long rail or road journeys for their newspapers.

Because of distribution and plant arrangements, daily and even weekly newspapers work to tight schedules which, under the changes described in the last chapter, require ever closer liaison between the editorial and the printing and publishing side. Missed deadlines can mean either material not getting into the right edition or the paper coming out late and some areas getting the wrong edition.

The purpose of this chapter is to look at the printing arrangements in the modern newspaper and to examine how they have come about.

The hot metal legacy

The typographical style of newspapers as they look today was developed during the long years of 'hot metal' technology, rooted in Caxton and perfected during the 19th century, which was employed by all newspapers until the late 1950s and by Britain's big circulation national papers until the mid-1980s. Molten metal (an alloy of 4 per cent tin, 12 per cent antimony and the rest lead) was used to set text and headlines in type and to mould the final printing plates used to print the newspaper by the letterpress method mainly on rotary presses, though in some cases on sheet-fed flat-bed presses.

The text was set from the writers' copy, containing instructions by the sub-editor, on manually operated automatic line casters, of which the commonest used was the Linotype machine. These set lines to the required width with the letters 'justified' by the operators so that they filled the line. The operator keyboarded the text into the machine in which the letters, or matrices, came together mechanically to form a line. The machine injected hot metal to take an impression of the line. As they cooled, the lines, or *slugs*, ejected into a tray in sequence until the entire story was set. Usually several operators set parts of each story.

Headlines were set on separate machines by operators who hand-selected letters from cases of metal type and arranged them on a metal 'stick' into which hot metal was injected creating, when it cooled, a metal slug of the headline reading in reverse. In the case of both headlines and text the type matrices were returned to their cases from which they would be used again and again for casting lines.

The setting of type and its arrangements into pages was called *composing* and the printer who did this was a compositor. The room in which this work was carried out was the *composing room*, or sometimes the case room, from the cases in which the type matrices were kept.

When each story was set the slugs of text and headlines were gathered on to metal trays, or galleys, from which were pulled inked proofs, called *galley proofs*. These were circulated to proof readers for setting errors to be corrected, and to the editorial for checking and reference. The galleys of type were assembled on a metal-topped bench called a *random*, from which they were transferred to another bench called a *stone* (originally topped by stone) on which the pages were made up.

The pages were put together from the lines of type, together with metal 'blocks' of pictures and adverts, in metal frames, or chases, by a compositor called a *stone-hand*. He (women stone hands were almost unheard of in hot metal print) fitted the materials in accordance with a page layout, or *scheme*, supplied by the editorial. The *half-tone* blocks by which photographs were reproduced in pages cast under the hot metal process posed an interesting example of an optical illusion. Finely screened raised dots of varying size, each taking ink and surrounded by white space, represented the varying range of tones between black and white in a mono picture so effectively that the fact that a picture was simply a collection of dots was apparent only by the closest inspection. Drawings, on the other hand, were reproduced as *line blocks* in which the lines printed as continuous black.

The completed page with all the stories, pictures and adverts in position – or pair of pages in the tabloid format – was referred to as a *forme*.

The printing plate. To achieve the curved metal plate from which the page was printed a *mould* was first taken from the forme in a papier-maché material called *flong*. This was laid across the forme so that it made contact with the raised type and blocks. The forme with the flong in contact with it was then placed under a moulding press in which the page impression was transferred to the flong under heavy pressure. The page mould, after being checked to see that it was free from faults, was put into a plate caster where hot metal was injected upon it while it was inside a drum. The resulting curved cast of the page, this time with the type raised up in relief but in negative, was called a *stereotype* plate. The plate was then attached to the rotary press along with other stereo plates for the paper to be printed by the letterpress, or direct impression, method.

The rotary press, the standard printing press in newspaper technology until the web offset press came along, and still used in some newspaper offices, comprises a roll-stand for carrying the roll of newsprint, a device for inking the plates as the machine operates, together with plate cylinders on which the stereotype plates are locked, and impression cylinders which press the printing paper against the stereotype plates. The ink is mechanically spread on the drum and thence by a series of distributing rollers to the printing plates and from there directly to the paper. The unit prints the paper on both sides, cuts the newsprint into pages and folds the product. The number of pages printed can be increased by using more printing units linked. Modern multiple-unit rotary presses can deliver up to 60,000 copies an hour.

The presses are located in the *machine room*. From here, conveyors take continuous streams of papers to the warehouse, or publishing room, where they are bundled and labelled for distribution. A machine room of a big circulation daily might use up to twenty-four rotary presses in order to achieve its printing 'run'. The number of plates needed for all editions runs into many hundreds an issue.

The computer

The revolution brought about by the computer has resulted in hot metal being abandoned at all stages in newspaper production to be replaced by computer-generated type and graphics, leading ultimately to page make-up on screen, with the page image being transferred to smooth polymer plates running on web-offset presses instead of on rotaries (letterpress).

It was a revolution not without its human problems. The use of VDUs (visual display units) or terminals meant that reporters and writers could keyboard their text directly into the computer, whence it could be recalled for checking and editing and then stored till needed. This meant the end of printers as such.

Cut-and-paste. In the early stages, once pages had been drawn and types and setting chosen, text and headlines were set from type 'masters' inside computer-driven photosetters in response to keystrokes by the sub-editors. These were output on bromide paper along with laser prints of the photographs, artwork and adverts and pasted on to page make-up cards, which had columns and depth marking in non-reproducing pale blue. The process was known as cut-and-paste and is still used on some newspapers.

At a stroke, typesetting, as it was known under hot metal had gone and the writers' keystrokes, subject to editing, were being used to set the newspaper in type. Direct input had arrived.

There still remained a composing room in which the pages were being put together on make-up frames rather like artists' easels by paste-up compositors using a wax adhesive. An editorial production editor would be on hand to see that the layouts were being precisely followed and that everything fitted. On completion, each page was photocopied for final checking and then photographed to produce a page negative. This was transferred by being 'burnt' into a smooth polymer plate to be printed by web-offset litho, or to a heavy polymer relief plate for printing by letterpress.

The cut-and-paste system worked well enough. A good paste-up compositor could do a faster job than under hot metal and produce an attractive result, with deft touches on features display, although a rushed page could betray spacing faults where text had been cut up to fit.

The end of even paste-up composing for most newspapers, however, was just a matter of time. By the mid-1980s a number of provincial papers and two new national dailies, *Today* and *The Independent*, were being made up on screen, although difficulties of graphics generation were resulting in pages having to be printed out with 'windows' to take laser-printed photographs and adverts before being consigned to negative.

There was still a fear by editors that screen make-up would impose modular shapes on newspapers that wanted to keep the free-style approach that hot metal and paste-up had allowed them. But the change to the total system was just round the corner.

Web-offset.[1] The consequence – and to some extent the aim – of photo-composition was a considerable cost-saving through doing away with traditional typesetting and block-making. Also, typesetting became much faster and less prone to error since texts could be checked on screen for keyboarding mistakes before being consigned to the photo-setter.

Manual speeds on a Linotype machine were about five lines a minute. An intermediate stage introduced in the 1960s in which line-casters were driven by computer-justified tape increased output to 14 lines a minute. Early photo-composition in the mid-1960s lifted speeds to 80 lines a minute, while by the 1980s laser-powered photosetters using cathode ray tubes (CRTs) were able to set at more than 1000 lines a minute from stored signals.[2]

A big attraction, however, was the interfacing of photo-composed pages with web-offset litho which, with the demand for colour and finer screen reproduction and generally cleaner operation, had moved into the van of press development. Photo-composed pages transfer easily to the smooth surfaces of web-offset pages. The thin photo-sensitive offset plate is applied directly to the page negative under bright light by a process in which the image is burned into it and the waste polymer washed away. The image is then transferred to newsprint by means of a chemical solution which creates areas that attract and areas that repel ink, using a fine balance between ink and water. The plate picks up ink from a bath which it offsets to a rubber blanketed cylinder which makes the actual contact with the paper, thus offsetting the ink impression on the paper. In letterpress the plate prints directly by impression on to the paper.

The dual method of web-offset printing linked to photo-composition appealed initially to smaller papers to whom the limited printing capacity of the early offset presses was no disadvantage. Starting in America as early as 1961, the new technology spread rapidly across the country. The system packages, designed primarily for smaller American papers, were soon taken up by some British provincial papers and some European ones as the first stage of the computer revolution.

The advantages were: better quality picture reproduction due to the method's acceptance of a finer screen (i.e., the number of dots making up the tones of a picture); easy adaptation to colour printing, with its attraction to advertisers; cleaner operation and less ink 'mist' than with letterpress printing; easier utilization for commercial printing, plus the very considerable savings on space and labour. The disadvantages were: higher operating and maintenance costs; greater waste of newsprint compared to letterpress especially at start-up (up to 3 per cent instead of 1 per cent); higher plate costs than for stereotype plates, limited types available in the early photo-setters and – probably the biggest item – the high cost of press replacement for the bigger newspapers with banks of rotary presses which might have left a life of as much as twenty-five years.

With the improvement in efficiency of web-offset presses for newspaper printing, and of photo-setting facilities, their use spread to the bigger American papers,[3] particularly those faced with the need to re-equip their machine rooms, and likewise spread further in Britain.

One thing that commended the new technology to bigger newspapers who were not ready to replant their machine rooms was the fact that they could continue to use their rotary presses by converting the page negative derived from paste-up, or from screen, to polymer relief plates. There was an interim stage where a low relief metal plate was made from a polymer pattern plate derived from the page negative, the thinking being that polymer could not on its own sustain a heavy print run. The trouble was that the extra processing added to plate-making time and costs, and this method was dropped when, in the mid-1980s, a new type of hard polymer appeared which made relief plates durable enough to stand long-run letterpress printing. To give them the right thickness to make them acceptable to the rotaries they were mounted on metal 'saddles'. They had the advantage that they were considerably lighter than the 40lb (18kg) conventional stereo plate. Thus the durability and cheap running costs of the rotary presses could be married to the cost-saving of photo-composition and a company's investment in its traditional machine room not thrown away.

By 1983 more than 130 out of approximately 200 newspaper production centres in England and Wales were using photo-setting. Eighty were printing by web-offset and the others on rotary presses with the use of polymer or low relief metal plates, or by the direct litho method in which rotary presses were converted to the use of smooth printing plates. Forty-two out of Britain's seventy-five evening papers were being produced by these new methods along with several hundred weekly and bi-weekly papers. Of the thirty biggest provincial newspaper companies only eight were not using some form of computerized technology, although disputes existed with the print unions as to who handled the new electronic equipment. Fleet Street, with its high circulation national daily and Sunday papers, remained a lone bastion of hot metal with only the Daily Mirror Group and *The Times* and *Sunday Times* photo-setting some or all of their pages, and using pattern plates to produce flongs from which conventional stereo metal plates were cast.

Within five years, spurred on by News International's move to Wapping in 1986, the whole of the British press, national and provincial, had thrown out hot metal and moved into the computer age, direct copy input by journalists had become established and the traditional craft printers had departed from the scene. In the case of the nationals it meant the abandonment of the centuries-old presence on Fleet Street as companies raced to sell their inconvenient city centre properties and build new hi-tech plant in Dockland and the suburbs of London.

Colour. The inability of newspapers to accomplish anything but rather primitive spot colour or pre-printed colour on rotary presses made the move into web-offset printing inevitable once computerized systems had become universally accepted. The gradual replanting of machine rooms means that most titles can now offer full run-of-the-press colour to advertisers and for selected editorial use by being able, through the use of colour separations electronically scanned, to print from colour positives and prints. Colour picture coverage can thus be given edition by edition in the same way as black and white.

Since pages have to make four passes through the press to receive each of the four principal source colours printing in register, special pages are nominated to accept colour so that extra press time can be set aside for them and publishing delay minimized.

The debate on how successful or desirable colour is on editorial pages, as opposed to advertising, continues. Meanwhile, on many national papers, and some provincial ones, some of the demand for colour advertising is being met by separately printed gravure colour magazines distributed as supplements without extra charge.

The total system

The ultimate development had always been the total system in which the text was entered by writers at the front end and emerged at the back end, after editing, planning and page design, as a printing plate, thus doing away with a composing room. The solving of the problems of screen geometry and graphics generation have now made this possible and electronic pagination as it is called is now becoming the norm.

Early fears that it might force inflexible modular shapes on to editors have abated as a result of the development of PC-linked systems in which (principally) Apple-Macintosh page-making terminals interact with office mainframe systems.

By early 1993 a growing percentage of provincial titles had moved into electronic pagination using a variety of page-makers. Meanwhile, most national titles both popular and quality, having evolved Apple Mac-based systems to suit their more complex requirements, and using QuarkXpress software, were ready for the plunge into full electronic pagination (see Figure 21). Trial runs showed that the final stumbling block – the layout demands of the popular tabloids – had been overcome by the flexibility and on-screen facilities of these hybrid systems, and editors were no longer in danger of having to change their presentation to suit the systems.

The movement into the total system was not a uniform progress. In 1995, despite the breakthrough in national newspaper offices, cut-and-paste was still being used by more than half Britain's newspapers for all or part of their page production. At the same time electronic pagination was being increasingly used alongside it in most centres. In some cases the cost of re-equipping was the problem.

Typical were examples in provincial papers where, through problems of graphics generation or advertising input, a page could not be completed on screen and had to be printed out as a bromide with spaces to take pasted-on material. It was then photographed to produce the negative for plate-making. Thus a camera-driven composing room still remained the interface between the editorial department and the presses.

Yet after nearly fifteen years of dominance the writing for cut-and-paste was on the wall. The concentration of printing by leading provincial newspaper companies into fewer strategically placed centres released the capital needed to re-equip and replant. By 1996 the bigger companies had joined the national papers in installing advanced page-making systems which cut out even the RIPS and page negative stage as well as the composing room by allowing for the outputting pages direct from screen to plate. The total system had truly arrived.

Other uses. The bigger newspaper computer systems can perform a variety of additional tasks such as accounting, auditing, purchasing and stock control. Tele-ad girls taking down classified advertisements can type them straight into the computer and recall them in the required measure while the system works out the charge, gives a credit check on the customer's account, classifies the advert into its section, arranges the number of insertions and bills and invoices the customer.

The Financial Times keyboards its stocks and shares prices into the computer which adjusts the price and yield and calculates the changes from the previous day's prices. Football league tables can be automatically updated simply by keying in the latest results, and the form record of thousands of racehorses kept up to date.

Page facsimile transmission

In multi-centre production, newspaper pages can be transmitted in facsimile from the main production centre by means of scanners which miniaturize the data so that it is compatible for sending by microwave, for short distances, or by broadband telephone lines or earth satellite for longer distances. Receivers at the various production centres unscramble the signal to re-form the pages and turn them into printing plates. The newspaper is then printed by web-offset or letterpress according to the system in use, without the need for any typesetting or any editorial intervention.

Figure 21 Electronic pagination arrives: a *News of the World* page one awaiting changes on screen on an Apple Macintosh PC in a standard production run. Alongside is the first edition. A special program enables the PC to interact with and use data from the paper's Atex mainframe system

The earliest use of this method was for the projected 'home facsimile' of newspapers to subscribers. This was tried experimentally by the *St Louis Post-Dispatch* in America in 1938, using radio signals, but was introduced first in Japan after the war by the *Asahi Shimbun* to 100,000 potential subscribers near Tokyo. The idea was to use a tele-newspaper receiver, but the cost of the machine and the paper proved to be uneconomic from the subscriber's point of view and the idea was dropped.

The Guardian, in Britain, began in 1949 to investigate the possibility of using the method for wiring pages for printing from Manchester to London but ran into union problems and dropped it. Japanese papers eventually established its regular use for multi-centre production in the 1960s. The first British paper to use it successfully was the *Daily Mirror* for its Ulster edition, printed in Belfast from 1966 to 1971 when the plant was bombed by the IRA and abandoned.

Today, Britain's national papers print by facsimile transmission in a variety of centres around the country and abroad. At Canary Wharf, in East London, where many of the titles are now located, there are no actual newspaper presses in use. The whole of their print runs are decentralized to strategically placed publishing plants and distribution centres chosen for ease of delivery to wholesalers.

The Financial Times, the *Daily Mirror*, *The Sun*, the *News of the World*, *The Economist* and the *Wall Street Journal* all use earth satellite for simultaneous production of editions abroad. It takes about three minutes a page to transmit an entire newspaper.

Page facsimile transmission makes it possible for a newspaper to extend its circulation area without heavy production and labour costs at secondary centres (which are not necessary with modern technology). It is suited to countries in which the geography and transport structure normally make it impossible to circulate a newspaper to all areas on the same day.

Looking ahead

Newspaper technology, despite the great breakthrough of the last decade, continues to develop. While there is little likelihood of machines doing away with reporters, feature writers or sub-editors, or for the need for considered page design, the mechanics of printing production keep being refined. Several British newspapers, we have seen, have installed equipment that can receive pages abroad by satellite transmission as offset plates ready for the press.

Even more advanced are the experiments in plateless printing. One version of this is ink-jet printing in which a computer-controlled ink gun sprays the letters on as the paper moves. The aim, by eliminating plates, is to reduce mechanical pressures, thus simplifying press design.

More revolutionary are the developments in picture transmission. It is now possible to set up an electronic picture desk in which a picture editor can call up a picture straight from a transmitter on to a screen, crop, size and adjust the tones of the image, and output it to an electronic page make-up system. To phase in with this there is a video still camera on the market which can capture fifty images on a 2-inch floppy disk, which is inserted by the photographer straight into a portable still video transmitter. This has its own CRT monitor which enables the photographer to select which pictures to transmit. The transmitter is then linked to a telephone line by means of a modem and a picture can be on the picture editor's screen within two minutes by simply dialling.

With the arrival of the electronic picture desk, staff and agency pictures, using digitized transmission can be fed straight into the system in which computerized storage and retrieval allows up to 300 pictures to be stored in negative form on a disc from which they can be chosen by monitor for printing. The aim is to capture late-breaking news on picture right up to page deadlines – in the case of electronic pagination without even taking time printing out. Meanwhile, newspapers have begun to store archive picture material on disc for feeding into the electronic system.

On the text side, and looking even further into the future, experiments are being carried out by the Americans and Japanese into voice character recognition machines which could in the end do away with keyboarding by writers.

A ten-year forecast for Britain by the Printing Industries Research Association (PIRA) issued in 1982, which visualized the general acceptance of direct inputting and page make-up by non-printing personnel, the increasing interfacing of word procesors with photo-setting systems, and an advance in the regional printing of newspapers from centralized editing and make-up facilities, had achieved its targets within five years.

A press release from the Printing and Publishing Industries Training Board, which sponsored the report, underlined the consequences of the changes in printing technology: '. . . The demand for old production skills – composing, retouching, page make-up, plate-making – is diminishing. There is a pressing need for new computer-related skills in data processing, systems management and computer science.'

In order to keep up with the latest technology many newspaper companies in Britain and the rest of Europe are members of IFRA, the international newspaper research organization based at Darmstadt in West Germany. It publishes a monthly magazine called *Newspaper Techniques*, evaluates new systems and carries special reports on all aspects of newspaper technology.

Electronic text

The abandonment of the 'home facsimile' newspaper idea led, in its place, to the use of television sets for electronic news transmission in America and Britain as an alternative to printed newspapers. The British systems have made more progress. There are two sorts.[5] Under the Prestel Viewdata system, owned by British Telecom, telephone subscribers pay for access to pages of information on an adapted television screen connected by telephone by a BT computer. Information providers, which include newspapers, travel companies and other advertisers, lease page space and have direct access to the system via special keyboards. The pages on offer include classified advertisements, financial information, home and sports news, holiday and car buying guides and games and quizzes.

There have been problems over copyright of material run on Prestel, in which British Telecom is in the position of being a carrier service. Questions have also been raised about the need for some form of control over the acceptance of material and of the confusing of editorial with advertising material.

The other system is operated by the BBC under the name of Ceefax and by ITV's Teletext (formerly Oracle). A decoder in the TV set makes use of redundant lines so that the viewer can call up pages of information. Here, control of material rests with the bodies controlling the BBC and ITV.

Ceefax and Teletext were slow to take off in the early years but are now standard on most TV sets though, despite criticisms, the page files remain thin and the 'pages' slow to call up on the electronic calibrator.

In 1993, after 20 years of transmitting, Prestel still had a modest 100,000 subscriber terminals, 60 per cent of them business, although pages of information had grown substantially in number.

There were also recurring complaints to Prestel and Teletext about the allegedly porn content of some late night advertisements.

Compaine, the American media technology authority, quotes the (admittedly partisan) views on electronic news pages of Jules Tewlow, an American Newspaper Publishers' Association director: 'It would appear unwise, if not patently foolish, to bet on the facsimile technology which offers only a limited potential for future growth as a principal carrier of information into the home ... Sheer bulk of product, logistics and limited selectivity capabilities preclude this.'

Further reading

See F. W. Hodgson, *Subediting: A handbook of modern newspaper editing and production* (Focal Press, 2nd Edition, 1993). Paul Williams's *The Computerized Newspaper* (Butterworth-Heinemann, 1990) is an essential text. The National Union of Journalists outlines some of the practical and human problems in *Journalists and New Technology* (NUJ, London, 1980). Ruari McLean's *Typography* (Thames and Hudson, London, 1980) has a useful chapter on the artistic and technical implications of photo-setting. See also Giles and Hodgson: *Creative Newspaper Design* (Focal Press, 2nd Edition, 1996) for utilization of the new systems.

The American view is given thoroughly in Benjamin M. Compaine's *The Newspaper Industry in the 1980s* (Knowledge Industry Publications Inc., New York, 1980), though it is now dated.

References

1 'Web' refers to the continuous run of paper from a reel as opposed to sheet-fed lithographic printing.
2 COMPAINE BENJAMIN, M.: *The Newspaper Industry in the 1980s* (Knowledge Industry Publications Inc., New York, 1980) p. 115.
3 Between 1963 and 1978, hot metal line-casters in the US declined from 11,175 to 1,158, and photo-composition units increased from 265 to 3,090. Source: SMITH, Anthony: *Goodbye, Gutenberg* (Oxford University Press, London, 1980).
4 COMPAINE, *op. cit.*, Chapter 7.
5 SMITH, Anthony, pp. 249–60, gives a detailed assessment.
6 COMPAINE, *op. cit.*, p. 156.

9 Running a newspaper

'I believe that financial strength and commercial stability are the best guarantees of a free press and it is management's task to use the resources with which it has been entrusted to make this possible.' *Lord Thomson of Fleet*[1]

Newspapers in Britain are owned by a great variety of companies from small family firms to big industrial conglomerates which control some of the national daily and Sunday papers. Despite the spread of companies in the provinces, four of them, Trinity International (formerly Thomson Regional Newspapers), Associated Newspapers, United Newspapers and Westminster Press control 30 per cent of the titles. The biggest of these, Trinity, is Britain's fastest growing newspaper chain.

The shift in ownership of national titles in recent years, as we have seen, has been away from the old club of proprietorial families towards multinational companies and industrial groups, albeit some with powerful proprietor figures. With this shift has come a remoter, less personalized control and, from the late 1970s, tougher, more vigorous management and tight financial accountability.

The provincial companies are organized at employer level in the Newspaper Society, which was formed in 1836 and represents virtually all regional and local newspaper publishers in England, Wales and Northern Ireland. The society negotiates wage agreements with the newspaper unions on behalf of members and offers a variety of services covering industrial relations, advertising, training, distribution and technical advice.

The Newspaper Publishers Association (NPA), formed in 1906, carries out a similar function in London and Manchester for the publishers of the national dailies and Sunday papers. The NPA is a looser organization since the more competitive national newspapers tend to take their own decisions on technology and production methods, are not involved directly in training, and carry out a good deal of in-house negotiation with the unions, though by 1990

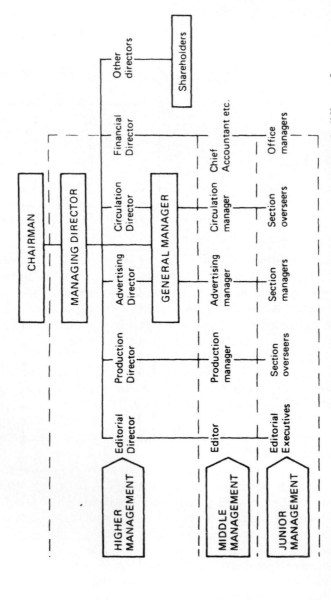

Figure 22 The management structure of a big or medium-sized newspaper company is not much different from any company structure. Here is a general model of the sort of titles that might be found

personal contacts had come to be used for many editorial staffs. The unified distribution arrangements organized between the NPA and British Rail have given way to a variety of individual arrangements mainly using road transport. As with the Newspaper Society, the NPA has a committee which advises on advertising standards.

Newspaper publishers in Scotland are served by two similar organizations, the Scottish Newspaper Proprietors Association and the Scottish Daily Newspaper Society.

Management

In the smaller provincial companies management is still a personal thing and follows a traditional pattern with relatively few titles, and a consultation procedure suited to the size of the newspaper.

In national papers and the bigger provincial centres control is exercised from the top through a number of executive or working directors each responsible for departments of the paper. Their twofold job is to provide a boardroom window on departmental activity to facilitate control and to offer specialist advice for the formulating of policy. The working directors play an important role in maintaining the financial viability of the company in initiating and imposing budgets and taking decisions, within a company's agreed policy, on such things as expenditure on capital equipment and its renewal, preparing trading statements, statistics and forecasts and controlling departmental activities. They also make the main appointments in their department (see Figure 22).

An average board has working members with such titles as editorial director, production director, advertising director and circulation director. In some cases there may not be an editorial director, in which case the editor (if there is only one paper, for example) is sometimes a director. In other cases advertising and circulation might come under one marketing director. Some companies also appoint a financial director to co-ordinate accounts, budgeting and the business side. On smaller groups these activities might be carried out by the company secretary.

Such directors, either alone or together with the managing director, are the stage of final appeal iñ departmental disputes, as with those concerning staff or workforce where the trouble has failed to be resolved at a lower level. This can be time-consuming activity on national papers when there is in-house bargaining over wages and conditions.

Budgeting and financial forecasting by departmental directors are helped in the more efficient offices by day-to-day checks and reports from line managers – overseers in charge of the various processes covered by the department. Where firm budget control is the rule any exceptional departmental expense has to be authorized at board level.

The structure just described comprises higher management. Below, and reporting to the departmental directors, come the managers who control the day-to-day activity of the departments. There is usually an overall general manager, who is sometimes also a director. The duties here vary from paper to paper but general managers tend on the whole to be involved more with mechanical production and administration, and with the workforce, and seldom with editorial or financial matters. The production side can include the maintenance and running of equipment and presses, plate making and the actual printing and publishing of the paper. Here there is an elaborate middle management structure with a production manager, deputy production manager, usually several assistants and, on national dailies, a night production manager. It is in this area, where the main mechanical workforce is concentrated, that problems of quality and work flow are most likely to arise, and where the maintenance of work schedules and quality control is vital. Here a regular physical managerial presence is necessary.

The advertising and circulation departments also have their managers and deputies, and there is sometimes a manager in charge of personnel and another in charge of publicity and promotions.

The role of middle management just described is to see that departments run smoothly, are properly manned, and that the work is completed on time to the required quality. The managers and their deputies are responsible for departmental appointments, budget control, duty rostering and work planning. In the case of disputes they are the intermediate stage in the procedure.

Below middle management, and reporting to them, come the line management, the heads or overseers of sections within the department. Titles again are more prolific on the production side, including plate room manager, machine room manager, systems manager, warehouse manager and so on. Their job is principally quality control, organizing the actual work 'on the line' and making sure there is someone competent there to do the job. The line managers are the first stage if any problems or disputes crop up.

The editor and his (or her) deputy run the editorial function as a department of the newspaper, though with more 'pull' in terms of authority than other department heads, delegating responsibility to their own departmental executives, appointing staff and dealing with problems. The administration side of the department is usually delegated to the deputy editor or to a managing editor.

Changes. Managements in the national newspaper industry as well as the unions came under criticism in the report on the industry published in 1966 by the Economist Intelligence Unit, and again in the reports of the 1976–77 Royal Commission on the Press. The principal grounds were the lack of outside expertise at higher management level and the lack of corporate planning objectives in industrial relations and, in some cases, marketing and budgeting objectives. Roderick Martin, an academic who published *New Technology and Industrial Relations in Fleet Street*, in 1981,[2] said of the management of the 1970s: 'The limiting effects of restricted recruitment were not alleviated by systematic career development, or by the wide use of outside training courses. . . . Excessive preoccupation with the practical and the customary resulted in an inadequate sense of perspective.'

By 1978, however, there were signs (noted by Simon Jenkins)[3] that this situation was changing. The onset of new technology, though still of modest proportions, was the principal agent, coupled with the need for stringent measures to deal with the trade recession which from 1978 began to bite into advertising revenues. Agreements on photo-setting at the Mirror Group and at *The Times* and *Sunday Times* enabled managements to buy out expensive old piecework practices and to restructure the production side. A tougher approach on annual wage negotiations, with agreements linked to manning cuts, helped to control the crippling yearly increases in wage costs.

The need for computer-based skills at the top resulting from the new technology brought in new blood and began a modest flow of appointments from company to company. Accountants and directors from outside the newspaper industry began to appear on boards. The unions, faced with changes in skills and job descriptions, responded with mergers to enable them to preserve their power and presence. Most important, the computerization of the editorial functions and many of the commercial functions of newspapers brought within reach the possibility of cost savings, though at first the attitudes of the unions, with their concern with jobs, made the full utilization of the new systems impossible and equipment remained mothballed for long periods while talks went on.

The unions

Two important union mergers in 1982, arising from the need felt by the members for a unified policy with which to grapple with the problems of computerized technology, reduced to six the number of trade unions representing the majority of employees of national and provincial papers.

The National Graphical Association (NGA), itself formed from the amalgamation of seven unions, and representing skilled printers, stereotypers, proof-readers and machine managers, merged with the second biggest craft union, the Society of Lithographic Artists, Designers, Engravers and Process Workers (SLADE) to form one union representing all craft workers. The new union chose the title of the National Graphical Association '82.

In the same year the two biggest unions representing the mainly semiskilled newspaper workers, the National Society of Operative Printers, Graphical and Media Personnel (NATSOPA) and the Society of Graphical and Allied Trades (SOGAT) merged under the title of SOGAT '82. The combined union represented engineers' assistants, printing assistants, cleaners, clerks, editorial messengers, copy readers, firemen, commissionaires, drivers, loaders and pressroom workers, but also circulation representatives and advertising staff and, in Scotland, some skilled printers.

Journalists were still represented in the main by the National Union of Journalists (NUJ) but also by the smaller Institute of Journalists (IOJ).

The remaining two unions were the Amalgamated Engineering Union (AEU) which represented newspaper engineers, and the Electrical, Electronic, Telecommunications and Plumbing Union (EETPU) which took in electricians and their assistants, in both of which unions members were trying to bring about a merger. A few members, mainly nurses, canteen workers, painters and some drivers, belonged to other unions.

The practice in newspaper offices was that each union (and in some cases separate sections of unions based on their original entity) formed a 'chapel' of its members for the purpose of negotiation with the management over house pay agreements, demarcation and other disputes and working conditions. Chapel officials, elected annually, consisted of a father of the chapel (FOC) or mother (MOC), who was chairman; a deputy FOC; a clerk of the chapel (COC), who was secretary and kept the minutes, and a committee, whose members were, in effect, shop stewards and represented the union presence on the floor.

This was the background against which the move into new technology in the 1980s took place. The disputes and demarcation problems, and the creeping opposition to change in newspapers that had beset union-management relations in the trouble-ridden 1970s, had been only a symptom of the real issue. The unions' worries over new technology were well founded in that they could see that it spelt the end of the livelihood of many of their members, but it took the breakthrough into direct input keyboarding in the provinces, first by a strike-breaking management at Nottingham, and later by agreement at Portsmouth and Wolverhampton to demonstrate the inevitability of what lay ahead.

The watershed of 1986 with Eddie Shah's new colour daily, *Today*, and the News International's move to Wapping was, in effect, merely the climax of a technological revolution that was already banishing for ever the place of hot metal and old printing skills in the making of newspapers. Of the jobs represented by the skilled craft union NGA '82, gone were line-casting, stereotyping, metal page composition, process engraving, plate casting and even proof-reading. The computer and the electronic processes it controlled, together with polymer printing plates, had replaced everything. By the end of the 1980s the NGA '82 had ceased to be a significant force in newspaper production, its position being taken on some papers by the electronic union, the EETPU.

In 1991 the craft-orientated NGA '82, faced with plummeting membership and the inexorable march of technology, threw in its lot with SOGAT '82 to become the Graphical, Paper and Media Union, the GPMU, the catch-all remnant of the once powerful printing unions.

The EEPTU, which ousted the NGA from composing rooms when the computer replaced hot metal, was itself subsumed in 1992 by the engineers into the Amalgamated Engineering and Electrical Union, the AEEU, and made its peace with the Trades Union Congress with which its member-poaching tactics had brought it into conflict. Electronic pagination, by building pages totally on screen, signified the end of composing rooms altogether.

Though all this simplified relations with managements, the changes in technology and job descriptions and the techniques of new-style managers had ushered in an entirely different working environment which offered few opportunities for industrial muscle.

With the decline of union power came the end of some of the less desirable products of the old management–union relationship such as chapel control over the supply of labour, especially casual labour, many of the restrictive work practices enshrined in house agreements, and demarcation and inter-chapel disputes. The beneficiaries of all this were the newspaper managements who, fortified by the influx of new blood as well as of new technology, had become tougher and more efficient.

Costs and revenue

Newspapers are traditionally a high cost industry. Yet even at the height of the 'silly money' period, when printers and engravers on piecework were earning more than departmental heads, newsprint was identified by three postwar Royal Commissions as the biggest single expenditure, varying from 28 per cent to 33 per cent of operating costs under hot metal production. During 1970 to 1975, in national newspaper offices, according to evidence given to the 1976 Royal Commission, production wages averaged 24 per cent of costs; with distribution remaining at about 10 per cent and other costs negligible by comparison.

By the early 1980s newsprint prices began to ease slightly, though the fall was exceeded by a progressive reduction in wage costs which by then had begun to take place. This, in the view of the 1976 Royal Commission, was the only area where costs could be effectively reduced. The benefits varied at first from office to office, retraining and redundancy being heavy items in balance sheets, but the spread of direct inputting and the end of many traditional print jobs soon brought even loss-making newspapers into profit.

Newspaper revenue comes from two main sources: the cover charge of the newspaper and from advertising. Other income can arise from commercial printing, promotions, special offers and readers' services. On the whole advertising is the main source, through varying in percentage from paper to paper.

A small provincial paper with a high advertisement contents quota is in a strong position now that it is computer-set and web-offset printed. Its newsprint and distribution costs are relatively low and its production costs modest compared with other papers. Some local weeklies have up to 70 per cent advertising.

A popular national daily or Sunday paper is faced with a high newsprint bill for its millions of copies plus high distribution costs, but this is offset by the fact that its circulation brings in a good cover charge income. In the populars a target advertising content to ensure reasonable profit is between 35 and 45 per cent. The cover charge is kept as low as possible and a balance achieved between circulation and advertising income, with advertising bringing in about a third of the total revenue.

Quality national dailies and Sundays find that despite a substantially higher cover charge (sometimes more than twice that of the populars) their smaller circulations and high newsprint bills for thicker papers make it necessary to carry between 50 and 70 per cent advertising to produce a profit. Advertising accounts for about 60 per cent of the revenue.

With a greater area of type through having more pages and less space given to display, quality papers have made greater economies of scale by the adoption of computer-setting through direct input, especially for classified advertising, on which they depend more than do the populars. With the popular tabloids, where the actual amount of keyboarding is less, display more complex and the income from circulation more important, the change-over has been less spectacular in cost-saving.

The 30 per cent rise in the cost of newsprint in 1995, however, posed a threat to this careful balancing of costs and revenue and was one of the factors in the demise of *Today* in that year.

Advertising

There are two main sorts of advertising carried by newspapers: *display* and *classified*. Display advertisements are those in which design plays the main part in attracting the customer. They consist of a slogan or selling line, usually a photograph or a drawing, and an explanation of the product and its price and the reasons why you should buy it. Display advertising sets out to create an image of value or desirability or urgency. It aims to attract not only those whose are likely to be interested anyway but those whose eyes might alight upon the advertisement by reason of its visual appeal. Most branded products – cigarettes, cars, convenience foods, detergents, liquor and confectionery – appeal through display advertising, with the image the first consideration and information secondary.

Yet manufactured goods occupy only 40 per cent of national newspaper advertising and an even smaller percentage of provincial advertising. The biggest single advertiser is the Government. Here the aim is primarily to convey information and, while the method of display advertising is still used, there is less stress on image and more on urgency through the use of a large type slogan to attract attention, and sometimes of graphics to simplify complicated information relating perhaps to pensions or special facilities in new legislation. This sort of advertising is sometimes called semi-display.

Classified advertisements consist of information about jobs, holiday accommodation, houses for sale, births, marriages and deaths etc. They are set to a fixed measure and format and classified under headings, sometimes in alphabetic order, so that the potential reader can run swiftly through them. Entertainment and 'postal bargains' also come under this category.

Classified advertising is strong in local papers, which run columns of appointments, holiday accommodation and financial advertising. Popular national papers are stronger on display advertising, particularly for mass-produced popular goods or special 'bargains' in which price dominates the display.

It was in the important classified sections where the short-fall in revenue occurred in the late 1970s and early 1980s as a result of the decline in recruitment advertisements and the success of 'free sheets' (see p. 153). It was recruitment which had led the original boom in classified advertising in the 1960s.

Display advertising is the main area of competition between press and television. 'Image' promotion is ideal on film, and in colour, and has the immediacy that black and white print cannot give. Yet on detailed information newspaper advertising scores on the old principle that it can be read at leisure, cut out and looked at again. Also, many products and services involving cutting out and filling in a coupon. By this means advertising response can be measured. In the case of some branded goods, TV and press advertising are used in joint campaigns. In the case of classified advertisements, newspaper and magazines are the ideal medium.

Rate cards. Advertising rates are based on column centimetres depending on sizes with discounts for special arrangements, or premiums for prime positions. National papers lose sometimes through not being able to offer special rate regional advertising arrangements due to the cost and publishing problems involved in changing pages for special areas. Here the regional arrangements of television and local papers score with manufacturers who wish to market products on a regional or test basis.

A special calculation based on the cost per single-column centimetre per thousand readers, is used to measure the true cost of an advertisement. On a circulation basis this gives a lower cost per thousand in national populars than in qualities, although the qualities might have special readership factors that justify the higher cost per thousand. The relatively high cost of evening paper and local paper advertising on this basis is offset by the higher penetration per household in the area, with some local weeklies on solus sites having the highest penetration of all paid-for papers (but see Free Sheets, pages 153–6). In general terms the revenue yield per page to newspapers is higher with classified advertising since there are virtually no discounts to clients.

Advertising agencies. Nearly 90 per cent of all national newspaper advertising, including Government advertising and probably more than half provincial paper advertising comes through agencies. Originally these acted as space brokers selling space to advertisers in return for commission from the newspapers of usually 15 per cent. The commission system still largely persists but agencies today specialize in offering sophisticated services in media planning and creative design to advertisers in return for a contract to design and place their advertising.

Newspapers, in their turn, value agencies as a means of organizing the flow of business, providing the complete advertisement in acceptable form and guaranteeing the credit-worthiness of the advertiser.

Agencies vary in size from a few partners to offices employing as many as 200 people, and their services vary accordingly. They all, however, provide for clients a programme of media and consumer planning on which to base their advertising (and sometimes a market evaluation of the product), a studio equipped to do the sophisticated artwork used in modern advertising, and a team of copywriters whose job is to think up slogans, or selling lines, and the words that describe the product and persuade the potential buyer.

Accounts are agreed with clients usually on a yearly budget basis and an account executive takes charge. After the initial assessment has been made and the media programme has been decided, a creative team of artists and copywriters prepares the actual advertisements. Most agencies have special media buyers whose job is to know the readership pattern of each newspaper and magazine, the best times to advertise and the most economic space-buying arrangements.

The main source of research used by agencies in their media planning is the yearly *National Readership Survey*[4] which classifies readership in social groups according to the occupation of the head of the household and the family spending pattern (discussed in Chapter 4) and gives readership profiles of the bigger newspapers. Advertisers and newspapers themselves also institute surveys and there is a Market Research Society which lists more than 200 research companies carrying out various forms of commissioned research, though not necessarily for advertising purposes, and using a variety of sampling methods.

Readership profiles. The *National Readership Survey* profiles make interesting reading for editors as well as for advertising men. In addition to the social grades, the readership of national and principal provincial papers is listed in percentage age groups, 15–24, 25–34, 35–44, 45–54, 55–64 and over 65. Thus at a glance the age profile of each newspaper is revealed. The charts show the percentage of men, women and housewife readers and also the weight of ITV viewers among the various newspaper readers to help determine their response to television advertising. The *National Readership Survey* is thus the bible of the media space salesperson.

Direct advertising. Some companies deal directly with newspapers, especially in the regions, but the main form of direct advertising is classified, although a percentage of this comes from agencies. This might be prepaid on special forms or might be telephoned in to tele-ad girls who, on some papers, canvas regular clients intensively.

Internal set-up. Advertising revenue is vital to a newspaper. The only alternatives to it are Government support, private subsidy or vastly dearer newspapers. The promoting of advertising business, the collection of the money and the organizing of advertising production come under the advertising director who, on most newspapers, sits on the board. The advertising director might have personal dealings with important clients and agencies and he or she plans long-term strategy for the attracting and forward planning of advertising in the paper. This includes special drives to attract advertising at certain times of the year, especially the slack weeks at mid-year, rate concessions to attract certain business, and in promoting advertising supplements in which editorial participation is used to attract business.

The internal office arrangements are controlled by the advertisement manager who deals directly with agencies and clients, plots the placings of adverts and keeps accounts. Many offices sub-divide advertising among a number of executives who specialize in classified, holiday or property advertising. In addition outside representatives, or reps, promote the company's business in the circulation area by making contact with clients and provincial agencies, recording feedback from clients and advising on possible new advertising business. Weekly reports from reps are used in planning strategy.

The department also has its own production arrangements if typesetting of advertisements is necessary, supervises the making up of pages of advertising and of actual adverts, and sees that advertisements get into the right pages and editions. (See Advertising and Policy, pages 78–80.)

Circulation

The circulation of a newspaper is the number of copies it sells for each day or week of issue. This is not to be confused with readership which is the number of people who read the paper – or who are calculated to read the paper. According to the *National Readership Survey*, national dailies average 3.2 readers per copy and Sundays 2.9 readers per copy. General weeklies and colour magazines have an average of 3.9 readers per copy and some of the monthlies and specialist magazines more than nine readers per copy. From this the numbers of the population that read a Sunday or a daily paper, and so on, can be worked out.

The circulation and sale of a newspaper is the responsibility of the circulation department. The paper, once printed, is stacked – bundled, tied and labelled – in the warehouse, or publishing room, a job now accomplished in most offices by automated methods, and thence dispatched by road or rail. Local papers use vans to distribute to newsagents and points of sale and many have elaborate street sale and direct door delivery arrangements. National papers deal mostly through area wholesalers from whom retailers draw their supplies.

About three-quarters of the quality dailies are delivered to the door and about half the populars. In the latter case the importance of casual sales intensifies the competitiveness, especially among the tabloids, whose quarterly circulation figures returned by the Audit Bureau of Circulation (ABC) hinge very largely on capturing such sales. The cost and difficulty of home delivery has led to experiments in distribution and several household magazines and specialized news sheets in recent years have been launched through supermarkets and grocers and even filling stations.

The wholesaler's discount on national newspapers averages about 8 per cent per copy and the retailers 28 per cent, depending on the part of the country. The remaining average of 64 per cent is the newspaper publisher's share of the cover price.

The circulation department of most newspaper offices also plays a part in publicity and promotions to further the sale of the paper, and distributes bills to points of sale. The promotion of sports events and circulation drives in special areas such as holiday towns during the summer is often arranged through the local circulation representatives (reps) working with the newspaper's promotions department, where there is one. Promotions, publicity, transport and circulation usually come under a circulation director at board level.

Editionizing. Distribution of all papers, local and national, is based on editions planned editorially to phase in with the distribution system to the circulation area. Editions can contain special news together with area sport. The earliest editions (unless printing is decentralized) go to the areas furthest from the production centre, and the latest being the city, town or London editions. In the case of national Sunday papers heavy editionizing of sports takes place to match in with these editions. Occasionally 'slip' pages for special news events are inserted to replace existing pages between editions where production and cost allow this. There is a limited amount of editionized advertising in national papers and rather more of it in provincial papers, especially for area retailing.

Free newspapers

A controversial development – and a threat to many hitherto prosperous newspapers – has been the emergence of the free-sheet or controlled circulation newspaper which makes its income entirely from advertising revenue which it attracts by means of a 'guaranteed' penetration of households in a given area. It nominates its circulation and then achieves it by unsolicited letterbox delivery using services of the kind used in leafleting, though some free-sheets have their own delivery or are given away in supermarkets and garage forecourts. Viability is achieved by fixing an advertising ratio which covers production and distribution costs and leaves a profit. Early free-sheets consisted almost entirely of advertising, though some had a few items of local editorial news, but later and more successful ones have introduced or improved their editorial content in an attempt to make them acceptable alternatives for readers to the local paid-for paper, and thus build up readership as apart from circulation.

The distribution methods of free-sheets have made them most effective for retailing and classified advertising in closely-knit urban areas or in the more populated counties. It is here that they have provided competition for advertising and, to a lesser extent, editorial content, with old established paid-for weeklies in a limited geographical area.

A study by IPC Marketing Services in 1968 suggested that there were then between 100 and 150 free-sheet titles, most of recent origin but seven dating back to the 1920s and three to before 1910. A report prepared for the 1976–77 Royal Commission, *Concentration of Ownership in the Provincial Press*, showed that numbers had grown from 65 in 1970 to 154 in 1974 but had thereafter declined to 133 in 1976, at which total circulation was estimated at 5,899,000. The report remarked that fewer than 10 per cent of the titles had more than a fleeting existence and observed that competitive free-sheets launched by the publishers of paid-for newspapers were used to wrest the initiative from independent free-sheets, followed sometimes by the closure of both free-sheets. Nevertheless, in evidence to the Commission, provincial proprietors quoted competition for advertising revenue from free-sheets as one of several factors forcing them to 'use newsprint more productively, reduce unit costs, create more marketing opportunities and establish industrial relations policies and practices that will encourage employees to accept inevitable changes.'[5]

From 1977 free-sheets began to boom, however, and by 1982 the recently formed Association of Free Newspapers (AFN) was claiming, on the basis of figures from the Advertising Association, that free titles had risen from 201 in 1977 to 250 in 1978, 315 in 1979, 325 in 1980 and, in a sudden urge, to 494 in 1981. Thereafter, and climbing more slowly, the total had reached 530 by 1988.

By the end of 1982, according to the AFN, free sheet distribution had reached 20 million. Of this, fifty-six titles, representing 20 per cent of the circulation, were owned by the then top four paid-for newspaper companies, Thomson, Westminster Press, Associated Newspapers and United Newspapers, with the rest mainly owned by new companies. By 1988 the association was claiming that distribution had increased in the six years to more than 29.5 million, or by nearly 50 per cent – which suggested increased printing of existing titles since the actual number of free sheets had risen by only 7 per cent. By 1990, however, the dip in advertising spending had put some out of business, and by 1995 there had been a hefty decline in titles and profitability, soaring newsprint costs being one of the factors.

There was no disputing the increase in advertising income during the 1980s for free-sheets, however, which rose, according to Advertising Association figures, from £1 million in 1968 to £314 million in 1986. In 1981, when the number of titles had more or less peaked, free-sheets drew in £104 million against £187 million for provincial paid-for dailies and weeklies, which had been keeping steadily ahead. By 1986, paid-for papers in the provinces, though still showing steadily increasing revenues, had fallen some way behind their thrusting rivals in their share of the kitty, collecting £243 million in advertising income against the free-sheets' total of £314 million.

It is difficult to determine what percentage of this free-sheet advertising was 'new' spending (as opposed to revenue taken from paid-for papers) since provincial evening paper revenue increased each year throughout the period, and weekly paper revenue each year with the exception of a small fall in 1980. Yet it was clear that free-sheets represented a growing percentage of regional paper advertising.

Free-sheet advertising certainly increased faster than any other sort in the boom years from 1977 onwards despite the trend, encouraged by the Association of Free Newspapers, towards giving more space to editorial content. A point made by Tony Boullemier, organizer of the first AFN Design Content for free-sheets in 1982, was that editorial space, where allowed for, should be used more effectively.

The new free *Nottingham Trader* launched in March, 1982, promised a 40 per cent editorial content as well as a distribution of 160,000 copies a week – a better editorial ratio than some paid-for papers.

Whether free-sheets were taking circulation from paid-for papers was difficult to prove. The Audit Bureau of Circulation Review in the last few years up to 1982 showed a gradual but not spectacular decline in the circulation of the majority of those local weeklies which had audited figures. Weeklies in the North and in Wales and Scotland tended to be more stable than those in the Greater London and Home Counties area, yet falls in the circulations of Greater London weeklies could be attributed to the greater competition they faced from other established paid-for papers than was the case in the far provinces. Paid-for papers had, too, the benefit of a readership loyalty based on editorial content.

By the end of 1983 provincial newspaper publishers, under the Newspaper Society, were combining with newsagents to organize special campaigns to publicize the value to readers and advertisers of local paid-for papers.

Free-sheets were conscious of the need to authenticate their circulations and many of them began to do this through an organization called Verified Free Distribution, which was established as a subsidiary of the Audit Bureau of Circulations.

Despite their rapid growth, free-sheets were not without their problems. A difficulty existed in attracting advertising other than of the shopping-guide and property type due to the lack of a profile or figures of actual readers as opposed to distribution. Any move to increase 'readership' through editorial coverage could only be at the expense of advertising income and therefore of profits. Editorial space, in its turn, was linked to a worry first aired at the AFN conference in Birmingham in September 1982, that the Treasury might withdraw the newspaper industry VAT concession from free-sheets on the ground that they did not fulfil the role of paid-for newspapers.

At a Media Society seminar on free-sheets in London a little later, Nicholas Herbert, Editorial Director of Westminster Press, stirred the controversy by saying that free-sheets 'had come like a cold shower to the traditional local newspaper'. The industry needed the competition and 'although this may be fatal to the moribund it had an invigorating effect on the comatose and the hung-over'. The National Union of Journalists took a less sanguine view and deplored 'the uncontrolled growth of free-sheets', and particularly the conversion of paid-for to free newspapers, and instructed the National Executive Council to review policy on a matter which could 'in the long term lead to a loss of NUJ jobs and threaten press freedom'.

Things that concerned the union about free-sheets were the separation of editorial and advertising matter, the level of journalistic integrity and the proper training and payment of journalist staff. Compounding the problem here were not only free newspapers as such but a growing range of give-away publications from magazines for office girls and rail and air travellers to civic newspapers and 'news letters' of all types which had burgeoned with the spread of in-house printing facilities in the 1980s made possible by computerized technology, and which were taking root often in a non-unionized environment.

Further reading

The Interim and Final Reports of the Royal Commission of the Press of 1976–77, and its research papers, published by the Stationery Office (see bibliography) remain the best source material on the running of newspapers. John F. Goulden's *Newspaper Management* (Heinemann, London, 1967) gives the 'feel' of a newspaper but is very dated. Simon Broadbent: *Spending Advertising Money* (Business Books, London, 1975, 2nd Edn) looks at advertising and the media in close detail. A more general picture of advertising practice is given in *The Practice of Advertising* (Heinemann, London, 2nd Edn, 1983) edited by A. H. Hart and J. O'Connor. *Behind the Headlines – The Business of the British Press*, edited by Harry Henry (Associated Business Press, London, 1978) looks at the economics of newspapers, national and provincial, at the period.

References

1 In foreword to John F. Goulden's *Newspaper Management* (Heinemann, London, 1967).
2 MARTIN, Roderick: *New Technology and Industrial Relations in Fleet Street*, Clarendon Press, Oxford, 1981, pp. 47–9.
3 JENKINS, S.: *Newspapers: The Power and the Money* (Faber & Faber, London, 1979).
4 Published by the National Readership Surveys Ltd, London.
5 *Industrial Relations in the Provincial Newspaper and Periodical Industry*, a report by the Advisory Conciliation and Arbitration Service (HMSO, London, 1977) p. 10.

10 The press and society

Britain has a free press. There is no censor and no licensing, and anyone can publish a newspaper provided they do not break the law in doing so. The press is in private hands. There is no Government controlled newspaper, no Government shareholding in a newspaper, and the press gets no form of Government help other than exemption from VAT. The sessions of Parliament are open to the press and the workings of the Government are reported and commented on, as are the workings of all other public institutions.

The freedom of the press is not inscribed on tablets as it is in the American constitution; it exists by consensus, and the freedom British newspapers enjoy and for which journalists fought over the centuries has to be guarded by editors, by political parties and by the people who care about these matters. It was guarded until 1990 by the Press Council, the voluntary regulating body for the industry, in whose constitution this duty was spelt out, and which has been mentioned a number of times in these pages (but see pages 165–70).

This unwritten but generally accepted concept of press freedom is something Britain shares with most Western countries though in some, notably France, Germany and Sweden, Government help is accepted in various tax concessions or in newsprint subsidies.

Operating thus freely, British newspapers offer a wide spectrum of political and social views. Though there is only one party-aligned daily, the Communist *Morning Star*, the national press presents political standpoints ranging from the solid Right to the extreme Left (though with a bias in volume circulation to the Right). National newspapers serve a variety of social groups. There are also daily and weekly newspapers and magazines published in support of religions, political fringe groups, trade unions, the entertainment industry, homosexuals, even the brewing and licensing trade. And there are local papers of every kind, including free ones. Anyone who can find the money – and the readers – can start a newspaper.

It might be complained that the advertising, which enables the price of newspapers to be kept down (and produce profits) is not available to papers with sectional or extreme political viewpoints. The fact that such papers exist and continue to be launched, proves that this is a handicap that can be surmounted.

Newsprint is the biggest single item, so a slimmed-down paper in which a higher percentage of the space is editorial is one answer. Another is to have a higher cover charge. If there is a demand, of whatever size, for a paper's viewpoint, then provided proper economies have gone into production and it is not trying to emulate a rich national daily, the price should not be a deterrent.

An advantage of the new printing technology is that a small newspaper can in theory be produced cheaply with few staff and in a space consisting of a few rooms.

'Sponsored' newspapers run by political, social and even civic groups save on costs by voluntary distribution and low-cost contributions from members. Subsidy is a way of keeping going such newspapers to serve a special group or aim. Ratepayers' money has even been used for this purpose. Subsidy is not new. In substance there is no difference between the subsidy that Communist party members put into the *Morning Star*, by way of donations, to keep it going from that which its various owners, voluntarily or involuntarily, have put into *The Times* for years. Both papers have suffered from a shortage of advertising revenue, though for different reasons. Before Northcliffe put the industry on a business footing, newspapers in the eighteenth and nineteenth centuries often lived off subsidies from their various owners, which included political parties, and even Government subsidies in some cases.

There is thus no obstacle to the publication and circulation of newspapers that cannot be surmounted. Yet there are threats to newspapers' freedom to operate – threats that can involve a form a censorship.

The creeping censor

It can be argued that the working of some legislation passed to protect the individual, people's property and the security of the State can act as an indirect form of censorship.

The Official Secrets Act. This Act, passed in 1911 (and in 1989 replaced with a new Act) makes it an offence for anyone working for the Crown to disclose, either by word of mouth or by writing, information acquired as a result of his or her job. 'Anyone' includes not only civil servants, diplomats and members of the judiciary but soldiers, policemen and even gardeners and porters paid by the Crown. The Act can cover almost any area of Government activity.

After the 1939–45 War the Government set up a Services, Press and Broadcasting Committee to clarify the working of the Act to editors by issuing special notices of matters which were ruled to a secret for reasons of national security. These were known as D-notices and the committee, which still operates, came to be known as the D-notice Committee. A D-notice is a specific request, originating in a Government Department, for editors not to publish a certain matter.

Yet D-notices have been used for occasions which have had only a marginal connection with State security, as a celebrated case in 1967 concerning the *Daily Express* showed. In this instance a story by Chapman Pincher, who had discovered that copies of all overseas cables were collected and taken to the Ministry of Defence for vetting before being allowed to be sent, was made subject of a D-notice after the ministry had learnt that it was about to be published. The furore that followed its publication (despite the D-notice) resulted in a committee being set up under Lord Radcliffe, whose report later in the year led to a revision of the procedure and the issue of fewer notices.

In 1993 the D-notice system was further altered to reflect the new circumstances of the breakup of the Soviet Union and the Warsaw Pact, the UK's involvement in smaller-scale conflicts and the threats of terrorism. The eight existing D-notices covering important security matters were replaced by six DA-notices (Defence Advisory Notices). It was stressed by the committee, however, that contravening a DA-notice could still mean prosecution under the Official Secrets Act.

Libel. Where a person complains that his or her character or livelihood has been damaged as a result of statements made in a newspaper, the person may sue for libel and, in some cases, win substantial damages. An editor might plead the truth of the statements or the defence might be that they are not defamatory or that the story was 'fair comment made in good faith and without malice about a matter of public interest.'

Threats of libel made to newspapers are common. In proportion, few reach court. Yet they still cost money since some are settled out of court where the bill, though it can be heavy, is preferable to the risk of an adverse judgement and punitive costs.

The Press is regarded as a lucrative target for litigants and cases are not unknown where attempts have been made on flimsy or even dubious pretexts to 'con' a newspaper into paying damages out of court on the threat of action. To editors, fear of libel is frequently a factor in withholding a story which might otherwise have been published for the public good.

Personal stories told by a third party can cause trouble. The person who is the subject, if he or she is aware, can try to stop publication by serving a writ on the editor threatening action for libel, breach of confidence (under the various laws and precedents governing confidentiality) or even breach of copyright. Such 'stopper writs', sometimes with little justification, are a method used to try to prevent editors from running stories. They can be ignored if an editor feels on good ground, but if a threatened action proceeds and the paper loses, the decision to publish is deemed to aggravate the offence.

Another form of 'stopper' is the injunction, which is an order not to publish issued on application to a court. A person can apply to a judge in chambers (i.e. personally) for an interim injunction which holds up publication of a story until the court has heard both sides. It is usual for an editor to be represented at the application and an undertaking to justify the use of the story, should later action be taken, is often sufficient for the complainant's application to be refused. If the interim injunction is granted it can later be thrown out by the court (at which point the story can then be published), or extended into an indefinite injunction, which is binding upon the editor.

Whichever legal method is used or threatened, the pressure is heavy on editors.

H. A. Taylor[1] wrote in his book *The British Press, a Critical Survey* in 1961: 'The anomalies of the law are responsible for much evasive treatment of fact by newspapers, for timid writing where explicit statement would best serve the public interest, for woolly phrases casting suspicions on innocent parties, and for lack of candour in comments on the affairs of public companies, leading to losses by investors.'

Taylor's words still apply today.

Contempt of court. This, after libel, constitutes the editor's chief worry in handling crime and investigative stories, though there are some famous occasions – the Yorkshire Ripper case, for example – when the law has been flouted. Contempt of court means broadly any conduct or spoken or written words which might impede the working of the court. For example, a newspaper must not, in most cases, publish a photograph of an accused person before he or she has been identified in court. An exception would be where the police have issued a photograph in the public interest. Nor can a newspaper comment or adduce new facts in cases which are before the court, or criticize the judge or the proceedings of the court while the case is being heard.

The aim of the law is to avoid influencing the jury and prejudicing a fair trial. Yet refusing to disclose sources of information for a newspaper story – a hallowed privilege claimed by journalists for many years – was ruled to be contempt of court during the trial, in 1962, of William Vassall, the Admiralty clerk sentenced for selling secrets to the Russians. The decision resulted in two *Daily Mail* reporters being sent to prison by the judge.

Another disturbing use of the law of contempt arose four years later following the Aberfan disaster when a coal tip overhanging a Welsh mining village collapsed and buried 144 people, most of them children in a school. A tribunal was appointed under a judge to take evidence and apportion blame, if any. The Press were warned by the Attorney General, Sir Elwyn Jones, QC, on the day the tribunal was appointed, that any newspaper comments thereafter 'on the subject matter may constitute contempt of court'.

The Press reacted indignantly at this attempt to 'gag' it on a matter of great public concern. Yet subsequent law committees ruled and reaffirmed that the Tribunals of Inquiry (Evidence) Act of 1921 allowed for such tribunals to be subject to the law of contempt of court, and the restriction remains. Remaining with it is the discretion of the judge to apply the law (refined and widened in the 1981 Contempt of Court Act), to a wide range of matters which, in the judge's view, might prejudice procedures being carried out.

Reporting restrictions. The court reporter working for *The Times* or the *Daily Telegraph* in the late 19th century, when Press publicity was seen to be not only part of the punishment for crime but a democratic process by which the public could see justice being done, would be astonished at the restrictions that face court reporters in the 1990s.

The excessive printing of salacious details was the reason for regulations passed in 1926 banning newspapers from publishing evidence in divorce cases. Only the judge's judgement may now be given, alongside names, addresses and summary of accusations and counter accusations, although a distinguished barrister writing in the *Sunday Times* in 1944 commented that the secrecy shown in divorce reports had done more harm to marriages than the publicity had in earlier times. And, as court reporters know, some judges are more inclined than others to 'go to town' about details in their judgement in divorce cases.

In 1933 the restriction which editors had for years observed voluntarily of not identifying children and young people in juvenile court (now youth court) proceedings was made legally enforceable, thus taking from an editor the option of giving such details in cases which he considered warranted it in the public good.

The principle of open justice was widely breached by the Criminal Justice Act of 1967 under which the press were barred from reporting evidence in cases at magistrates courts where the accused, because of the seriousness of the charge, was committed to stand trial at a higher court. The reason given was that since only prosecution evidence was heard at the lower court it was unfair at that stage to give the cases publicity.

The provisions of this Act, and of three further Acts of 1980, 1981 and 1988 on the same subject, have become a source of headache to editors.

The arrangements for the press are anything but simple. Under the 1967 Act, reporters at committal hearings can give only details of a defendant's name and address, the charge, the names of counsel, the decision of the court and details of the arrangements for bail and legal aid. Restrictions on reporting the actual evidence, however, can be waived, first, where the defendant applies to have the hearing reported; second where the court decides not to commit the defendant for trial; third where the court decides to deal with one or more of a number of defendants summarily (i.e. at the lower court); and fourth once the defendants have had their trial before the high court, when committal evidence can then be published and treated as being contemporaneous.

In repeating and clarifying these provisions the Magistrates Court Act of 1980, in addition, allows magistrates in the lower court to dispense with oral evidence and to rely on written statements – but even if a defendant elects to have reporting restrictions lifted there is no provision for these written statements to be made available to the press.

Strictly, a reporter should sit through all lower court committal hearings and take a note of the evidence in case it can be reported at the time. Under the 1980 Act, for instance, if the court decides to deal with one or more of several defendants in a case on the spot, while committing others for trial, then cases dealt with on the spot can be reported, and the reporter has a story. If only one of several defendants wants reporting restrictions lifted and not the others, however, a ticklish situation arises. To deal with this a further refinement of the provisions was made under the Criminal Justice (Amendment) Act of 1981 by which the examining magistrate at the lower court may lift reporting restrictions only if he or she is satisfied, after hearing the representations of all the accused, that it is in the interests of justice to do so.

Having weighed up all these possibilities the chances are that a busy reporter might decide that it is a waste of time sitting through committal proceedings.

A committee which examined the need for the new law in 1967 rejected evidence submitted by newspapers who claimed the long-established freedom to report the deliberations of all courts for the public good and to ensure that justice is seen to be done. Many editors now feel that the public good is suffering as a result of the law. Fear of local publicity is no longer a deterrent to would-be wrongdoers. A newspaper cannot publicize the case, for instance, of a man who, at lower court committal hearing, loudly proclaims his innocence or complains of police treatment during questioning. Nor is there an opportunity for cases of wrongful arrest being brought to light at an early stage through the effect of local publicity.

An even greater threat to the principle of open justice arose from the Sexual Offences (Amendment) Act of 1976, which barred the press from mentioning the names of rape victims and also of the accused, except where there had been a conviction or if the judge decreed that the accused's name should be mentioned. The law was strongly opposed at the time by the Law Society, the Press Council and the Guild of British Newspaper Editors on the ground that it was the beginning of the path to secret courts. Critics pointed out that even if a dangerous psychopathic sex killer was on the loose a newspaper would be committing an offence under the act if it named him, described him or published his picture if he had previously been accused but not convicted of rape.

A further anomaly was outlined in a letter entitled 'Secret Jailings' which appeared in *The Times* on December 3, 1979, above the name of Walter Greenwood, joint editor of *Essential Law For Journalists*. In it he quoted the case of a man who had been jailed for 18 months at St. Albans Crown Court and had his car forfeited after being found guilty of an indecent assault, but whose identity could not be revealed because he had been acquitted of a rape charge under the Sexual Offences (Amendment) Act. No order had been made by a judge permitting publication of his name. Said the letter: 'An important principle is thus breached that the identity should be known of those who lose their liberty.' Under the Criminal Justice Act of 1988, however, you can now identify the accused in such cases at all times. Further categories were made subject to restrictions in the Sexual Offences (Amendment) Act of 1992.

Even more worrying, as far as day-to-day editing of a paper is concerned, is a provision of the Race Relations Act, which came into force in 1977, which makes a newspaper and its staff liable to conviction for reporting an inflammatory speech or election manifesto, such as that of an extremist politician, where it contains anti-immigrant sentiments, even though there is no intention by the newspaper of stirring up race hatred.

The growth of all this legislation, however justified in law, has made the job of the editor more difficult and has resulted in accusations by some critics of an anti-Press bias by governments.

Union action. Trade union action in pursuit of disputes with managements or with each other has been, until the last few years, a source of censorship when it involved preventing or impeding the publication of a newspaper. In November 1970, for example, the house chapel (branch) of the National Society of Operative Printers, Graphical and Media Personnel (NATSOPA) threatened to stop *The Observer* being printed if it used a story about dissension in the Society of Graphical and Allied Trades, of which it formed part. The stoppage was averted by a meeting between the union and the Newspaper Publishers Association at which the NPA stuck by the editor's right to decide what appeared.

In December the same year, production was halted at the *Evening Standard* because print workers objected to an anti-trade union cartoon by Jak and was resumed only after the management agreed to publish a letter from the printing chapels objecting to the cartoon. This led to the Press Council issuing a statement affirming 'the importance to the public . . . of the right of a newspaper to publish lawfully what it may.'

In 1976 the *News of the World* lost two million copies due to chapel action over an article by Lord George Brown which alleged overmanning in the industry. In March the same year, the *Financial Times* lost an entire day's issue because the NGA printers refused to set in type copy derived from the *Interim Report on the Royal Commission on the Press* which referred to earnings of some of their members.

In 1977 the Press Council condemned the action of printers at *The Times* who stopped the paper coming out because the editor refused to print a union disclaimer alongside an article by David Astor, former editor of *The Observer*, alleging 'censorship by unions'. Later, in 1982 some readers of *The Sun* failed to get their paper when railwaymen at King's Cross refused to handle it because it carried an interview which, they said, prejudiced their case in a dispute with British Rail.

One effect of the new climate in union–management relations (see pages 145–7) is that there has been no recorded case of union censorship or attempts at censorship since Fleet Street's move into new technology in the mid-1980s.

Complaints about the press

The fact that newspapers are produced at great speed, often under the stress of competition, and that reporters and sub-editors are working at pressure is an explanation rather than an excuse for mistakes that creep in. Industrial trouble within the production process can, on occasion, add to this problem.

Complaints made by readers can range from such niggling things as a misspelt name or a wrong date to serious allegations of bad taste, intrusion and actual defamation of character. If the complaint is made to the editor – which is the proper channel in the first instance – and it is a justifiable one, then in theory a reader can obtain some form of redress. There is no legal right of reply, however, and a Commons Bill to achieve this failed in 1983.

Here are ways in which a complaint might be dealt with:

By letter. Sometimes the matter can be settled by an exchange of correspondence in which an accepted explanation or apology is given.

Disclaimer. This is a printed statement in a newspaper explaining that the person/company etc. named is not the person/company etc. of the same or similar name involved in a story previously published in the paper. It is intended to mitigate unintentional offence caused through confusion of identity arising out of name or circumstance.

Correction. Where the offence has been caused by a straightforward mistake of fact, an agreed correction might be published. This is usually a brief printed statement putting the matter right and perhaps containing an apology.

Agreed statement. If the offence is greater, and the published inaccuracy more glaring, and counsel has perhaps been consulted, the solution might be the printing of an agreed statement written either by the newspaper or by the complainant or his or her lawyer, which might have to be given comparable prominence to the story complained about.

Damages. Where damage is alleged to a person's character or livelihood as a result of a newspaper's story the lawyers of the two sides might get together to agree a sum of money plus costs plus a printed apology acceptable as an out-of-court settlement in lieu of an action for libel. If such agreement is not possible, or where a newspaper contests either the claim or the amount, then the action proceeds to court.

In cases where an agreed settlement is not possible or satisfactory, or where recourse to the courts is not appropriate – i.e. principally in cases of refusal to correct, alleged intrusion or bad taste – then the complainant can take the matter to the Press Complaints Commission.

Press regulation

Since 1953 the British press, following the recommendations of the 1949 Royal Commission, has tried to maintain standards and deal with complaints by a system of self regulation, first through the Press Council and latterly through the Press Complaints Commission.

The Commission, the current regulatory body, was set up in January 1991, to deal solely with complaints against the press as one of the recommendations of the Committee on Privacy and Related Matters chaired by Mr (now Sir) David Calcutt QC. The Committee had been appointed by Margaret Thatcher's Government to report on the press following Parliamentary agitation in 1988–89 for new press laws on intrusion and right of reply by complainants following a number of court decisions adverse to the press.

The new Commission replaced the Press Council which had dealt with complaints against newspapers for 37 years along with other duties laid upon it by the three postwar Royal Commissions. The aims of the Press Council, in their final revised form, had been:

1 To preserve the established freedom of the Press.
2 To maintain the character of the Press in accordance with the highest professional and commercial standards.
3 To consider complaints about the conduct of the Press or the conduct of persons and organizations towards the Press; to deal with these complaints and record resultant action.
4 To keep under review developments likely to restrict the supply of information of public interest and importance.

5 To report publicly on developments that may tend towards greater concentration or monopoly in the Press (including changes of ownership, control and growth of Press undertakings) and to publish statistical information relating thereto.
6 To make representations on appropriate occasions to the Government, organs of the United Nations and to Press organizations abroad.
7 To publish periodical reports recording the Council's work and to review, from time to time, developments in the Press and factors affecting them.[2]

The Council had had to endure some criticism of its workings. The 1962 and the 1977 Royal Commission on the Press both attacked it, for instance, for failing to monitor problems arising from changes and concentration of ownership and the long-term consequences in the industry of poor union–management relations.

In some ways the Council was the victim of its own good offices since dealing with complaints was the more publicized side of its work. With a few fluctuations this work grew and took up an increasing proportion of its time. In 1975, for example, the Complaints Committee handled 440 complaints; in 1976 it handled 534. By 1980 the total had reached 632, in 1981, 813, and in 1982, 831. By 1989 the number of complaints had climbed to 1,871.

It would be wrong to assume that increasing complaints meant that the Press was more culpable; it could equally have been the result of an increasing public awareness of the Council's existence and activity.

In fact, the complaints that eventually came up for adjudication by the full Council remained throughout the period at an average about sixty to seventy a year. Of the ones originally received some were rejected by the Complaints Committee, a number duplicated others, and a growing number were settled by conciliation machinery by which the Council brought complainant and newspaper together. Nearly three-quarters of those received were in the end withdrawn for one reason or another.

The Council embodied its more important adjudications in Declarations of Principle circulated to editors on such things as chequebook journalism (see Chapter 3), intrusion (Chapter 2), misrepresentation, attacks on third parties, political partisanship in newspapers, and attempts by trade unions to stop material appearing.

Though editors, with rare exceptions, accepted their obligation to print in full adjudications made against them, the fact that acceptance of the Council's adjudications was voluntary led to charges that it was toothless. Yet a survey carried out by Social and Community Planning on behalf of the 1977 Royal Commission[3] among a sample of editors and journalists showed that the majority would regard it as an important matter if they were censured by the Council. The majority of those who had had dealings with the Council said it had dealt satisfactorily with the matter. One in ten favoured 'more teeth' for the Council.

The influence on editors of the Press Council's Declarations of Principle could be responsible for the fact that the majority of complaints received from the public in its later years concerned not important matters of principle but of simple inaccuracy or failure to print corrections or disclaimers.

The fact that the Council lacked powers to impose punishments on editors and journalists who stepped out of line found approval both in the industry and with many members of the bar; such powers could be the thin end of the wedge for press freedom, it was argued. The self-regulatory constitution of the Council and its terms of reference were favoured in a number of Commonwealth countries who adopted it as a model when setting up their own press councils.

Yet the danger to press freedom in the form of anti-press legislation by Governments was always present. The setting up of the Press Council in 1953 came just in time to avert the passing of a Labour Opposition Private Member's Bill to force a controlling body on the industry by law. It had reached Second Reading. The Council's early consideration of the problem of intrusion into people's private lives came just as the Porter Committee on Defamation was considering including intrusion in its terms of reference for reviewing the law. The action of the Press Council for rallying editors for its Declaration of Principle on chequebook journalism in 1966, in the wake of the Moors Murder coverage, almost certainly forestalled anti-press legislation. The adjudication over the Yorkshire Ripper coverage in 1983 was another reminder of the dangers of statutory legislation if the press did not respond to voluntary control.

The Press Complaints Commission

The two years run-up to the Calcutt Committee had seen unprecedented criticism of the press in Parliament with demands for legal curbs on intrusion and for the right of reply for complainants to newspapers. A number of high (and in some cases much criticized) libel awards had been made against the national tabloids, although many actions had been energetically defended.

The Committee completed its work in May 1990, and its report was published the following month. It was at once welcomed in principle by the Home Secretary, Mr David (now Lord) Waddington, who accepted its recommendations. Chief of these was that the Press Council be replaced by a new Press Complaints Commission to deal solely with complaints against the press, including complaints of unfairness and intrusion into privacy, that the new Commission should issue appropriate guidance to the editors and that it be properly funded by the industry.

The report announced: 'Our intention is to strengthen voluntary self-regulation to the maximum degree possible. The future of non-statutory regulation should, however, be dependent upon the press setting up and adequately supporting the Press Complaints Commission. If it fails to do so, an alternative statutory approach will be necessary. . . . If the press fails to set up and fund the Commission, or if the system of self-regulation seriously breaks down rendering the Commission ineffective, there will need to be a new statutory Tribunal to adjudicate upon breaches of the Code of Practice (see below) and, where appropriate, grant injunctions and award compensation.'

The report recommended that the Commission should consist of twelve members instead of the thirty-six of the existing Press Council. In the event it was set up with fifteen members and an independent chairman.

Press freedom – The Report excluded from the new Commission's purview matters of the freedom of the press. It said: 'In our view the two distinct functions of defending the freedom of the press and adjudicating on complaints sit uneasily together. Moreover, there is insufficient interdependence between these reponsibilities to make it necessary for one body to have to undertake both. We understand that a number of other groups already exist which bring together those working to defend the freedom of the press, for example the United Kingdom Committee of the International Press Institute.'

In providing effective redress for complaints against the press, said the Report, 'the Complaints Commission would in fact be serving press freedom better than it would by acting as an overtly campaigning body.'

Right of reply – 'We recommend against the introduction of . . . a statutory right of reply . . . We do not regard a right of correction as a practical proposition. We are not persuaded that disputes of fact could be resolved under a speedy and informal procedure.'

Intrusion – The Report recommended the creation of new criminal offences in England and Wales covering certain areas of physical entry into private property and the placing of bugging devices on private property.

Within seven months the plans for the new Commission had been broadly accepted by national and provincial newspaper editors, the funding was in place and the Commission had installed itself in the old Press Council offices in Salisbury Square, just off Fleet Street, and had begun its work.

In an article in *The Observer*, Mr Louis Blom-Cooper QC, last chairman of the Press Council, complained that the Council had been starved of funding by the industry for years and had been hampered and, in some cases, 'seriously undermined by prominent figures among the national newspapers.' He picked out, in particular, Andreas Whittam-Smith, editor of *The*

Independent, who had led the ombudsman movement by which newspapers appointed independent assessors to deal with readers' complaints. He also criticized the 'unhelpful attitude' of the National Union of Journalists, which had withdrawn its four nominees from the Press Council from 1981 to 1990.

A run of highly publicized stories about prominent people, including politicians and members of the Royal family, ensured that the new Commission had its work cut out from the start to fulfil its mission. Nevertheless, the new chairman, Lord McGregor of Durris, had praise for editors in the Commission's first annual report in May 1992, for their compliance with the Code of Practice.

The Commission had received 1396 communications from the public during the year, of which it had adjudicated on 91. Of these 43 were upheld, 14 against national dailies, 12 against national Sunday and weekly papers, 10 against regional papers, 1 against a free newspaper and 6 against magazines. Of the remainder of the complaints, 204 were not pursued by complainants, 113 were outside the Commission's remit, 49 were disallowed for unjustifiable delay, 519 were ruled to be not a prime facie breach of the Code of Practice, 387 were resolved by conciliation between newspaper and complainant, and 33 were still being investigated.

'I am sure,' said Lord McGregor in a statement to journalists, 'that the ethical standards embodied in the Code will now be observed cumulatively, expansively and irreversibly.'

By early 1993, however, yet another Private Member's Bill – Clive Soley's on 'Freedom and Responsibility of the Press' – was working its way through Parliament in the wake of a spate of stories about the marriage troubles of the Prince and Princess of Wales, and Sir David Calcutt was calling for statutory controls.

The Commission's retiring Director, Ken Morgan, had warned the previous year against being complacent. He told editors prophetically: 'I don't think the threat of statutory legislation will ever go away.'

The Complaints Commission, just completing its second year of operation and backed by editors and a united press establishment, responded to the criticisms by defending its record vigorously while at the same time unveiling improvements in its procedures.

Its funding body, the Press Standards Board of Finance (Pressbof) published a powerful document in May 1993, entitled *Strengthening of Self-Regulation*, which listed a wide-ranging series of measures designed to reinforce public confidence in the authority of the Commission and 'the serious application' of the newspaper and periodical industry's Code of Practice.

A few days later the Commission announced that 'to meet any misconceptions regarding their independent status the membership of the Commission will be altered to ensure a lay majority consisting of the independent chairman, eight non-press members and seven editors.' At the same time membership of the Appointments Committee (which appoints members of the Commission) would be increased from three to five, three of them independent members who, along with the Commission's chairman, would give a clear lay majority.

The Code of Practice (see Appendix B) was further revised and a new section promised on the use of long-range cameras, with a further clause covering the term 'public interest' under examination. Also reinforced was the commitment by editors to maintain the Code, the contents of which would be kept under continuous review by the Code Committee of Pressbof.

In June the Commission finally announced the start of the long promised public Helpline (Tel: 0171-353-3732) to advise the public and expedite the reporting and handling of complaints.

At the same time, with the question of privacy in mind, the Commission issued an important reminder to likely complainants that in the case of third-party complaints (i.e. general complaints by the public) 'the PCC cannot adjudicate when only one side of the story is available to them and they must ascertain and respect the wishes of anyone who would be involved were a third party complaint to be pursued.'

The Commission also announced a nationwide publicity campaign, supported by posters and events, to publicize its work and procedures. By July, with its campaign in full swing, the Commission's battle for survival – and with it important principles of press freedom – had been won.

(See Appendix B for full Code of Practice.)

Other safeguards for the public

In the relations between Press and public the Press Complaints Commission is seen as a guarantee of fair dealing. Here are some other safeguards:

The office lawyer. The legal editor or the office lawyer (see Chapter 7: Legal Checks) has a useful watchdog role. He or she sees, as far as possible, that the law is not broken by reporters and other writers and in this sense the public interest benefits. Though rulings on whether or not a story is legally permissible are not binding, it is not usual for an editor to flout them.

The Code of Professional Conduct, to which members of the National Union of Journalists subscribe, can be invoked on ground of conscience by a journalist who is asked to obtain information or photographs by methods against 'the over-riding considerations of the public interest'. The Code stipulates the duty to avoid falsification, distortion, misrepresentation, intrusion into private grief and distress, and the 'suppression of the truth because of advertising or other considerations'. It specifies standards in circumstances which might involve race or sex discrimination or the acceptance of bribes (see pages 188–9).

The Advertising Standards Authority, which is a voluntary body sponsored by the various sides of the advertising industry, controls standards in advertising and deals with complaints from the public. Its address is Brook House, Torrington Place, London WC1. It has formulated a British Code of Advertising Practice covering such things as misleading statements, wrongful descriptions and various forms of visual offence, and it lays down standards of practice for those engaged in the profession. It is signed and subscribed to by the professional bodies federated into the Advertising Association.

Advertising standards committees are operated both by the Newspaper Society, for provincial papers, and the Newspaper Publishers Association, for national papers, to which members can refer advertisements where there are doubts about their ethics or legality. The committees also advise on any companies whose business should not be handled for various reasons.

A more general protection for the public, in respect of advertisements, exists in the provisions of the Trade Descriptions Act of 1968.

A Broadcasting Complaints Commission was set up in 1981 to consider complaints from people who felt they had received 'unjust or unfair treatment' in sound or TV programmes.

Like all voluntary controls, these safeguards are not foolproof (even the law cannot guarantee a totally law-abiding community) but they are intended to show that the industry takes seriously the defining and maintaining of standards and the consideration of complaints.

The press and politics

The Victorians regarded the press and the enlightenment it gave to people as a factor in the development of political parties and of universal suffrage. Since the 19th century, however, there has been a change both in the polarization of political parties and in the place of newspapers in society.

A recurring charge in recent decades has been that the press influences the vote against the Left at election time. The evidence does not support this, but points rather to a decline in political influence.

In 1945, when the then biggest selling daily, the *Daily Express*, fiercely supported the Conservatives and Churchill, Britain's successful war leader, the General Election resulted in a landslide victory for Labour. In 1964 Labour were voted to power 'to end 13 years of Tory misrule' at the same time as their champion, the *Daily Herald*, in which the TUC had a half share, reached its lowest circulation since the 1930s and was sold to the International Publishing Corporation.

A. C. H. Smith, in a study of the popular press[3], regarded the working-class partisanship of the *Daily Mirror* as one of the factors in the 1945 vote. The *Mirror* was very popular with the Forces. Yet Smith adds: 'All the evidence suggests that Labour would have won heavily whatever any newspaper said . . . Beaverbrook's papers (the *Daily and Sunday Express*) never had an ounce of real influence.' By 1964, however, the *Mirror's* grassroots identity with Labourt had declined, according to Smith, and 'instead of a voter hearing a candidate on the hustings we have arrived at the public opinion poll addressed by party spokesmen on television'.

Media sociologist Colin Seymour-Ure[4] noted, in 1959, 'a decline in newspapers' unwillingness to recognize merit in opponents and faults in their own party'. By 1970, he was saying that the media had detached itself as never before from the party system and might take an anti-Government stance regardless of party.

Charges of political bias continued to be made, however, and the Press Council, in response to a complaint about the provincial *Burton Daily Mail* in 1971, ruled that 'freeeedom of the press includes the freedom to be partisan . . . a newspaper is entitled, if it wishes, to make itself an instrument of propaganda for any cause. It may be better that it should not; but if it does so it is quite impossible to say that its attitude involves any lowering of professional standards'. It was a fallacy, said the Council, 'to assume that a newspaper had a duty like the BBC or ITV to give equal time to both parties'. It depended on the editor.

Ian Jackson found that the non-partisan view dominated in the provincial press. In a sample of attitudes at the General Election of 1970 he noted that of twenty-five evening papers, 40 per cent had Conservative views, 16 per cent Liberal, 4 per cent Labour and 40 per cent were non-partisan, while of twenty-five weeklies nearly 90 per cent were non-partisan.[5]

Speaking at a Media Society Seminar in London in July 1974, TV personality and some-time Fleet Street editor Alastair Burnet remarked that 'it has been doubtful for . . . (some years) . . . that readers' views are regularly altered by newspapers. It appears rather that newspapers tend to confirm their readers' views; that is if the readers want to have views and are not just reading for entertainment'. He also compared the decline in press political influence with the growth in the importance of TV and local radio at election times.

Non-media based opinion polls, too, have become an important element in people's voting intentions.

In general, papers like the *Daily Herald* (later relaunched as the non-political *Sun*) and the Communist *Morning Star*, each with contents dominated by party loyalties, have shown up poorly in postwar circulation figures. Such party-motivated papers have been of the Left. Yet the failure to attract readers has been at variance with the pendulum swing of General Elections which has indicated an electorate fairly evenly balanced between Left and Right.

One is led to two conclusions: 1. newspapers, in Britain at least, do not appear to influence voting intentions, or to reflect them to any degree; and 2. people on the whole do not seem to buy newspapers for political reasons.

Why bother with newspapers?

A newspaper's personality, as noted by the 1947–49 Royal Commission, would appear to be the vital factor in choice by readers. This personality is the product of a unique, if fragile, partnership between editor and reader. If the partnership breaks down, then the paper fails. Loyalty might count for a while but it is not sufficient on its own.

As for the threat of rival communications media, take the case of radio. Its arrival in the 1920s drew pessimistic forecasts from editors and proprietors, yet the avid listening to news broadcasts during the war was followed after the war, when newsprint restrictions were relaxed, with the fastest and highest circulation gains in British newspaper history.

Television inspired even greater foreboding, yet a study of the Audit Bureau of Circulation's six-monthly figures for national daily newspapers showed that between 1962, when television set ownership reached its natural peak, and 1969, two years after colour television was launched, overall daily circulations rose marginally from 14,616,831 to 14,863,881. The National Readership Survey for 1968 showed that while 69 per cent watched television on an average day, 81 per cent read a national newspaper.

One effect of colour television was that a number of newspapers rushed into expensively produced pre-printed colour pages on the theory that colour was what people were going to want. Yet the past decades showed that *The Sun*, for instance, which was late into running colour, gained circulation rapidly at the expense of the *Daily Mirror* and the *Daily Express*, both of which went early into pre-printed colour.

By 1977, the electronic news sheet had begun to reach the home via television under the names of Prestel, Ceefax and Oracle. Though it was at first expensive its future provoked new messages of doom on Fleet Street. Yet, six years later, in 1983, when the new method had grown much cheaper, the ABC half-yearly circulation returns showed that total daily sales of the national dailies had actually risen in the period from 13,913,196 to 14,992,953. By 1992, despite teletext, TV, video and computer games the total daily sales of the nationals were still running at 14,113,000 in a period of deepest recession.

The conclusion one is forced to draw is that one medium feeds on another, that a newspaper's story sends people to television news or radio, or teletext to see the latest developments; and that a Ceefax or radio newsflash sends people to newspapers to get the details. That the expansion of the media, especially television, and perhaps of travel, is augmenting people's insatiable curiosity about the world and its happenings.

A survey commissioned by the 1976–77 Royal Commission reported that its findings 'do not suggest that television and radio news are seen as alternatives to newspapers. If anything, regular watching of television news is more common among regular newspaper readers than among others.[8]

There is, in fact, no statistical evidence to suggest that newspapers face any intrinsic danger from rival news media, despite the fact that to watch television or listen to the radio you have merely to turn a knob.

Any danger to newspaper buying was always more likely to come from within. Heavy production or newsprint costs could force up the cover charge of newspapers so that people might find them too expensive to buy. It is here that computerized technology has served the press well by helping to bring about economies.

Further reading

Roper Mead's *The Press Council* (Media Guide Series, 1978) summarizes the work of the Council up to the late 1970s. A. C. H. Smith and others, *Paper Voices: The Popular Press and Social Change* (Chatto and Windus, 1975) is a perceptive study of the social and political attitudes of the *Daily Mirror* and *Daily Express*. Charles Wintour's *Pressures on the Press* (Andre Deutsch, 1972), though becoming dated, is still relevant in its field.

References

1 TAYLOR, H.A.; *The British Press, a Critical Survey* (Arthur Barker, London, 1961).
2 Press Council's Articles of Constitution (revised), July 25, 1978.
3 SMITH, A.C.H.: *Paper Voices: The Popular Press and Social Change* (Chatto & Windus, 1975) pp. 61 and 204.
4 SEYMOUR-URE, C.: *The Political Impact of the Mass Media* (Constable, 1974) p. 234.
5 JACKSON, I.: *The Provincial Press and the Community*, pp. 271–8.

Appendix A:
A career in journalism

The skills in journalism, as our examination of them has shown, are varied and need to be learned systematically. In Britain this means in most cases starting a career on one of around 1300 provincial newspapers. Here, however modest the range, the work is a microcosm of the pattern of news and the procedures that will be used wherever a trained journalist puts finger to keyboard in the town and city papers of Britain, in national newspapers, in the rest of the world.

Industry and jobs and the industrial relations that derive from them start once the local factory gates open. Trade and business begin where goods and money change hands. Guilt and innocence become issues the moment a court sits anywhere. The arts, religion, sportsmanship, tragedy and human achievement all play their part in the pages of the local paper.

No job is so insignificant that the best possible techniques should not be applied to it. The training of a journalist begins the day he or she compiles for the first time a list of mourners at an ex-mayor's funeral – a lesson in accuracy and human contact. The tentative report of a parish council meeting is the start of a monitoring of the democratic process that will go on throughout a journalist's life as a news gatherer. The deadline by which the first inquest verdict is filed is the mother and father of 10,000 deadlines.

What then of the journalist? There is no stereotype to call upon. The profession probably attracts more varied entrants than professions such as law, accountancy, entertainment and the various branches of technology. Journalists combine an ability with words with a more than average curiosity about the world. They are interested in the workings of institutions and the law and have the historian's flair for analysis of motives and events. A journalist is conscious not only of news but of the context in which it happens, has a strong creative urge, is gregarious by habit and therefore is interested in people.

A journalist is a political creature and, though able to subordinate personal views during work (Lord Beaverbrook had a number of socialist leader writers for his Right-wing *Daily Express*), is well equipped to operate in the world of politics. Of 640 members of the House of Commons one in ten list themselves as journalists or journalist/authors or as ex-journalists.

A journalist will probably have A-levels in such things as English, modern languages, history or economics, but will probably have shone at sports and group activities as well. A trainee is increasingly likely to have taken a degree before entering the profession. How, then, to begin?

Newspaper training

Academic syllabuses have at last caught up with newspaper practice. BA degrees in journalism are now available at a number of universities in addition to the often sociologically based degrees in media studies which have been with us since the 1970s. Entry into the profession, however, whether for graduates or for those with A-levels, is subject as in other professions to a period of industry-based training. This usually means getting a job first.

Breaking into journalism remains, as it ever was, a matter of personal approach between the aspirant and the editor, depending on a vacancy existing or being advertised. At least two A-levels, preferably in English with economics or a modern language, are usually asked for. Having a suitable degree will count with many editors. A file of work – for example contributions to youth or school magazines, or typewritten articles whether published or unpublished – can be a big help. Once a job is secured the training programme begins from day one.

The NCTJ

The main training body, and the one that since 1952 has regulated training for the industry, is the National Council for the Training of Journalists, which operates from the Latton Bush Centre, Southern Way, Harlow, Essex. The council, which is funded by per capita payments from member newspapers in the Newspaper Society and recently formed itself into an industry-based limited company, runs courses, sets examinations and awards a National Certificate to candidates after an approved course of study and the successful passing of examinations.

More than 750 students, half of them female and more than half graduates – making up the main annual intake of newspaper journalists in the UK – enter the NCTJ training scheme each year. They do this in one of two ways: either as direct entrants, having found themselves jobs on newspapers, or as full-time students on a one-year pre-entry course run at colleges accredited by the NCTJ. For the pre-entry course a student does not have to find a job first, although a few are sponsored on half pay by their newspapers.

Direct entrants, whether graduate or non-graduate, are registered with the NCTJ upon joining their newspaper and are sent a distance learning pack. This is a basic foundation course consisting of three ring binders containing fifteen units of printed learning material covering the reporter's job, the elements of newswriting, interviewing and other aspects, together with self-assessment instructions, eight audio tapes and a newspaper style book.

As a student journalist you are expected to complete this course while working on your newspaper during your six-month probationary period. On completing this successfully you are sent by your editor on a twelve-week course at a college accredited by the NCT. These are located at Darlington, Harlow (Essex), Edinburgh, Portsmouth and Sheffield. Here you are assessed on the results of your foundation work and you take seven preliminary examinations in newspaper journalism, law, public administration and shorthand.

After passing these examinations and completing two years of on-job training in full employment you are entitled to sit the NCTJ's National Certificate examination. This has four main sections: a face-to-face interview with telephone follow-through to produce a story; speech reporting, the write-up to include follow-up ideas; newspaper practice Part 1, a major journalism exercise; newspaper practice part 2, with practical questions including some on law and public administration.

The National Certificate qualifies the trainee as a fully trained senior journalist. The Open University allows it as one credit towards a degree.

Pre-entry students, graduate or non-graduate, are accepted by the NCTJ for a one-year course of full-time study, with examinations, at one of nine accredited colleges situated at Darlington, Redruth, Pontypool, Harlow, Gloucester, Portsmouth, Preston, Sheffield and Lambeth (ethnic minorities only). You then have to find a job (in which successful completion of the pre-entry course usually helps) in order to complete your training and proceed to the National Certificate examination. Local council grants are available in some areas for the pre-entry course.

In-house training schemes

Whichever of the above two routes you take, a good deal of your training, it will be seen, takes place while serving your newspaper in your first job. The facilities available from your company are thus of importance, and there is an increasing stress on in-house training arrangements.

More and more provincial newspaper groups have been developing their own staff training programmes. Many of these are accredited by the NCTJ and are run in conjunction with their examinations. Since 1986, however, it has been possible for newspaper groups to run their own schemes and some now do so, issuing certificates on completion of training, and thus providing an alternative route for students wanting to be journalists. To qualify for entry to these schemes you have to have obtained a job on one of the company's newspapers.

The principal in-house training schemes are:

Trinity International, Groat Market, Newcastle upon Tyne;
The Training Centre (Independent), St Leonard's-on-Sea, Sussex;
United Provincial Newspapers, Leeds;
Eastern Counties Newspapers, Rouen Road, Norwich;
Midland News Association, Old Hill, Tettenhall, Wolverhampton;
Trinity Newspapers (Southern), Chester;
Southern Newspapers, 1 High Street, Christchurch, Dorset;
Emap Group Training Scheme, Peterborough, Northants.

There is some direct entry into national newspapers in specialized fields such as politics, leader writing and financial journalism, but national newspapers in Britain on the whole draw their staffs from the provincial training grounds and have no training facilities of their own.

An advantage with provincial and local papers is that they offer a wide variety of work for the young reporter, with training usually including three months' experience of sub-editing, thus providing the first step to a career in the editing and production side of newspapers where promotion into executive areas can be more rapid.

NVQs

A new factor from 1992 has been the introduction of the Government's National Vocational Qualifications which have been accepted by the newspaper industry as they have by other industries. These, whatever the job or profession, specify certain necessary standards of competence and knowledge based on in-house assessment by an approved training officer.

The aim of the NCTJ and the independent in-company schemes is to provide the training to enable students to qualify for their NVQ in newspaper or periodical journalism at the same time as they undergo their professional training leading to their company or NCTJ certificate. The hope within the industry is that training might be simplified in future by merging the two qualifications in one.

The need for a single transferable qualification has been pointed by the added complication of the Government's **Modern Apprenticeships** scheme introduced in September 1995, to help industry train school leavers. For those in journalism to whom this applies companies have to some extent built facilities on to the existing NVQ training structure. For further details of this scheme write to:

Training and Education Department,
The Newspaper Society,
Bloomsbury House,
74–77 Great Russell Street,
London WC1B 3DA

Journalism degrees

BA degrees in journalism are now available at City University, London; the London College of Printing, the London Institute, the City of Liverpool Community College; at the universities of Wales (Cardiff), Central Lancashire (Preston), Liverpool John Moores, Bournemouth, Luton, Teesside, and Napier (Edinburgh); and at the Falmouth School of Art and Design and the Southampton Institute of Higher Education. Nottingham Trent lists a BA in broadcast journalism.

These new degrees combine a practical induction into journalism with an academic study of newspaper practice and attitudes. The journalism content is in some cases offered alongside a subsidiary subject such as film studies, English, economics, sociology or a modern language.

While, as with other vocational degrees such as those in law, economics and commerce, a journalism degree does not qualify a person for a career, it does provide a broad base on which to build for the professional training and examinations that follow, and it can allow exemptions from part of the training. It also offers an attractive choice to students wishing to take a first degree before starting career training, and to Commonwealth or foreign students wishing to acquire a graduate qualification in journalism rooted in British newspaper practice.

Other media-related degrees

There is a great number of BA degree courses in media studies and other media-related subjects such as typography and graphic design, broadcasting and film studies and public relations which can offer a useful basis for career training in journalism. The linguistic or sociological bias of some media studies courses can be a disappointment to students interested in a job in the media and looking for a more vocational approach, but many courses do include a useful grounding in print and broadcast journalism techniques.

The ones at Sussex, East Anglia and Glamorgan universities and North East Wales Institute of Higher Education include modern language studies. Leeds Metropolitan University and the College of St Mark & St John, Plymouth offer public relations alongside a variety of subjects. Bradford University includes media technology; Glasgow Caledonian has communication and the mass media; Brighton, information and media studies; Lancaster, culture and communication media. Greenwich combines media and communication studies; Westminster (formerly the Polytechnic of Central London) has an old-established communication studies course with a useful content in print journalism and broadcasting. Stirling University, which houses the John Grierson Film Archive, specializes in film studies.

Typography, graphics and media design are given prominence in degree courses at Reading and Portsmouth Universities and at London University's Royal Holloway and Bedford College. The one at Reading is of particular value for students interested in the graphic design side of newspapers and magazines.

A number of other universities offer degree courses in media studies of one slant or another. Study the syllabuses carefully to ensure you are getting the course you want.

Postgraduate courses. For those already with degrees there are one-year postgraduate diploma courses in newspaper journalism and radio or TV journalism on offer at City University, London; the University of Central Lancashire, Preston; the University of Wales, Cardiff; De Montfort University, Leicester; the City of Liverpool Community College, and one run jointly by Glasgow Polytechnic and Strathclyde University. Harlow College and Cornwall College, Redruth, offer twenty-week postgraduate courses.

HNDs. At the other end of the scale, new school leavers can take a two-year Higher National Diploma in journalism at Napier University, Edinburgh; at Surrey Institute of Higher Education, and at Bell College of Technology at Hamilton. HNDs in journalism are also on offer at the London Institute (388–389 Oxford Street) and at Barnsley College, Yorks. HNDs, in advertising are available at West Herts College and in broadcasting and advertising at Falmouth School of Art and Design. The London Institute has HNDs in advertising, marketing and public relations; editorial practice; and press and public relations as well as their BA journalism degree.

Short courses. There is an assortment of short courses available aimed mainly at those who have started their career. The NCTJ offers a wide variety at centres in London, Harlow and Rugby, open to all-comers and designed to help working journalists acquire specialist skills. These include media law, PR and the press, sub-editing, feature writing, layout skills, interviewing techniques, using QuarkXpress in page production, privacy and the journalist and 'sharpening your English'. NCTJ tutors will also present courses to suit in-company. For details write to the NCTJ (address on page 176).

The Newspaper Society offers residential short courses for senior staff in editorial law and management, marketing and promotions for editorial and in advertising and the commercial side of newspapers. For details apply to the society (address above).

An important specialism is covered by the NCTJ's Distance Learning foundation course in Sub-editing which offers ten tutor-based modules for completion in three to six months of study.

Access courses. For mature students seeking entry into newspaper journalism the NCTJ supports one-year Access courses at Lambeth College, London; Handsworth College, Birmingham; Sheffield College; Highbury College, Portsmouth; Swansea College; Calderdale College, Halifax, and City of Liverpool Community College. Those successfully completing a course get a certificate equivalent to A-levels and are given access to the selection procedure for the NCTJ Pre-entry course. The colleges will supply details.

Periodicals

There are about 4000 periodicals in Britain including general interest and women's magazines and covering almost every subject, trade, occupation and hobby, a great number of them based in London. Work on many periodicals is similar to procedures in newspaper journalism but different in content, and tends to appeal to those with specialized interests. Great writing skill and originality can be needed, with an awareness of other people's tastes and opinions. In addition to those taking jobs there is a body of young entrants operating on a freelance basis.

Most of the big magazine companies run in-house training schemes monitored by, and run in conjunction with, the Periodicals Training Council. About 80 per cent of entrants are graduates or have had some full time education beyond A-levels.

A main source of entry is through specialisms undertaken on the one-year postgraduate courses at City University, London, the University of Wales at Cardiff, the University of Central Lancashire, or the postgraduate course run by Glasgow Polytechnic and Strathclyde University. The London College of Printing offers a one-year pre-entry course in periodical journalism for A-level students and a two-year HND course in business studies which includes journalism. Reed Business Publishing offers a seven-week pre-entry training course at Sutton, Surrey, which takes external applicants.

For those not able to attend a full-time college based course, the NCTJ's Distance Learning programme offers, by post, tutor-based foundation courses in writing for the periodical press and in media law for periodical journalists. Satisfactory completion of the modules of work entitles students to sit the NCTJ's preliminary examinations in the subjects.

Press photography

Some in-company schemes include courses in press photography, with a yearly intake of fifty to sixty mostly by direct entry into jobs on local papers. Educational requirements are the same as for trainee reporters, though two years' experience of photographic techniques or a completed further education course in photography will be accepted by editors.

There is a one-year pre-entry full-time course in press photography at Sheffield College, sponsored by the NCTJ, who also run a tutor-based distance learning course in photojournalism for press photographers who want to write feature articles to accompany their work.

The London College of Printing runs evening courses in photojournalism.

Appendix B:
Code of Practice for the Press

The Press Complaints Commission Code of Practice for the Press.

The Press Complaints Commission are charged with enforcing the following Code of Practice which was framed by the newspaper and periodical industry and ratified by the Press Complaints Commission in 1993.

All members of the Press have a duty to maintain the highest professional and ethical standards. In doing so, they should have regard to the provisions of this Code of Practice and to safeguarding the public's right to know.

Editors are responsible for the actions of journalists employed by their publications. They should also satisfy themselves as far as possible that material accepted from non-staff members was obtained in accordance with this Code.

While recognizing that this involves a substantial element of self-restraint by editors and journalists, it is designed to be acceptable in the context of a system of self-regulation. The Code applies in the spirit as well as in the letter.

It is the responsibility of editors to cooperate as swiftly as possible in PCC enquiries.

Any publication which is criticized by the PCC under one of the following clauses is duty bound to print the adjudication which follows in full and with due prominence.

1   Accuracy

(i)   Newspapers and periodicals should take care not to publish inaccurate, misleading or distorted material.
(ii)   Whenever it is recognized that a significant inaccuracy, misleading statement or distorted report has been published, it should be corrected promptly and with due prominence.
(iii)   An apology should be published whenever appropriate.
(iv)   A newspaper or periodical should always report fairly and accurately the outcome of an action for defamation to which it has been a party.

2   Opportunity to reply

A fair opportunity for reply to inaccuracies should be given to individuals or organizations when reasonably called for.

3   Comment, conjecture and fact

Newspapers, while free to be partisan should distinguish clearly between comment, conjecture and fact.

4   Privacy

Intrusions and enquiries into an individual's private life without his or her consent including the use of long-lens photography to take pictures of people on private property without their consent are not generally acceptable and publication can only be justified when in the public interest.

Note – Private property is defined as any private residence, together with its garden and outbuildings, but excluding any adjacent fields or parkland. In addition, hotel bedrooms (but not other areas in a hotel) and those parts of a hospital or nursing home where patients are treated or accommodated.

5   Listening devices

Unless justified by public interest, journalists should not obtain or publish material obtained by using clandestine listening devices or by intercepting private telephone conversations.

6   Hospitals

(i) Journalists or photographers making enquiries at hospitals or similar institutions should identify themselves to a responsible official and obtain permission before entering non-public areas.
(ii) The restrictions on intruding into privacy are particularly relevant to enquiries about individuals in hospital or similar institutions.

7   Misrepresentation

(i)   Journalists should not generally obtain or seek to obtain information or pictures through misrepresentation or subterfuge.
(ii) Unless in the public interest, documents or photographs should be removed only with the express consent of the owner.
(iii) Subterfuge can be justified only in the public interest and only when material cannot be obtained by any other means.

8   Harassment

(i)   Journalists should neither obtain nor seek to obtain information or pictures through intimidation or harassment.
(ii) Unless their enquiries are in the public interest, journalists should not photograph individuals on private property without their consent; should not persist in telephoning or questioning individuals after having been asked to desist; should not remain on their property after having been asked to leave and should not follow them.
(iii) It is the responsibility of editors to ensure that these requirements are carried out.

9   Payment for articles

(i) Payments or offers of payment for stories, pictures or information should not be made directly or through agents to witnesses or potential witnesses in current or criminal proceedings or to people engaged in crime or to their associates – which includes family, friends, neighbours and colleagues – except where the material concerned ought to be published in the public interest and the payment is necessary for this to be done.

10   Intrusions into grief or shock

In cases involving personal grief or shock, enquiries should be carried out and approaches made with sympathy and discretion.

11   Innocent relatives and friends

Unless it is contrary to the public's right to know, the Press should generally avoid identifying relatives or friends of persons convicted or accused of crime.

12   Interviewing or photographing children

(i)   Journalists should not normally interview or photograph children under the age of 16 on subjects involving the personal welfare of the child, in the absence of or without the consent of a parent or other adult who is responsible for the children.
(ii)   Children should not be approached or photographed while at school without the permission of the school authorities.

13   Children in sex cases

(1)   The press should not, even where the law does not prohibit it, identify children under the age of 16 who are involved in cases concerning sexual offences, whether as victims, or as witnesses or defendants.
(2)   In any press report of a case involving a sexual offence against a child:
   (i)   The adult should be identified.
   (ii)   The terms 'incest' where applicable should not be used.
   (iii)   The offences should be described as 'serious offences against young children' or similar appropriate wording.
   (iv)   The child should not be identified.
   (v)   Care should be taken that nothing in the report implies the relationship between the accused and the child.

14   Victims of crime

The press should not identify victims of sexual assault or publish material likely to contribute to such identification unless, by law, they are free to do so.

15   Discrimination

(i)   The press should avoid prejudicial or pejorative reference to a person's race, colour, religion, sex or sexual orientation or to any physical or mental illness or handicap.

(ii) It should avoid publishing details of a person's race, colour, religion, sex or sexual orientation, unless these are directly relevant to the story.

16   Financial journalism

(i) Even where the law does not prohibit it, journalists should not use for their own profit financial information they receive in advance of its general publication, nor should they pass such information to others.

(ii) They should not write about shares or securities in whose performance they know that they or their close families have a significant financial interest, without disclosing the interest to the editor or financial editor.

(iii) They should not buy or sell, either directly or through nominees or agents, shares or securities about which they have written recently or about which they intend to write in the near future.

17   Confidential sources

Journalists have a moral obligation to protect confidential sources of information.

18   The public interest

Clauses 4, 5, 7, 8 and 9 create exceptions which may be covered by invoking the public interest. For the purposes of this code that is most easily defined as:

(i) Detecting or exposing crime or a serious misdemeanour.

(ii) Protecting public health and safety.

(iii) Preventing the public from being misled by some statement or action of an individual or organization.

In any cases raising issues beyond these three definitions the Press Complaints Commission will require a full explanation by the editor of the publication involved, seeking to demonstrate how the public interest was served.

Comments or suggestions regarding the content of the Code may be sent to the Secretary, Press Standards Board of Finance, Merchants House Buildings, 30 George Square, Glasgow G2 1EG, to be laid before the industry's Code Committee.

Appendix C:
The National Union of Journalists Code of Professional Conduct

Like other trade unions, formed for mutual protection and economic betterment, the National Union of Journalists desires and encourages its members to maintain good quality of work and high standards of conduct.

Through the years of courageous struggle for better wages and working conditions its pioneers and their successors have kept these aims in mind, and have made provision in Union rules not only for penalties on offenders, but for the guidance and financial support of members who may suffer loss of work for conforming to Union principles.

While punishment by fine, suspension or expulsion is provided for in cases of 'conduct detrimental to the interests of the Union or of the profession,' any member who is victimized [Rule 20, clause (g)] for refusing to do work . . . 'incompatible with the honour and interests of the profession' may rely on adequate support from Union funds.

A member of the Union has two claims on his/her loyalty – one by his/her Union and one by his/her employer. These need not clash so long as the employer complies with the agreed Union conditions and make no demand for forms of service incompatible with the honour of the profession or with the principle of trade unionism.

1 A journalist has a duty to maintain the highest professional and ethical standards.

2 A journalist shall at all times defend the principle of the freedom of the Press and other media in relation to the collection of information and the

expression of comment and criticism. He/she shall strive to eliminate distortion, news suppression and censorship.

3 A journalist shall strive to ensure that the information he/she disseminates is fair and accurate, avoid the expression of comment and conjecture as established fact and falsification by distortion, selection or misrepresentation.

4 A journalist shall rectify promptly any harmful inaccuracies, ensure that correction and apologies receive due prominence and afford the right of reply to persons criticized when the issue is of sufficient importance.

5 A journalist shall obtain information, photographs and illustrations only by straightforward means. The use of other means can be justified only by overriding consideration of the public interest. The journalist is entitled to exercise a personal conscientious objection to the use of such means.

6 Subject to justification by overriding considerations of the public interest, a journalist shall do nothing which entails intrusion into private grief and distress.

7 A journalist shall protect confidential sources of information.

8 A journalist shall not accept bribes nor shall he/she allow other inducements to influence the performance of his/her professional duties.

9 A journalist shall not lend himself/herself to the distortion or suppression of the truth because of advertising or other considerations.

10 A journalist shall only mention a person's race, colour, creed, illegitimacy, marital status or lack of it, gender or sexual orientation if this information is strictly relevant. A journalist shall neither originate nor process material which encourages discrimination on any of the above-mentioned grounds.

11 A journalist shall not take private advantage of information gained in the course of his/her duties, before the information is public knowledge.

12 A journalist shall not by way of statement, voice or appearance endorse by advertisement any commercial product or service save for the promotion of his/her own work or of the medium by which he/she is employed.

Bibliography

The following books have been read or consulted:

ADAMS, James R. *Media Planning* (Business Books, London, 2nd Edition, 1977).

ARNOLD, Edmund C. *Modern Newspaper Design* (Harper and Row, New York, 1969).

AYERST, David. *The Guardian: a Biography* (Collins, London, 1971).

BAGNALL, Nicholas. *Newspaper Language* (Focal Press, 1993).

BOTTOMLEY, Ted and LOFTUS, Anthony. *Journalists' Guide to the Use of English* (Express and Star Publications, Wolverhampton, 1971).

BOYD, Andrew. *Broadcast Journalism* (Focal Press, 1993).

BOYD-BARRETT, Oliver. *The International News Agencies* (Constable, London, 1980).

BREWER, Roy. *An Approach to Print* (Blandford Press, London, 1971).

BROADBENT, Simon. *Spending Advertisers' Money* (Business Books, London, 2nd Edition, 1975).

CENTRAL OFFICE OF INFORMATION. *The British Press* (pamphlet) (HMSO, London, 1976).

CHRISTIANSEN, Arthur. *Headlines All My Life* (Heinemann, London, 1961).

COMPAINE, Benjamin N. *The Newspaper Industry in the 1980s* (Knowledge Industry Publications, New York, 1980).

CRONE, Tom. *Law and the Media* (Butterworth-Heinemann, 3rd Edition, 1995).

CUDLIPP, Hugh. *Walking on the Water* (Bodley Head, London, 1976).

DALLEY, Terence (ed). *The Complete Guide to Illustration and Design* (Phaidon Press, London, 1980).

DAVIS, Anthony. *Magazine Journalism Today* (Focal Press, 1994).

DOBSON, Christopher. *The Freelance Journalist* (Focal Press, 1994).

DODGE, John, and VINER, George. *The Practice of Journalism* (Heinemann, 1963).

DURRANT, W. R. *Printing* (Butterworth-Heinemann, 1990).

ECONOMIST INTELLIGENCE UNIT. *The National Newspaper Industry: A Survey* (EIU, London, 1966).

EVANS, Harold. *Editing and Design: Book One, Newsman's English; Book Two, Handling Newspaper Text; Book Three, News Headlines; Book Four, Pictures on a Page; Book Five, Newspaper Design* (Heinemann, London, 1974–78).

EVANS, W. A. *Advertising Today and Tomorrow* (Allen & Unwin, London, 1974).

FINCHER, Terry. *Creative Techniques in Photo-Journalism* (Batsford, London, 1980).

GILES, V. and HODGSON, F. W. *Creative Newspaper Design* (Focal Press, 2nd Edition, 1996).

GOULDEN, John F. *Newspaper Management* (Heinemann, London, 1967).

GRAHAM, Betsy. *Magazine Article Writing* (Holt, Rinehart and Winston, New York, 1980).

HARRIS, G. and SPARK, D. *Practical Newspaper Reporting* (Focal Press, 2nd Edition, 1993).

HART's *Rules for Compositors and Readers* (Oxford University Press, 39th Edition, 1983).

HENRY, Harry. *Behind the Headlines* (Associated Business Press, London, 1978).

HENNESSY, Brendan. *Writing Feature Articles* (Focal Press, 3rd Edition, 1995).

HOBSON, Harold (and others). *The Pearl of Days: an Intimate Memoir of the Sunday Times, 1822–1972* (Hamish Hamilton, London, 1972).

HODGSON, F. W. *Subediting* (Focal Press, 2nd Edition, 1993).

HUTT, Alan. *Newspaper Design* (Oxford University Press, 2nd Edition, 1967).

JACKSON, Ian. *The Provincial Press and the Community* (Manchester University Press, 1971).

JENKINS, Simon. *Newspapers: The Power and the Money* (Faber & Faber, London, 1979).

KEENE, Martin. *Practical Photojournalism* (Focal Press, 2nd Edition, 1995).

LEVY, H. P. *The Press Council: A History* (Macmillan, London, 1967).

McLACHLAN, Donald. *In The Chair: Barrington Ward of The Times* (Weidenfeld, London, 1971).

McLEAN, Ruari. *Typography* (Thames and Hudson, London, 1980).

McNAE, L. C. J. *Essential Law For Journalists* (Butterworths, London, 8th Edition, 1988).

MARTIN, Roderick. *New Technology and Industrial Relations in Fleet Street* (Clarendon Press, Oxford, 1981).

MEAD, Roper. *The Press Council* (Media Guide Series, London, 1978).

MEDINA, Peter. *Careers In Journalism* (Kogan Page, London, 1981).

NATIONAL UNION OF JOURNALISTS. *Journalists and New Technology* (NUJ, London, 1980).

ROYAL COMMISSION ON THE PRESS, Reports: Report 1947–49 (HMSO, London, 1949).

Report 1961–62 (HMSO, London, 1962).

Interim Report 1976 (HMSO, London, 1976).

Final Report, 1976–77 (HMSO, London, 1977).

Working Papers, 1976–77: *News Technology and the Press* by Rex Winsbury (HMSO, London, 1975). *Review of Sociological Writing on the Press* by Professor Denis McQuail (HMSO, London, 1976).

Research Series, 1976–7: *Industrial Relations in the National Newspaper Industry* (HMSO, London, 1976). *Industrial Relations in the Provincial Newspaper and Periodical Industries* (HMSO, London, 1977). *Attitudes to the Press* (HMSO, London, 1977). *Analysis of Newspaper Content* (HMSO, London, 1977). *Concentration of Ownership in the Provincial Press* (HMSO, London, 1977). *Periodicals and the Alternative Press* (HMSO, London, 1977).

SCHOENFELD, A. C. and DIEGMUELLER, K. S. *Effective Feature Writing* (Holt, Rinehart and Winston, New York, 1982).

SELLERS, Leslie. *Simple Subs' Book* (Pergamon Press, Oxford, 1968) and *Keeping Up The Style* (Pitman, London, 1975).

SEYMOUR-URE, Colin. *The Political Impact of the Mass Media* (Constable, London, 1974).

SMITH, Anthony (ed.). *The British Press Since the War* (documents) (David and Charles, Newton Abbot, 1974) and *Goodbye Gutenberg: The Newspaper Revolution of the 1980s* (Oxford University Press, 1980).

SMITH, A. C. H. (and others). *Paper Voices: The Popular Press and Social Change* (Chatto & Windus, London, 1975).

SOMERFIELD, Stafford. *Banner Headlines* (Scan Books, Shoreham-on-Sea, 1979).

STRUNK, William and WHITE, E. B. *The Elements of Style* (Macmillan Publishing Co., New York, 1979).

TAYLOR, A. J. P. *Beaverbrook* (Hamish Hamilton, London, 1972).

TAYLOR, H. A. *The British Press: A Critical Survey* (Arthur Barker, London, 1961).

THOMSON OF FLEET, Lord. *After I Was Sixty* (Hamish Hamilton, London, 1975).

TREWIN, Ion. *Journalism* (David and Charles, Newton Abbot, 1975).

TUNSTALL, Jeremy. *The Westminster Lobby Correspondents* (Routledge and Kegan Paul, London, 1970); (ed.) *Media Sociology* (Constable, London, 1970) and *Journalists at Work* (Constable, London, 1971).

WATERHOUSE, Keith. *On Newspaper Style* (Viking, 1989).

WHALE, John. *Journalism and Government* (Macmillan, London, 1972 and

The Politics of the Media (Fontana Books, London, 1977).

WILLIAMS, Paul. *The Computerized Newspaper* (Butterworth-Heinemann, 1990).

WINSBURY, REX. *New Technology and the Journalist* (Thomson Foundation, 1976) (see also under Royal Commission 1976–7).

WINTOUR, Charles. *Pressures on the Press: An Editor's View of Fleet Street* (André Deutsch, London, 1972).

Glossary

ABC Audit Bureau of Circulations, the body that authenticates and publishes newspaper circulation figures.

Ad Advertisement.

Ad dummy The blank set of pages of an edition with the shapes and positions of advertisements marked in.

Ad rule The rule or border separating editorial matter from advertisements on a page.

Add Copy added to a story already written or sub-edited.

Advance Printed hand-out of a speech of statement issued in advance to the press.

Advertising agency An organization that prepares and designs advertisements for clients, and buys advertising space.

Agony column A regular feature giving advice on personal problems to the mainly young; hence agony aunt.

Alts Alterations made to copy or edited matter.

Angle A particular approach to a story.

Angling Writing or editing a story from a particular angle, i.e. to bring out a particular aspect of its news content.

Art Pertaining usually to design and layout of pages, the use of pictures and typography in newspaper display.

Art desk Where page layouts are drawn in detail and the pictures edited.

Art editor The person responsible for the art desk and for design of the newspaper.

Artwork   Prepared material for use in newspaper display.

Ascender   The part of a letter that rises above its x-height, as in h, k, l and f.

Assignment   A story which a journalist has been assigned to cover: a briefing.

Author's marks   Corrections of amendments by the writer on an edited story, either on screen or on proof.

Advertorial   Advertising disguised as editorial material.

Back bench   The control centre for a newspaper's production, where sit the night editor and other production executives.

Backgrounder   A feature giving background to the news.

Back numbers   Previous issues of a newspaper.

Bad break   Ugly or unacceptable hyphenation of a word made to justify a line of type. See *Justify*.

Banner   A headline that crosses the top of a page – also *streamer*.

Bastard measure   Any typesetting of non-standard width.

Beat   An exclusive story or one that puts a newspaper's coverage ahead of another's.

Big quotes   Quotation marks larger than the typesize they enclose, used for display effect.

Big read   A long feature covering many columns – usually an instalment of a series.

Bill   A newspaper poster advertising the contents of the paper at selected sites.

Black   A copy or carbon of a story, an electronic duplicate of a story; also used to describe certain boldface types.

Blanket   Newspaper page proof.

Bleach-out   A picture overdeveloped to intensify the blacks and remove the tones – useful in producing a motif to use as a display label on a story.

Blobs   Solid black discs used in front of type for display effect, or for tabulating lists.

Blow-up   Enlargement of a picture or type.

Blurb   A piece of self-advertisement composed of type, and sometimes illustration, used to draw a reader's attention to the contents of other pages or issues to come.

Bodoni   A commonly used serif type, noted for clean lines and fine serifs.

Body   The space taken up by the strokes of a letter – the density of a letter.

Body matter   The reading text of a newspaper.

Body type   The type used for reading text.

Bold   Name given to type of a thicker than average body.

Border   A print rule or strip used to make panels for stories, or for display effects in layout – used in stick-on tape form in paste-up pages.

BOT   Type reversed as black on tone background.

Box   A story enclosed by rules on all four sides – also *panel*.

Break   1 Convenient place to break the text with a quote or crosshead; 2 The moment news happens.

Breaker   Any device such as a quote or crosshead which breaks up the text in the page.

Break-out   A secondary story run on a page with a main story, usually on a feature page. Also: a sidebar.

Brief   A short news story, usually one paragraph.

Briefing   Instructions for a journalistic assignment.

Bring up   An editing instruction meaning use certain material earlier in a story.

Broadsheet   Full size newspaper page approximately 22 in by 15 in, as opposed to tabloid, half size.

Bromide   Emulsioned stiff paper on which photographic material is printed; any photographically printed material.

Bucket   Rules on either side and below tying in printed matter to a picture.

Bureau   The office of a news agency; in the US any newspaper office separate from the main one.

Buster   Headline whose number of characters exceed the required measure.

By-line   The writer's name at the beginning, or near the top, of a story.

c & lc Capital letters and lower case of type.

Cablese Abbreviated text used in copy transmitted by telegraph, i.e. to save transmission costs.

Caption Line(s) of type identifying or describing a picture.

Caps Capital letters of type.

Caslon A traditional-style serifed type faced used for headlines.

Cast off To edit to a fixed length; (n) the edited length of a story as estimated.

Catchline Syllable taken from a story and used on each folio, or section, along with folio number, to identify it in the typesetting system.

CD-Rom Compact disk read-only memory used to hold computer-accessible data.

Centre spread Material extending across the two centre-facing pages in a newspaper. *Spread*: any material occupying two opposite pages.

Centred Type placed equidistant from each side of the column or columns.

Century Much used modern serifed type with bold strokes.

Change pages Pages that are to be given new or revised material on an edition, or on which advertising material is being replaced.

Characters The letters, figures, symbols, etc. in a type range, hence *character count*, the number of characters and spaces that can be accommodated in a given line of type.

Circulation The number of copies of a newspaper sold, i.e. in circulation; hence *circulation manager*, the executive in charge of distributing copies and promoting circulation, also *circulation rep* (representative).

City editor Editor of financial page; in US the name given to the editor in charge of news-gathering in main office.

Classifieds Small adverts gathered into sections.

Clean up Editing instruction to improve tone of copy.

Cliché A well-worn, over-used phrase.

Cliffhanger A story that still awaits its climax or sequel.

Close quotes Punctuation marks closing quoted material.

Close up To reduce space between words or lines.

Col Short for column.

Colour   Descriptive writing.

Column   Standard vertical divisions of a newspaper page; hence column measure.

Column rule   Fine rule marking out the columns.

Columnar space   Vertical space separating one column of matter from another.

Command   A keyboarded instruction to a computer.

Comp   Compositor; a printer who composes typeset material or makes up a page.

Compo   Composite artwork made up of type and half-tone.

Condensed type   Type narrower than the standard founts; hence *extra condensed* and *medium condensed*.

Contact book   A reporter's record of useful personal contacts and their telephone numbers.

Content   Material in a newspaper.

Contents bill   Bill or poster advertising a story or item in a newspaper.

Copy   All material submitted for use in a newspaper.

Copy-taker   Telephone typists who take down reporters' copy on a typewriter or VDU (US telephone reporter).

Copy-taster   Person who sorts and classifies incoming copy in a newspaper.

Copyright   Ownership of written or printed material.

Corr   Short for correspondent.

Correct   To put right typesetting errors.

Correction   Published item putting right errors in a story.

Count   The number of characters in a line of type.

Coverage   The attendance at, and writing up, of news events; also the total number of stories covered.

Credit   Usually the photographer's or artist's name printed with an illustration; hence *credit line*.

Crop   To select the image of a picture for printing by drawing lines to exclude the unwanted area; also to exclude unwanted area on screen.

Crosshead   Line or lines of type to break the text, placed between paragraphs.

Cross reference   Line of type referring to matter elsewhere in the paper.

CRT   Cathode-ray tube, used as a light source to create the type image in a photosetter (in cut-and-paste make-up).

Cursive   Any flowing design of type based on handwriting.

Cursor   Electronic light 'pen' on VDU screen, used to manipulate text during writing and editing.

Cut   To reduce a story by deleting facts or words.

Cut-off   A story separated from the text above and below by type rules making it self-contained from the rest of the column; hence *cut-off rule*.

Cut-out   Half-tone picture in which the background has been cut away to leave the image in outline.

Cuttings   Catalogued material from newspapers cut out and stored in a cuttings library for future reference (in US clippings).

Cuttings job   A story based on cuttings.

Cypher   A type character which represents something else, i.e. ampersand (&) and £ and $ signs.

DA-notice   An official instruction to editors that a story is subject to the Official Secrets Act and therefore should not be used.

Database   Stored material to which a computer gives access.

Dateline   Place and date of a story given at the top.

Dead   Matter discarded and not to be used again.

Deadline   Latest time a story can be filed, accepted or set.

Deck   One unit of a headline.

Decoder   A device for turning transmitted material into usable form, i.e. pictures or text.

Default-setting   Standard typesetting in a given computer program unless overriden by a keyboard command.

Define   To specify on a computer screen the material a command is intended to cover.

Delayed drop   An intro which reserves the point of a story till later.

Descender   The part of a letter that projects below the x-line.

Diary   1 The newsroom list of jobs for the day or week; 2 A gossip column in a newspaper.

Direct input   The inputting of material into a computer by writers for the purpose of screen editing, i.e. by the use of VDUs.

Directory   A list of stories of a given classification held in a computer and available to those with access.

Disaster caps   Large heavy, sanserif type, used on a major (usually disaster) page one story.

Disclaimer   A printed item explaining that a story printed previously has nothing to do with persons or an organization with the same or similar name as used in the story.

Display ads   Advertisements in which large type or illustration predominate.

District reporter   Reporter working from a base away from the main office.

Double   The same story printed twice in the paper.

Double-column   Across two columns.

Dress   Redress or revision of a story; also *rejig*.

Drop letter   An outside initial capital letter on the intro of a story; also *drop figure*.

Drop quotes   Outsize quotes used to mark off important quoted sections in a story.

Dummy   Blank copy of the paper, sometimes half size, showing the position and sizes of the advertisement and space available for editorial use; mock-up of editorial pages for a new format. Can be *electronic dummy* on screen.

Edit   Prepare copy for the press.

Edition   An issue of the paper prepared for a specific area; hence *editionize*, to prepare such.

Editor   Chief editorial executive who is responsible for the editing and contents of a newspaper.

Editorial   The leading article or opinion of the paper; also *leader*.

Editorialize   To insert, or imbue with, the newspaper's own opinion.

Editor's conference   Main planning conference of a newspaper.

Egyptian   A type family which has heavy 'slab' serifs.

Ellipsis   Omission of letters or words in a sentence, represented by several dots.

Em   Unit of type measure based on the standard 12 pt roman lower case letter 'm'; called a *mutton* (in US a pica).

Embargo   Request not to publish before a nominated time.

En   Half an em – based on the standard roman lower case letter 'n'.

EPD   Electronic picture desk.

Exp   Expanded (of type).

Execute   Computer command meaning to put into effect.

Facsimile   Exact reproduction of an original, as in facsimile transmission of pages from one production centre to another by electronic means.

Family   All the type of any one design.

Feature   Subjective articles used in newspapers, as opposed to objective news material; newspaper material containing advice, comment, opinion or assessment; sometimes any editorial content other than news.

File   A reporter's own computer input; to send or submit a story; a writer's or agency's output.

Files   Back issues.

Filler   A short news item of one or two paragraphs.

Filmset type   Photoset type (as used in paste-up pages).

Fit-up   Artwork involving several elements joined together.

Flash   Urgent brief message on agency service – usually an important fact.

Flashback   A story or picture taken from a past issue.

Flatbed press   Small, mostly old-time, press that prints from a flat surface, i.e. not rotary.

Flat plan   A single-sheet plan (on paper or screen) showing all newspaper pages with advert position.

Flimsy   Thin paper carbon copy of story.

Flush   Set to one side (as of type).

Fold   Point at which the paper is folded during printing; hence *folder*, a device attached to the press which does this.

Folio   Page.

Follow-up   A story that follows up information in a previous story in order to uncover new facts.

Format   1 The shape and regular features of a newspaper; its regular typographical appearance; 2 Any pre-set instruction programmed into a computer.

Forme   The completed newspaper page or pair of pages when ready to be made into a printing plate.

Fount   All the characters in a given size of any type (sometimes *font*).

Frame   The adjustable easel at which paste-up pages are made up from photoset and photographic elements.

Freebie   Free trip, services, entertainment offered to a journalist.

Freelance   Self-employed person, i.e. journalist.

Free sheets   Newspapers that rely solely on advertising income and are given free to readers.

Front office   Usually the advertising and editorial part of a newspaper office to which the public are admitted.

Fudge   Part of the front or back page of a newspaper where late news is printed from a separate cylinder 'on the run', sometimes called the 'stop press', i.e. the presses are stopped so that the late news can be fudged in.

Full out   Type set to the full measure of a column.

Galley   Shallow long metal tray on which metal type was gathered and proofed before being taken to the page; hence *galley proof*.

Gatekeeper   Sociologist's name for the copy-taster.

Gatherers   Journalists who gather and write material for a newspaper – a sociological term.

Ghost writer   One who writes under another's name; one who writes on behalf of someone else.

Good pages   Pages that do not have to be changed for later editions.

Gothic   Family of sanserif type with a great variety of available widths – medium condensed, extra condensed, square, etc.

Graphics   Usually any drawn illustrative material used in page design.

Grot   Abbreviation for Grotesque, a family of sans headline type.

Gutter   The margin between two printed pages.

Hack   Slang term for journalist – sometimes used by journalists.

Hair space   The thinnest space used between letters in typesetting systems.

Half lead   The second most important story on a page.

Half-tone   The reproduction process, consisting of dots of varying density, by which the tones of a photograph are reproduced on a page.

Handout   Pre-printed material containing information supplied for the use of the press.

Hanging indent   Style of typesetting in which the first line of each paragraph is set full out and the remaining lines indented on the left.

Hard copy   Typewritten or handwritten copy, as opposed to copy entered into a computer.

Hard news   News based on solid fact.

Head, heading   Words for headline.

Header   The part of a VDU screen in which menus and basic instructions are entered, and in which the computer communicates with the user.

Heavies   Name sometimes given to the quality or serious national press as opposed to the popular press; newspapers that specialize in serious news.

H & J   Computer term for 'hyphenated and justified', meaning that the material has been prepared on the screen in the length and sequence of equal lines in which it will be typeset.

Hold   To keep copy for use later; also *set and hold*.

Hold over   To keep typeset matter for later, also to *HO*.

Hood   Lines of type above a picture or story and attached by rules top and side.

Hook   A term used in some computer system for a queue or desk to which stories can be sent after tasting to await possible use.

Horizontal make-up   Page design in which stories and headlines cross the page in several legs as opposed to being run up and down.

Hot metal   The now disused printing system in which type was cast from molten metal into 'slugs' for assembly into pages.

House style   Nominated spellings and usages used to produce consistency in a given newspaper of printing house.

Imprint   Name and address of the printer and publisher, usually found at the bottom of the back page of a newspaper.

Indent   Material set narrower than the column measures, leaving white space either at the front or at both sides.

Ink fly A fine spray that can hang in the air in rotary printing operations.

Insert Any copy inserted into a story already written or edited.

Intro The introduction or beginning of a story.

Investigative journalism A form of reporting in which a news situation is examined in depth by a team of reporters under a project leader, i.e. as an investigation of all aspects.

Issue All copies of a day's paper and its editions.

Italic Type characters that slope from right to left.

Jack line See *widow.*

Job A journalistic assignment.

Journalese Newspaper-generated slang; shoddy, cliché-ridden language.

Justify To space out a line of type to fit a nominated width.

Kerning The adjustment made to the spacing between letters in a line of type.

Keyboard The panel of keys on a typewriter or VDU by which copy is entered on to paper or a screen.

Kicker A story in special type and setting that stands out from the main part of the page.

Kill To erase or throw away a story so that it cannot be used.

Label A headline without a verb.

Layout The plan of a page.

Lead (pronounced leed) The main story on a page; the page lead.

Lead (pronounced led) The space between lines of type under the hot metal system, achieved by using strips of metal, or leads, of set points width (term still used on computer systems).

Leader Editorial opinion, or leading article.

Leg Any portion of text arranged in several columns on the page.

Legal kill A legal instruction not to use.

Legman A journalist who assists with gathering the facts but does not usually write the story; hence leg work.

Letterpress A method of printing from a raised or relief surface, as with metal or polymer stereo plates on rotary presses (no longer common in newspaper production).

Letter-spacing Space the width of an average letter in a given type.

Lift To use, and keep in a page, matter that has appeared in a previous edition.

Light box A device consisting of a ground glass screen illuminated from below through which prints of pictures can be viewed face downwards so that they can be manually cropped and scaled on the back.

Light face Type of a lighter weight or character than standard.

Lineage Computation of lines used as a basis of payment to writers; sometimes used for payment of non-staff newspaper contributors.

Line block An engraved plate, as in the hot metal printing system, which reproduced the lines of a drawing in continuous black, as opposed to the half-tone block which rendered tones by means of dots of varying density.

Line drawing Drawing made up of black strokes, as with a cartoon or comic strip.

Literals Typographical or keyboard errors.

Lithography Printing by means of ink impressed on a sheet.

Local corr A district correspondent.

Logo Name, title, recognition word, as of a regular column or section of newspaper.

Long primer Old name for 10pt type; also 1p.

Lower case Small, as opposed to capital, letters of an alphabet.

Machine room The room or hall containing the presses used to print a newspaper or magazine.

Make-up The act of making up a page, sometimes the page plan.

Masking Excluding part of a photograph by paper overlay to indicate area to be used.

Master The basic type shape inside a photosetter from which printed type is generated for cut-and-paste production.

Masthead The name or title of a newspaper at the top of page one.

Measure Width of any setting.

Medium   A weight of type between light and bold, or heavy.

Memory   The part of a computer that retains information fed into it; where written and edited stories are stored.

Merchandizing   Information about price and place of purchase in consumer journalism features.

MF   Abbreviation for more to follow.

MFL   More to follow later.

Milled rule   A Simplex rule or border with a serrated edge as on the edge of a coin.

Montage   A number of pictures mounted together.

Mood picture (or shot)   A picture in which atmosphere is more important than content.

Mop-up   A story that puts together information already used in separate ways, or on separate occasions.

Morgue   Old name for newspaper picture and cuttings library.

Motif   An illustration used to symbolize a subject, or to identify a feature or story.

MS   Manuscript of any text before printing.

Mug shot   Picture showing only a person's head.

Must   An item that must be used, and containing *must* in its instructions.

Mutton   Printers' old name for an em.

Nationals   Newspapers on sale all over the country.

New lead   A version of a story based on later information.

News agency   An organization that collects, edits and distributes news to subscribing newspapers.

News desk   The newsroom, where the collection of news is organized, and where reporters are based (in US, city desk).

Nibs   News in brief.

Night editor   The senior production executive of a daily paper.

Nose   The intro or start to a story; hence to *re-nose*.

NS   Newspaper Society, an association for provincial newspaper proprietors in Britain.

Nuggets Small items of news; separate sections of a story.

NUJ National Union of Journalists (in Britain).

Nut Printers' name for an en; hence *nutted*, type indented one nut, or nut each side.

Obit Obituary item.

Offset Printing by transferring the page image from smooth plastic printing plate to a rubber roller which then sets it off on to paper.

Off-stone When a page is ready to be made into a printing plate – a hot-metal term that has lingered on in some offices.

Open quotes Punctuation marks denoting the start of a quoted section.

Overline A line of smaller type over a main headline; also a *strapline*.

Overmatter Left-over in-type material not used in the edition.

PA Press Association, home national news agency in Britain.

Page facsimile transmission Method by which completed pages are digitized and reduced to an electronic signal for transmission by wire or satellite to another printing centre for simultaneous production.

Pagination The numbering of pages; the number of pages of a publication.

Panel Story enclosed in rules or borders; see *box*.

Paste-up The method of making up pages from photoset material by attaching them to a page card.

Personal column Regular colomn signed by writer (i.e. with a by-line).

Photoset The name given to photocomposed type output to cut-and-paste page make-up, hence *phototypesetter*.

Pica 12 pt type; unit of measurement based on multiples of 12 points (pica = one em).

Picture desk Where collecting and checking of pictures is organized; hence *picture editor*.

Plate Printing plate, made of polymer, derived from the page image.

Platen Surface which holds the paper in a typewriter or printing press and presses it against an inked surface.

Point   Unit of type measurement. The British-American point is 0.01383 in, or about one seventy-second of an inch. The size of type is measured by depth in points.

Populars   Mass circulation newspapers of popular appeal.

Press release   Official announcement for use by press.

Print   Total number of newspapers printed of one issue; also a picture or bromide printed from a photographic negative.

Print order   The number of copies of an issue ordered to be printed.

Print-out   A copy of material in a computer printed out for reference in advance of page make-up or printing. Print-outs sometimes show the type as it will look when set.

Printing plate   The plate, metal or polymer, from which the page is printed.

Processor   The part of a typesetter that produces the bromide print of the type for paste-up; or equipment that produces the print from a photographic negative for paste-up.

Projection   The display and headline treatment given to a story in the page.

Promotion   Any form of planned publicity that has a specific aim.

Proof   An early impression of typeset material.

Proof reader   Person who reads and corrects proofs to ensure that copy has been accurately followed; hence *proof marks*, corrections marked on a proof.

Publishing room   Where the newspapers are counted, wrapped and prepared for distribution.

Puff   An item in a newspaper which publicizes something or somebody.

Pull-out   Separate section of a newspaper that can be pulled out, often with separate pagination.

Pundit   A regular newspaper columnist who dispenses opinion.

Qualities   Serious, as opposed to popular, newspapers.

Queue   A collection, or directory, of stories held in a computer – features queue, newsroom queue, etc.

Quire   Unit of freshly printed, ordered newspapers, usually twenty-six copies.

Quotes Raised punctuation marks to indicate quoted speech.

Qwerty Standard keyboard layout as on a typewriter or VDU, based on the first five characters of the top bank of letter keys.

Ragged (left or right) Copy set justified on one side only, sometimes used in captions.

Range The number and variety of characters available in a type.

Rate card List of newspaper advertising charges based on specific sizes and placings.

Reader A proof reader.

Reader participation Editorial material or items which involve contributions by readers, such as readers' letters, competitions and articles based on invited opinions.

Readership The total number of people who read a newspaper – not the number of copies in circulation. The estimated number of readers per copies of magazines and newspapers can vary considerably.

Readership profile A tabulated analysis of the sorts and ages of readers that buy a newspaper or magazine.

Redress See *rejig*.

Reel Spindle holding a roll of newsprint; sometimes, a roll of newsprint; hence *reel room*, where rolls of newsprint are stacked for use.

Register The outline of printed matter as it appears on the paper; important in colour printing where the main colours are printed separately on to the picture image.

Rejig The revision of a story in the light of later information, or a change of position in the paper, often between editions.

Release The date or time handout material becomes available for use.

Re-nose To put a new intro on to a story, using different material or a different angle.

Re-plate To replace a printing plate to allow a later version of a page on to the press.

Reporter Person who gathers and writes up news.

Retainer Periodic payment made to retain someone's services, as with local correspondents; see *stringer*.

Retouching Improving the quality of a photograph in the scanner, or of a print by the use of a brush or pen.

Reuters   British based international news agency.

Revamp   General change given to a story or page in the light of a reconsidered approach.

Reverse   Type printed white on a black or tone background; can be done in a photosetter for paste-up as *reverse video*.

Reverse indent   See *Hanging indent*.

Review   Assessment of arts production.

Revise   To check and correct, or improve, edited material.

Rewrite   To turn a story into new words rather than to edit on copy.

RO   Run on (on typed copy).

Roman   The standard face of a type.

ROP   Run of press. For instance spot colour is printed during run of press rather than as a separate or additional process.

Rota picture   A news picture obtained under the rota system, in which limited coverage of an event by newspapers is allowed on a shared basis.

Rotary press   Press on which newspapers used to be printed by the letterpress method from curved metal or polymer relief plates. Some still in use.

Rough   Outline sketch of page layout.

Rule   A printed border of varying width.

Run   Length of time taken to print an issue of a newspaper.

Running story   A story that develops and continues over a long period.

Run on   To carry on printing without changing plates for an edition.

Rush   Second most urgent classification of news agency material after *flash*; hence *rushfull*, a full version based on rushes.

Sans   Sanserif-types without tails, or serifs, at the end of the letter strokes.

Satellite printing   Printing at subsidiary production centres by the use of page facsimile transmission.

Scaling   Method of calculating the depth of a picture to be used.

Scalpel   Used to lift, cut up and place material in paste-up pages.

Schedule   List of reporting or feature jobs being covered for an issue of a newspaper.

Scheme To plan and draw a page; also a *page layout*.

Scoop Exclusive story.

Screamer Exclamation mark.

Screen The density of dots in half-tone reproduction of photographs.

Screen The part of a VDU on which stories held in the computer are projected for reading or editing; hence *screen subbing*, subbing by electronic means by use of a cursor.

Scroll (up or down) To display material on to a VDU screen so that it can be read in sequence.

Seal Standard words, often in spot colour, at the top of a page indicating the edition; also a logo.

Section A separately folded part of a newspaper; hence sectional newspapers.

Send A command to transfer material in a computer to another queue or desk, or to the page or a typesetter.

Separation The separate elements of a colour picture by which the colour is transferred to the page.

Sequence The order in which a story is presented (in subbing).

Series Range of type sizes, or of types.

Serif Type characterized by strokes that have little tails or serifs.

Service column An advice, or consumer, column.

Set and hold Edited and put into type for use later.

Set flush To set full to the margin.

Set forme The last forme (or page or pair of pages) to go to press.

Set solid To set without line spacing.

Setting format Setting of a nominated size, width and spacing that is programmed into the ·computer, i.e. where such setting is regularly used.

Shorts Short items of edited matter, usually of one, two or three paragraphs.

Sidebar Story placed alongside a main story to which it relates.

Side-head A headline or cross-head set flush left, or indented left.

Sign-off The name of the writer at the end of a story.

Situationer A story giving background to a situation.

Sizing See *scaling*.

Slab-serif Type with heavy square-ended serifs.

Slip To change a page between editions, hence *slip edition*.

Slug-line Catchline (in US).

Snap Piece of information in advance of full details in news agency story.

Spike Home for unwanted stories. Computers also have an electronic *spike* to which stories can be sent.

Spill To run down and fill space (of type).

Splash The main page one story.

Split screen The use of a terminal to display two stories at once.

Spot colour Non-processed colour applied to the page during run of press.

Spread A main story that crosses two adjoining pages.

Squares Black or open, a species of type ornament used to mark off sections of text.

Standfirst An explanation in special type set above the intro of a story, i.e. it stands first.

Stand-up drop An initial letter in large type that stands above the line of the text at the start of a story.

Star Type ornament; hence *star-line*, a line of stars.

Star-burst Headline or slogan enclosed in star-shaped outline, used in blurbs and advertising.

Start-up When the presses begin to print.

Stet Proof mark meaning 'as it stands'.

Stock bills Newspaper display bills on fixed subject such as 'today's TV', 'latest scores', etc. ·

Stone Bench where pages were made up under hot metal system; hence *stone sub*, the journalist who supervised this work; *stone-hand*, the printer who worked on the stone (terms still used in some cut-and-paste page operations).

Stop press Late news printed from a separate cylinder on to the page while on the press, or afterwards.

Strap-line Headline in small type that goes above the main headline; also *overline*.

Streamer Headline that crosses the top of the page, also a *banner* headline.

Stringer A local correspondent.

Sub-editor Person who checks and edits material for a newspaper to fit a set space, and writes the headline (US deskman).

Subhead Secondary headline.

Subst head Headline in place of another.

Syndication The means by which a newspaper's material is offered for a fee for use in other publications or countries.

Tabloid Half size (newspaper).

Tag-line An explanatory line or acknowledgement under the bottom line of a headline.

Take A piece of copy, part of a sequence.

Tear-out A picture printed with a simulated torn edge, usually a flash-back of a printed picture, or a part of a document; also *rag-out*.

Telephoto lens Camera lens that magnifies an image telescopically.

Teleprinter Machine that prints text received by telegraphic signal.

Terminal The part of a video display terminal on which electronically-generated text is displayed and monitored; also any VDU or VDT.

Textsize A broadsheet, or full-size newspaper page.

Tie-in A story that is connected with one alongside.

Tie-on A story that is connected with the story above.

Tip-off Information from an inside source.

Top A top of the page story; mostly any story of more than three paragraphs in length that merits a good headline.

Trim To cut a story a little.

Turn head A head covering a story that has been continued from another page (US a *jump head*).

Typebook Catalogue of types held.

Typechart A tabulated list giving character counts for given types.

Underscore To carry a line or rule under type.

Update To work in later information.

Visualize   To plan and work out how a page or display will look.

VDU   Visual display unit, a device with a screen and keyboard used to display and enter text into a computer; also VDT, visual display terminal.

Web-offset   A system of printing in which the inked page image is transferred from a smooth printing plate on to a rubber roller and then offset on to paper, as opposed to being printed directly on to paper by relief impression.

Weight   The thickness of a type.

Widow   A short line left at the top of a column of reading type (usually avoided in page make-up).

Wing in   To place a headline within the top rule of a panel or box, leaving a piece of rule showing on either side.

Wire   A means of transmitting copy by electronic signal which requires a receiver or decoder.

Word processor   Electronic system by which text can be keyboarded into a computer, stored, edited, amended and finally printed (i.e. processed) when required.

Work station   A special video display terminal used at a distance from the main computer, with access and facilities to enable work to be done over a telephone line away from the main centre.

WOB   White on black type.

WOT   White on tone type.

x-height   The mean height of letters in a type range, exclusive of ascenders and descenders.

Index

VDUs (VDTs), 21, 131
Verified Free Distribution (VFD),
    155
Victims of crime, 186

Waddington, Lord, 167
Wall Street Journal, 137
Wapping, 146
Ward, Stephen, 49
Waterhouse, Keith, 126
Web-offset, 132–4, 126–8
Westminster Press, 141, 155
Whitaker's Almanack, 112
Whitehall PROs, 39
Whittam-Smith, Andreas, 168
Who's Who, 111

Wilson, Harold (Lord), 42, 49
Wintour, Charles, 40, 71, 79
WOBs, 94
Words:
    foreign, 7
    little used, 7
    shorter, 7
Women's pages, 44
Writers' and Artists' Yearbook, 37
Writs, 159

X-height, 101

Yorkshire Post, 4, 51
Yorkshire Ripper, 51–2, 160, 167